EASTERN CUSTOMS

EASTERN CUSTOMS

The Customs Service in British Malaya and the Opium Trade

Derek Mackay

The Radcliffe Press
LONDON • NEW YORK

Published in 2005 by The Radcliffe Press
6 Salem Road, London W2 4BU

In the United States and in Canada
distributed by Palgrave Macmillan, a division of St Martin's Press
175 Fifth Avenue, New York NY 10010

ISBN 1 85043 844 7
EAN 978 1 85043 844 1

A full CIP record for this book is available from the British Library
A full CIP record for this book is available from the Library of Congress

Library of Congress Catalog card: available

Typeset in Sabon by Oxford Publishing Services, Oxford
Printed and bound in Great Britain by MPG Books Ltd, Bodmin

Contents

List of illustrations

Acronyms and abbreviations

ADC	aide-de-camp
ADO	assistant district officer
AIF	Australian Imperial Force
BMA	British Military Administration
BOAC	British Overseas Airways Corporation
CO	commanding officer
Dalco	former name of Dalforce
Dalforce	special group made up of mostly communist Chinese volunteers
DOM	brand name of liqueur
FMS	Federated Malay States
FMSVF	Federated Malay States Volunteer Force
FOB	free on board
HDML	Harbour Defence Motor Launch
HE	His Excellency
HMS	His Majesty's Ship
ICI	Imperial Chemical Industries
JP	justice of the peace
KL	Kuala Lumpur
KPM	Koninklijke Paketvaart Maatschappij
M$	Malay dollars
MAS	Malay Administrative Service
MCA	Malayan Chinese Association
MCS	Malayan Civil Service
MI5	Military Intelligence (the security service dealing with subversion and espionage)
MPAJA	Malayan People's Anti-Japanese Army
MT	Mechanical Transport
ODO	outdoor officer (rank applied to the most junior customs officer on the Malayan mainland)
PODO	preventive outdoor officer
POW	prisoner of war
PWD	Public Works Department
Q	query, hence camouflaged or disguised (as in Q-boat)

RA	Royal Artillery
RAF	Royal Air Force
RAOC	Royal Army Ordnance Corps
RN	Royal Navy
RNVR	Royal Naval Volunteer Reserve
RO	Revenue Officer
RSPCA	Royal Society for the Prevention of Cruelty to Animals
S$	Straits dollars
SEDO	Supervisor of Export Duties Office
SOE	Special Operations Executive
SS	steamship
UMNO	United Malays National Organization
USIS	United States Information Service
VE	victory in Europe
VHF	very high frequency

Glossary

Ad valorem	descriptive of a customs duty calculated as a percentage of the assessed value of dutiable goods
amah	Chinese nurse or female servant
atap	thatching
ayah	Indian or Malay nurse or female servant
bendahara	Malay chief and principal minister of a Malay state
bersanding	part of a wedding ceremony when the guests file past the seated bride and groom
bhang	Indian hemp
blukar	jungle undergrowth
boy	male servant
bumboat	generally applied to a small craft selling its wares to ships in harbour
bunga mas	traditional tribute, literally 'gold flower'
chandu	opium prepared for smoking
chest	standard container in which raw opium was shipped. In the late nineteenth century it appears to have contained 150 lbs
chichak	lizard
chinting	Malay term for a customs officer
dato	Malay equivalent of a knight
dato bandar	see under *shahbandar*
deepavali	Hindu festival of lights
dollars	the Spanish dollar was used in the early days of British Malaya. The Straits dollar (S$) and the Malayan dollar (M$) were set at 2/4d (11.7 p) from 1906
East Indiamen	ships of the British East India Company
Enche (*Che*)	polite form of address equivalent to Mr or Mrs
Indian hemp	source of hashish or marijuana
jamban	privy or closet
Jawi	Arabic script modified for Malay

kain songket	gold and silver threaded textiles
kampong	rural village
kangchu	headman
kangka	Chinese settlement (lit. river foot)
kebun	garden, used colloquially to mean 'gardener'
Kempetai	Japanese special police
koleh	small Malay boat, oared or sailed
kongsi	Chinese group engaged in collective action
krait	poisonous snake
kuali	shallow conical metal dish
lascar	Malay sailor
mangrove	tree growing on muddy swamps covered at high tide
mentri	vizier
merdeka	independence
missy kesihatan	travelling health sister
munshi	Malay teacher
Negrito	type of aboriginal people
padang	an open area, often set aside for sport
padi	rice plant
penghulu	headman or local chief
preventive officer	customs officer equivalent to a police inspector
punkah	fan, manual or electric, suspended from the ceiling
raja	ruler or landlord
resthouse	government 'hotel' providing simple accommodation and food for travelling civil servants
revenue officer	rank applied to the most junior Customs officers
rickshaw	small two-wheeled carriage drawn by a man
ronggeng	folk dance
Sakai	type of aboriginal people
sambal	spicy condiment from Malaysia
sampan	small Chinese boat, usually propelled by oars
samsu or *samsoo*	liquor distilled from rice
serang	Malay coxswain

shahbandar	harbour master
Shanghai jar	large stone water jar
songkok	Malay man's formal headgear
syce	chauffeur
Temenggong	Malay chieftain and minister in Johore
toddy	drink fermented from palm juice
tongkang	Chinese lighter or sailing vessel
topi	sun helmet
trishaw	bicycle rickshaw
tuan	sir
twakow	Chinese sailing vessel
ubat	medicine
wayang	Malay theatre
weights	local measures were 10 *hoon*s = 1 *chi*; 10 *chi* = 1 tahil (1¹/₃ oz);16 tahils = 1 katti (1¹/₃ lbs); 100 kattis = 1 pikul
Yang di-Pertuan Agong	official title of the head of state of Malaysia
Yang di-Pertuan Negara	head of state of Singapore

Foreword

This history of the Malayan Customs and Excise Service is a welcome and valuable addition to the published history of government in Malaya down to 1957. When in 1874 the Sultan of Perak signed the Pangkor Engagement, which became the model for all states, he agreed that 'the collection and control of all revenues [should] be regulated' under British advice. In the event the new regime retained for a generation much of the traditional practice, including the subletting of most customs and excise duties to Chinese 'tax farmers'. It was a policy that illustrates the theme that, with abundant data collected by careful research, runs through this book. In the work of revenue collection, it is always necessary to understand and adapt one's methods to the economic system, especially when it is so complicated and increasingly sophisticated as it was in Malaya. Among other things this book is excellent economic and social history.

The taxation of opium yielded a substantial portion of total revenues but raised an obvious moral issue. The customs service was first established, in 1910, after the demise of the now obsolete tax farming system, and in the acceptance that gradually a way must be found to eliminate the opium trade that was a source of social evil but entrenched in the Chinese way of life. Derek Mackay describes, in fascinating detail, how the service (in which he held a senior position) did its work, in strenuous, demanding and sometimes dangerous circumstances. His narrative reproduces first-hand accounts from customs staff at all levels of their experiences, not least in enforcing taxation by effective 'preventive' work. The smuggler and other masters of evasion were formidable opponents. This descriptive material is well supplemented, both in the main text and in comprehensive appendices, with statistics on revenue, trade and production, and also departmental staffing. But, as the author plainly intends, it is very much a story of men at work, and of the life that they – and their wives – lived in Malaya and Singapore in the first half of the twentieth century.

J. M. Gullick

Introduction

The British established a presence in Malaya very gradually. Although the three Straits Settlements were acquired by 1824, a further fifty years were to pass before the home government reluctantly authorized intervention in the neighbouring native states, and the last of the treaties by which, one by one, they accepted British protection was signed only in 1919. Almost forty years later those same states became members of an independent Federation of Malaya. Throughout this period of foreign rule the commercial and industrial development of the country took place within the framework of an increasingly sophisticated administrative structure, provided by government departments undertaking a variety of responsibilities and staffed largely by locally recruited civil servants.

The senior appointments in these departments were initially given to British expatriate officers. Generations of young Britons made their careers in Malaya and learned to admire the country and its many different peoples and cultures. They were privileged to live in a place of great beauty and to share in a society of colourful variety, hospitality and tolerance. Those who scaled the dizzy heights of the administrative service are well recorded in the formal histories. Many, indeed, have left us their personal memoirs. The great majority, however, served their time in departments of government whose activities have largely been unremarked.

The Customs Departments in British Malaya had a brief but unusual history. Long opposed by the powerful merchant community in the free port of Singapore, a customs service was finally introduced in 1910 to take over the monopolies hitherto granted to private revenue farmers. Of these by far the most important, providing more that 50 per cent of government revenue in the Straits Settlements, was the opium monopoly. For the next three decades the service was responsible for the importation, processing and distribution of opium throughout Malaya and the conduct of a not inconsiderable export trade. As international opposition to drugs hardened, the service supervised the introduction of a system of registration and rationing designed to control and eventually to eliminate the vice. In 1946, following a total ban on drugs, the service assumed the role of an anti-narcotics force while also coping with the collection and protection of customs and excise revenues and preparation for the independence of Malaya. The work was demanding but seldom dull.

It was three ex-officers of the Malayan customs service who conceived the idea of this book, J. F. M. Roualle, K. S. Hellrich and the late J. S. A. Lewis. My task has been to try to fulfil their concept, to trace the history of the service, to explain its part in the administration and to capture, through their personal accounts, a glimpse of the experiences of some of those expatriate officers who served in it. I can claim no credit for the conception of the book but I accept full responsibility for its inadequacies.

All three of the founding fathers provided me with extensive material, advice and guidance, particularly John Lewis whose essays on various topics laid the foundation for several chapters. My former colleagues, their wives or, in some instances, their widows, responded generously to my pleas to put their memories on paper and I have been able to quote many of them at length. They have hunted out old documents, newspaper cuttings and photographs and have shown a keen interest in the project and great patience at its slow progress.

Their names are recorded in the list of sources at the back of this book.

John Lewis gave me an introduction to Tony Kirk-Greene of St Antony's College, Oxford, who proved a source of much wise advice and provided a signpost to my further research. Professor A. J. Stockwell of Royal Holloway University of London gave generously of his time, drew up a reading list and made me a copy of the Report of the Straits Settlements and Federated Malay States Opium Commission 1908, a crucial document in the foundation of the Malayan Customs Service. It was Mr J. M. Gullick, a former member of the Malayan Civil Service and scholar of Malayan history, who drew my attention to the work of Margaret Lim, and kindly made available a copy of the relevant passages in the Report of the Committee on Malayanization of the Public Service 1956. As the work progressed I received valuable support and advice from Simon Boice of the British Empire & Commonwealth Museum at Bristol, to whose archives I was welcomed.

I must also acknowledge the friendly reception and helpful attitude of the staff at other locations I visited; the Public Record Office at Kew; the Foreign & Commonwealth Office Library; the London School of Economics; the School of Oriental and African

Studies; the Imperial War Museum; Newington reference library; Cambridge University Library; Rhodes House Library, Oxford and the High Commissioners for Singapore and Malaysia.

This book is not a definitive history of the Customs Service. Such a work would demand a level of scholarship to which I cannot aspire. It is perforce an unbalanced account. My sources are, like myself, former British officers of the service and it is their stories that form a substantial element in the narrative. Thus the tale is incomplete, for the development of the service, its increasing sophistication and its success in coping with a multiplicity of roles, depended ultimately on the work of the locally recruited staff. Drawn from all the races of a multicultural society, Malays, Chinese, Indians, Eurasians and others, those men and women undertook duties that were often arduous and not infrequently hazardous. It is they and their successors who have inherited the traditions of the service to whom, with fond memories of many good friends, and colleagues, this book is dedicated.

Derek Mackay

Map of Malaya

Part One:
The Setting

1. A toddy tapper climbs a tree in Singapore.

1
A tropical peninsula

The southernmost part of the Asian mainland, the Malayan peninsula stretches nearly 500 miles, from the Thai border on the narrow isthmus of Kra to within two degrees of the equator. It stands between the South China Sea to the east and the Indian Ocean to the west, and covers an area a little larger than England without Wales. For centuries ships of many nations have navigated the narrow waters between Singapore and the Indonesian islands to the south, and sailed through the long Straits of Malacca, which divide Malaya from the huge island of Sumatra to the west. In the path of both the southwest and northeast monsoons the country has no distinct seasons and its proximity to the equator precludes any observable variation in the timing of sunrise and sunset. It is wet and warm. At sea level the temperature is generally maintained between 70° and 90°F (21–32°C). Rainfall overall averages about 100 inches per year. The natural vegetation is lush forest, covering even the mountains of the main ridge that runs down the centre of the peninsula and splits the country in two – a blue backdrop to the rich green scenery. The principal rivers flow from the hills to the east and west coasts. Facing the South China Sea are extensive sandy beaches. The west coast has fewer such attractions and for much of its length consists of mangrove swamps.

In the heart of Malaya there still live survivors of earlier cultures, usually referred to as 'aborigines', but it is the Malays who gave the country its name, 'Negri (or 'Tanah') Melayu', the Land of the Malays, a description transmuted by Europeans into 'Malaya'. They are believed to have migrated from Yunnan about 2000 BC, spreading throughout the peninsula and the adjacent islands that now form Indonesia. They settled on the coasts and the banks of the rivers as subsistence farmers and fishermen, sharing a rich culture and a fragmented, shifting political structure of numerous small tribal states. In a forestland they built in wood, often decorating their houses in distinctive styles. They wove and dyed colourful sarongs and manufactured elegant silver ornaments. Their language is well suited to the composition of poetry.

The arrival of Indian traders from the Coromandel coast, probably in the first century AD, brought about cultural and political changes, including the spread of Buddhism and the institution of *raja*s as rulers of the petty tribal communities.[1] There are references in Malay records to a larger state called Langkasuka, which may have been located astride the present Thai border. By the ninth century the dominant power was Sri Vijaya, an Indo–Malay kingdom that finally lost Malaya to the Javanese Hindu empire of Majapahit in the fourteenth century. Among the dependencies of this new conqueror was the island city of Tumasik ('Sea Town'), better known by its Indian name Singapore ('Lion City'). In about 1403 it was from Tumasik, now under the domination of Siam, that a Palembang prince, married to a Majapahit princess, fled north to found a new realm at Malacca. Although his successor claimed the title of Maharaja and introduced a constitution based on Hinduism, the flourishing little port was to be the place from which Muslim missionaries went forth to convert the Malays of the peninsula and the Indonesian archipelago to Islam. It remains their religion to this day.

The prosperity of Malacca attracted visitors from China, in 1408 the famous eunuch-admiral Cheng Ho,[2] who was to return several times. Although Malacca had to pay an annual tribute to Siam its rulers were soon sufficiently powerful to exact similar payments from smaller states such as Pahang, Indragiri and Kampar in return for their protection. Merchants from Gujerat, Coromandel, Java and China maintained warehouses in the port, to which the southwest monsoon brought trading ships from China and the northeast those from India. There were cargoes of sugar, textiles, porcelain, spices, incense, silver and opium. Officials collected the port fees and export duties in accordance with established rules and procedures. Following a *coup d'état*, engineered by Muslim Tamil merchants in about 1450, the rulers of Malacca adopted the title of sultan. The last to do so, Sultan Mahmud, exercised power over most of Malaya and, while acknowledging the ultimate suzerainty of China, ceased to pay tribute to Siam. He was eventually to find himself in conflict with a far more dangerous power.

The Portuguese expansion in Asia proceeded very rapidly. It was in 1488 that Bartolomeu Dias rounded the Cape. Only ten years later Vasco da Gama arrived at Calicut. On 1 August 1509 a small fleet dropped anchor in the Malacca roads and sent envoys ashore. Local Indian merchants, aware of the activities of the Portuguese in India, encouraged a plot to seize the ships while the visitors were entertained on land. It is said that one of the sailors had already acquired a lover ashore and that she swam out to his ship to warn him of the danger. The Malaccans captured a party of Portuguese who had landed to buy cloves but the ships were secure. Unable to negotiate his men's release, the Portuguese commander Diego Lopez de Sequeira took his fleet back to India. His brief visit had not been fruitless. It afforded an excuse for conquest.

In June 1511 Alfonso d'Albuquerque reached Malacca with a fleet of 15 ships, carrying a force of 800 Portuguese and 300 Malabaris. Although he was said to have 20,000 warriors to defend his city Sultan Mahmud attempted to placate the Portuguese, returning his prisoners and offering to provide a location for a fort. His offer was in vain. It took d'Albuquerque and his men five days to overcome his resistance and to seize his realm. It was to remain in Portuguese hands for almost 130 years.

They have left their mark on Malacca. The remains of their great fortress 'A Famosa' are still a tourist attraction. So too is the ruined church on the hill where the body of St Francis Xavier,[3] once an inhabitant, lay in state. The College of St Paul was founded as early as 1548. Above all there is the local community of Portuguese Eurasians, who preserve the colourful folk customs imported by the conquerors. But the Malays did not accept their conquest. Throughout their occupation of Malacca, which they extended over the adjacent territory once ruled by the sultans, the Portuguese faced intermittent warfare. Sultan Mahmud still possessed lands from which he could carry on the struggle to restore his power. After his death his descendants sat on the thrones of Johore and Perak. In the sixteenth century local armies besieged the city several times, but like Sultan Mahmud before them, the Portuguese were finally to fall to a challenge from Europe.

By the beginning of the seventeenth century the Dutch were already a substantial presence in the archipelago. In 1619 the Dutch East India Company, empowered to found settlements and negotiate treaties on behalf of the Dutch government, established its capital at Batavia in Java, and took measures to eliminate its rivals. An offer to amalgamate was rejected by the English East India Company,[4] which was then driven from the area following the massacre of its settlers at Amboyna[5] in the Moluccas. The Portuguese trade was gradually strangled as the Dutch intercepted their ships at sea and seized their cargoes, which fetched high prices at ports such as Amsterdam. Finally, with the support of Johore they attacked Malacca. The siege lasted from early in June 1640 to 14 January 1641, when A Famosa was finally taken by storm. Thousands had died on both sides through disease, famine and battle.

The Dutch were determined to profit from their prize. They claimed to have inherited by right of conquest the system of tolls and licences imposed by the Portuguese, and sent out their patrol vessels to enforce the decree that no ships should sail through the Malacca Straits without calling at Malacca to obtain a pass. Their attempts to maintain a monopoly in tin and other exports led to frequent conflict with Malays who were reluctant to accept the company's low prices. On occasion they had to compromise. The Sultan of Kedah at the northern end of the strait was prepared to offer only half of his tin output to the company and with this it had to be content. A further dispute arose when the Minangkabau people of Naning, a territory under the jurisdiction of Malacca, refused demands for a tithe of their rice crop, and waged war so fiercely that the Dutch were forced to accept an annual tribute of just 400 quart measures of rice. Plagued by such problems and the corruption of its agents, the company was virtually bankrupt when in 1798 its possessions passed into the hands of the Batavian Republic.

Meanwhile, events at the northern end of the strait had further compounded Malacca's woes. Following the massacre of its agents at Amboyna in 1623, the English East India Company abandoned its factories to the east of India and withdrew from Malaya, Japan and Siam. In the following century, however, its now dominant position in India and the declining power of its Dutch rival encouraged the company to look once again at the rich spice market of the archipelago. The conflict with the Dutch and the French in 1782 revealed the need for a base on the far side of the Bay of Bengal, where its ships could be repaired and which would serve as a port of call for the East Indiamen engaged in the growing traffic with China. Attempts to negotiate the purchase of a suitable location in Rhio and Trengganu foundered when their rulers demanded a promise of military support. In 1771 a treaty negotiated with the Sultan of Kedah by Francis Light,[6] the captain of a ship engaged in local private trade, was similarly rejected by the Madras Council when found to include a commitment to support the sultan in his current conflict with Selangor. Unwilling to become involved in the tangled politics of Malaya, the company backed off. Indeed, it was in 1784, the year in which the Dutch seized Rhio from its Bugis rulers, that Pitt's Act[7] expressly required the company to refer to the British government any agreement that might lead to war.

Nevertheless, in 1785 when Light presented a fresh agreement to lease the island of Penang from the Sultan of Kedah, the company accepted it, despite its provision that the company would help the sultan against any enemy with men, arms and money. On 17 July 1786 Light, whom the company had appointed as superintendent, hoisted the British flag over Penang. In his new role he soon had to explain to the sultan the implications of Pitt's Act, while conveying to the company the sultan's expectation that it would assist him against potential aggression by Siam. In 1788 he had to inform his royal friend that the East India Company's support would be confined to the exercise of its influence. Not surprisingly, the sultan tried to recover his island by force, but in 1791 he had to accept a new treaty increasing his rent to S$ 6000 a year, raised again to S$ 10,000 a year in 1800, when the company added to its new property a strip of the mainland since called Province Wellesley.

The sultan's anxieties were fully justified. His state was always dominated by Siam, to which he sent a triennial *bunga mas*, a symbolic tribute, and in 1816 he had no choice but to obey a command that he conquer his southern neighbour, Perak. His cooperation did not save him. In 1821 the Siamese invaded Kedah itself and the sultan fled to Penang with some 20,000 of his subjects. There for the next twenty years his schemes to recover his throne were a constant embarrassment to his hosts. He was not, however, without supporters among them. Such men as Robert Fullerton and Stamford Raffles[8] were highly critical of the company's role in the acquisition of Penang. The sultan's exile finally came to an end when, in 1842, Siam permitted him to return as ruler of Kedah, still under Siamese suzerainty.

Penang lies close to the mainland. The acquisition of Province Wellesley secured both sides of the narrow strait and brought some much needed agricultural land to feed the growing population. Although its trade grew rapidly its accounts were usually in deficit. It proved unsuitable as a naval shipyard and the navy's stores were soon transferred to Trincomalee. Initially a dependency of Bengal, it received a governor in 1805. In 1807 it introduced a legal system, based on British law but taking account of native religion and usages. Its fortunes were not enhanced by the outbreak of war against revolutionary France and the effect on trade of Napoleon's Berlin decrees.

Meanwhile, the French military successes in Europe could have opened Dutch overseas possessions to their navy and Britain moved to prevent this by occupying Malacca. After Napoleon's defeat in 1814 the little port was returned to the Dutch (although they did not resume responsibility until 1818). By that time both the Dutch and British had come to recognize that the ideal location for a trading settlement would be at the southernmost tip of the peninsula. Both were making preliminary moves to discover and acquire a suitable site. It was a race in which the Dutch appeared to have a head start. Although the Bugis had recovered Rhio, their leader, Raja Ali, accepted the role of 'under king' to Sultan Mahmud, whose dominions now comprised Rhio, Lingga, Johore, Singapore and Pahang. The *temenggong* exercised his authority in Johore and Singapore and the *bendahara* did so in Pahang. When Mahmud died in 1812 his eldest son, Hussain, was cheated of his inheritance and his younger brother, Tungku Abdul Rahman, succeeded. He entered into a treaty with the Dutch, whose influence was thus paramount in the southern peninsula and adjacent islands.

A very remarkable man was to upset these cosy arrangements. Thomas Stamford Raffles was the son of a sea captain and began his career as a clerk in the India Office at the age of 14.[9] Within ten years he was appointed assistant secretary to the presidency of Penang. He studied Malay, held strong views on Britain's moral responsibilities to her Asian subjects and was in favour of the abolition of slavery. In 1810 he headed the British expedition to secure Java and was lieutenant governor of that island until its return to the Dutch in 1814. Reduced in the aftermath of war to a far less impressive posting in Bencoolen, he visited Calcutta in 1818 and received from Lord Hastings[10] approval for his plans to curb Dutch expansion and to further British interests in Malaya. His first instruction was to seek a location for a post in Rhio, but in view of the Dutch treaty he was given authority to negotiate with 'the Chief of Johore'. On 28 January 1819 he landed at Singapore and signed a preliminary agreement with the *temenggong*. On 6 February Hussain was proclaimed Sultan of Johore. For ceding Singapore, the new sultan was to be paid S$ 5000 a year, the *temenggong* S$ 3000.

It was as well that Raffles had moved so quickly. Soon after he sailed from Calcutta Lord Hastings had second thoughts and sent a letter after him cancelling the mission. The receipt of Raffles's enthusiastic account of his purchase restored his courage. When the inevitable Dutch protest arrived he played for time, responding firmly to the criticisms of India House and ordering the pusillanimous Bannerman at Penang to send troops to assist in the defence of the new colony. What undoubtedly persuaded the company to defy the Dutch, however, was the extraordinary success of Raffles's venture.

The location of Singapore could hardly have been bettered. It stood on the shortest sea route between India and China, an advantage later enhanced by the opening of the Suez Canal. But it was Raffles's vision that ensured its prosperity. As he wrote to a friend in London: 'Our object is not territory but trade; a great commercial emporium and a fulcrum whence we may extend our influence politically.' To the government of India he wrote: 'I have declared the port of Singapore is a free port and the trade thereof open to ships and vessels of every nation, free of duty, equally and alike to all.'[11] The island proved a magnet for the traders of the East, particularly the Chinese. It was the British who provided a safe, orderly environment, the Chinese, and to a lesser extent the Indians, whose enterprise and industry was the foundation of its commercial success. By June 1819 it already boasted a population of 5000.[12] The imports and exports transported in local craft rose from some S$ 4 million in 1820, to S$ 8.5 million in 1822 and over S$ 13 million in 1823.[13] Although Raffles had to return to his post at Bencoolen in 1819, leaving the administration of Singapore to Major Farquhar, he was back in 1822 and did not take final leave of his beloved island until June 1823. His influence was everywhere. He prohibited slavery, introduced trial by jury, appointed magistrates from among the British merchants who were now active in the port and formed them into an advisory council. Before he left he founded the Singapore Institute, a college for higher education and a permanent centre for the study of the life and languages of the region. He sailed home to England and there, with Sir Humphry Davy, applied his restless energy to the foundation of the Zoological Society and its collection in Regent's Park, London.

The Treaty of London in 1824 settled the dispute with the Dutch. The British were to be the sole European power in the peninsula, including Malacca, which therefore reverted to the company. They ceded Bencoolen to the Dutch who remained paramount in the archipelago. That year the population of Singapore reached 10,000 and 35,000 tons of shipping made use of the port. Its first newspaper, the *Singapore Chronicle*, commenced publication.[14]

For more than thirty years the company continued to administer the three settlements and largely avoided any involvement in the affairs of the adjacent Malay states. In 1825 the British agreed to arbitrate in a boundary dispute between Perak and Selangor. The following year some troops were sent to persuade the Siamese to withdraw from the Perak River. In 1830 the company foolishly attempted to impose on the *penghulu* of Naning a variation in the assessment of his tithes and spent a great deal of money on a pointless war.[15] Some goodwill was recovered when the defeated *penghulu* was given a pardon, a pension and a house in Malacca. But time was running out for the East India Company. In the aftermath of the Indian Mutiny the British government assumed responsibility for its territories. These included the settlements, which became the subject of a lengthy dispute between the India and Colonial offices. It was in 1867 that the Straits Settlements, as they were now officially named, were transferred to the Colonial Office and the link with India was finally severed.[16] Apart from the temporary occupation of the Dindings these were to be the only British territories in Malaya.

The Colonial Office continued the company's policy of non-intervention[17] in the Malay states. In 1872 the Singapore Chamber of Commerce was advised that 'it is the policy of Her Majesty's Government not to interfere in the affairs of the Malay States unless where it becomes necessary for the suppression of piracy or the punishment of aggression on our people or territories.' It was an attitude that was becoming increasingly difficult to maintain. The frequent conflicts between the local rulers, civil wars over the disputed succession to their thrones and the growing violence arising from the presence of large numbers of Chinese tin miners in Larut were creating a situation bordering on anarchy. Piracy was rife and slavery extensive. Sir Harry Ord,[18] governor of the Straits Settlements from 1867 to 1873, described himself as the 'helpless spectator' of the growing disorder and disintegration to which most of the Malay states were prey. In 1871 he failed to persuade the chiefs of Perak to conduct a peaceful discussion of the succession to the throne. The Royal Navy had to take action against pirates who had seized a vessel under British colours.

Meanwhile, the rivalry of the Chinese secret societies in Larut spilled over into Penang where there were violent street fights. In 1873 248 Chinese, including every leading merchant in the Straits Settlements, presented a petition to Ord, pleading for steps to protect their trade.[19] As it happened, London had undergone a change of heart and Ord's successor, General Sir Andrew Clarke, arrived with authority for a change of policy.[20]

Clarke was instructed to ascertain 'the actual condition of affairs in each State' and to report what measures could be taken 'to promote the restoration of peace and order and to secure protection to trade and commerce'. Specifically, he was to 'consider whether it would be advisable to appoint a British officer to reside in any of the States. Such an appointment could, of course, only be made with the full consent of the native Government.' Clarke saw the situation in Perak as his opportunity to act on these instructions. He backed the legitimist heir, Raja Muda 'Abdullah, and at a meeting of chiefs at Pangkor secured an agreement embodied in a treaty signed on 20 January 1874.[21] It was the first of a series of such treaties under which Malay states agreed to accept British protection against foreign attack and to deal with foreign powers only through Great Britain. They also provided for the appointment of a British officer (in some states referred to as a 'resident' and in others as an 'adviser') whose advice must be taken and followed except in matters concerning Malay religion or custom.

The first resident in Perak, James Wheeler Woodford Birch,[22] was faced with a sensitive situation in which it would have been wise to proceed with caution. 'Abdullah was not universally popular and his rival Ismail was by no means satisfied with his compensation of a title and monthly pension of S$ 1000. The Mantri of Larut was displeased by his subordination to 'Abdullah and the presentation of a bill for the cost of suppressing the violence in his district. Many Malays saw the cession to Great Britain of the Dindings in western Perak[23] as the prelude to total annexation. Birch was well intentioned but impatient. He expressed contempt for local customs and initiated reforms without apparently recognizing the need to offer corresponding concessions. He abolished the chiefs' feudal dues without compensation. He attempted to protect debt slaves against their masters. The sultan was soon plotting against the resident. When magic proved ineffective the plotters turned to assassination and Birch was speared to death in his bathhouse on 2 November 1875. It had been an unhappy beginning for Clarke's new policy. The British response to the murder of their officer was predictable. The troops moved in, three chiefs were hanged and three banished, including 'Abdullah: a successor to the sultan was easily found. The successor to the unfortunate Birch, however, was to prove an inspired choice. Hugh Low was a botanist who soon won the confidence of the Perak Malays. He tackled the problem of feudal dues, providing compensation to the chiefs in the form of a percentage of the local revenue. He set up a state council over which the sultan presided, with the resident, major chiefs and prominent Chinese as members. It was to pass all legislation. In each district there were appointed Malay or British magistrates to administer the statutes. Slavery was a knottier problem. Debtor slavery was not finally abolished until 1884. It was Hugh Low who set the pattern for the British advisory role in the Malay states. He came to be regarded as the model of a successful resident.

Meanwhile, the new system was rapidly extended to other territories. In Selangor[24] it was introduced in the aftermath of an act of violence. In February 1874 pirates in the employment of a son of the sultan murdered eight British subjects. After a naval demonstration the sultan agreed to put the culprits on trial and to accept a British adviser. An informal visit by the young Frank Swettenham, already experienced in Perak, proved a great success. The sultan wrote to Clarke asking that Swettenham be sent to 'set my country to rights and collect all its taxes'. By April 1874 Clarke was negotiating with the chiefs of Sungei Ujong, the most important state of Negri Sembilan,[25] where Chinese tin miners were a prey to illegal 'tax collectors'. A bond signed by the chiefs of Sungei Ujong and Linggi brought these activities to an end and introduced an assistant resident (Captain Tatham). The *dato bandar*, the collector of the illegal taxes, rejected the deal but a brief intervention by a small British force easily suppressed a minor uprising. One by one the other states of Negri Sembilan accepted residents or advisers. In 1895 they were combined to form the modern state of the same name.

The *bendahara* still ruled Pahang,[26] but in 1887 he assumed the title of sultan and accepted a treaty offering British protection against external attack and the provision of a British agent. In 1888 a full resident replaced the agent.

The protected states were flourishing. Trade was developing, the population was increasing at a remarkable rate and communications were rapidly improving. The first railways were built in 1884. There was clearly a need for the administration to be rationalized and in 1893 Swettenham put forward a proposal for a federal constitution. In 1895 Perak, Selangor, Negri Sembilan and Pahang became the Federated Malay States,[27] with a resident-general to whom the state residents were subordinate. In 1909 a federal council was formed with power to override state legislatures. The federation prospered. Between 1891 and 1901 the population rose from 424,218 to 678,595. Revenue increased from just under S$ 8.5 million in 1895 to just under S$ 24 million in 1905. The FMS produced more than half the world's tin output. In 1904 the postal service handled ten million covers. There were 2000 miles of telegraph wires, 2400 miles of roads, 340 miles of railways. Some 13,000 children were at school and government hospitals treated thousands of patients.

Although the four sultans now enjoyed greater pomp and wealth they had surrendered much of their power. Not surprisingly, the rulers of other peninsular states were wary of involvement in the FMS and preferred to establish rather looser relationships with the British administration. In 1885 the Sultan of Johore placed its foreign affairs in the hands of the British government and agreed to accept a British agent when required to do so. In the event, it was not until 1910 that an adviser was appointed, and in 1914 that a general adviser took post. The country already enjoyed a constitution adopted in 1895. The remaining states – Kedah, Perlis, Kelantan and Trengganu – were the subject of a treaty with Siam signed in 1909. In both Kedah and Perlis there were advisers appointed by Siam to which they were heavily indebted. The FMS took over the debts and British advisers replaced the Siamese. Over Trengganu Siam exercised only a nominal overlordship, which it transferred to Great Britain under the treaty. The status of Trengganu was established in an agreement with Great Britain in 1910, amended in 1919 when a British adviser was posted there. The exact relationship between Siam and Kelantan was in dispute. In 1903 the *raja* accepted a British officer in Siamese service as his adviser. This curious arrangement ended when the provisions of the 1909 treaty took effect and a regular British adviser was appointed.

There were now three political groupings in Malaya – the Straits Settlements, the Federated Malay States and the unfederated states. These arrangements were to remain broadly unchanged until the Japanese conquest in 1942. In the Settlements Singapore now dwarfed its partners. By 1921 its population exceeded 350,000. Extensive docks included the largest east of Suez. With

Penang it handled over 50 per cent of the exports from the mainland. Two products, tin and rubber, dominated these.

The weakness of the Malayan economy had been its dependence on the sale of tin in a notoriously volatile market. Other products were tried but failed to make a substantial contribution to the export trade. Coffee was planted but could not compete with the Brazilian product. Tea is still grown in the hill country but production remains at a modest level. Oil palms, kapok and pineapples have all played their part but the need was for large-scale export commodity. Although the pertja is a Malayan tree, and a modest trade in gutta-percha had long been conducted with Britain, it was in 1873 that the first moves were made that were to transform the economy of the peninsula and much of its landscape. In that year Para rubber seeds were planted in Kew Gardens. In 1877 some plants were sent to the botanic gardens in Singapore where in 1888 its director, Henry Ridley, was the first to see their potential. It took him more than ten years to convince the sceptics. It was he who devised the method of 'herring bone' tapping, which turned an exotic curiosity into a commercial investment. By 1902 there were 16,000 acres under rubber, by 1909 200,000 acres. The invention of the motorcar created a worldwide demand for rubber and the plantations spread rapidly along the roads and railways of Malaya. International companies, British trading houses and Chinese entrepreneurs plunged into the new market. Malay smallholders joined in, converting their orchards into rubber estates. By 1937 53.7 per cent of the three-and-a-quarter million acres under rubber were owned by Asian estates and smallholders. Exports that year, including rubber imported from adjacent countries, were valued at £56½ million, almost half Malaya's total trade.

These changes in the country's economy were reflected in the composition of its population. The Malays were flourishing but immigrants dominated the new industries and the related commercial expansion. Among these the Chinese were by far the largest racial group. By 1921 they already amounted to 35 per cent of the population of Malaya. By 1941 they had reached 43 per cent and marginally outnumbered the indigenous Malays, 2.379 million against 2.278. Their circumstances extended over the whole range of prosperity, from the richest merchants and entrepreneurs to the poorest labourers.[28] Another wave of immigration followed the introduction of rubber planting, as large numbers of Indian labourers, mostly Tamils, were brought in to tap the trees. Following this initial surge their numbers settled as a proportion of the population, remaining at 14 per cent throughout the 20 years from 1921 to 1941.

This remarkable racial and cultural mix was the source of problems for the British administration, calling for different treatment in the settlements, the federated and the unfederated states. A legislative council, comprising the governor, 13 official and 13 unofficial members governed the Straits Settlements. The chambers of commerce nominated three of the unofficial members, and the governor nominated the other ten (five Europeans, three Chinese, one Indian and one Eurasian). The Singapore and Penang municipalities were, however, governed by commissioners with an Asian majority. In 1920 a select committee appointed by the council concluded that only Malays, Eurasians and Straits-born Chinese regarded Malaya as their native country and discounted the possibility of enfranchising a population of aliens. In the FMS the depression following the First World War led to charges of federal extravagance and in 1927 the rulers demonstrated their dissatisfaction with recent constitutional changes by withdrawing from the federal council. The British government reacted with another change of policy and, in 1932, a substantial measure of decentralization, restoring legislative powers to the state councils. In 1935 the Dindings reverted to Perak.

Meanwhile, the 1930s saw a growing political awareness among the immigrant peoples, particularly the Chinese. Reflecting developments in their home country the Kuomintang organizations engaged in 'anti-imperialist' propaganda and other more aggressive action. Even more militant was the Malayan Communist Party, which achieved some success in fomenting discontent among the Chinese labourers and organizing strikes. From the beginning of the Sino–Japanese War in 1937 it concentrated on Anti-Japanese action, but it was not until 1940 that it received instructions from Hong Kong to cease anti-British activities and to support the British war effort.

With its resources fully committed to the war in the West, Great Britain lacked the strength to defend Malaya against the Japanese attack in December 1941. Its totally inadequate air and sea forces were easily defeated and the conquest of the peninsula was completed in just ten weeks. The communists, who had played their part in the fighting on land, remained the only effective resistance and took to the jungle as the Malayan People's Anti-Japanese Army, supported by British agents and arms deliveries. It was to be three and a half years before the surrender of Japan brought the occupation to an end.

When the British returned to Malaya in September 1945 they found a people scarred by disillusion, oppression and privation. Clearly, the British had failed to protect the country. That the Japanese were not liberators soon became apparent. After the experience of a harsh military government, the effects of wartime shortages and the sufferings of those who fell victim to the conqueror's brutality, the restoration of a British administration came as a relief but was received with mixed feelings. The Chinese accused the Malays of collaboration, the Malays wanted no part of the MPAJA's dream of a communist state and the Indians were well aware of events in their homeland. There were serious shortages of rice and cloth, violence between Malays and Chinese and an urgent need to restore both the health service and the education system. Although the rubber plantations had survived and were soon back in production the rebuilding of tin dredges would take years. A temporary military administration struggled to cope with a host of such problems while the British government sought to impose its master plan to hasten progress towards a viable, united Malaya. The Malayan Union, which excluded Singapore, was conceived by a planning unit at the Colonial Office in 1943 and initiated on 1 April 1946.

It was opposed by the newly formed United Malays National Organization (UMNO) led by Dato Onn bin Jaafar, on whose advice the sultans boycotted the installation of Sir Edward Gent as governor. UMNO, boasting two million members, persuaded Malays not to serve on any council or committee. On 1 June 1946 Malcolm Macdonald, the governor-general, met the rulers at Kuala Lumpur and secured their agreement to a revised plan, a federation of nine states and two settlements. A committee of six Malays and five British officials worked out the details and on 1 February 1948 the Federation of Malaya was born. A British high commissioner presided over an executive and a legislative council. In each state there was a *mentri besar* appointed by the sultan and a British adviser.

Singapore remained a separate crown colony. Here a governor presided over a legislative council consisting of four ex-officio and five nominated official members, four nominated unofficial ones and nine elected members. The colony's first elections took place in March 1948 and the new council was inaugurated on 1 April.

Sadly, Malaya was now to be faced with a new crisis. A communist conference held in Calcutta in February 1948 resolved on a policy of armed struggle, and some 6000 to 8000 MPAJA, largely Chinese, vanished into the Malayan jungle with their leader Chin Peng. The murder of three British planters and two Chinese on 16 June set in motion the lengthy conflict officially dubbed the 'emergency'. The communist tactics were organized terrorism. They burned villages, attacked the rubber industry, destroying rubber stocks and slashing rubber trees, and they derailed trains and ambushed the security forces. Despite the deployment of some 30,000 special constables and an increasing commitment of troops the situation worsened. In May 1950 alone there were 534 'incidents'. Recalled from retirement, Lieutenant-General Sir Harold Briggs provided a positive plan of action, aimed at cutting off the guerrillas' supplies and support and protecting the villages against intimidation. It entailed the forcible removal of Chinese squatters into 'New Villages' where they were given land to cultivate. Following the assassination of High Commissioner Sir Henry Gurney in October 1951, his successor, General Sir Gerald Templer, proved a dynamic leader, whose sometimes draconian measures soon took effect. With better information and improved techniques the security forces were now winning the war.

Public support was the key to success. The people of Malaya were persuaded that the British offered a better future than the communists. Progress towards self-government was an essential part of that future and the process began during the emergency. In the federation Tungku Abdul Rahman, a son of the Sultan of Kedah and a former district officer, headed an alliance between UMNO and the Malayan Chinese Association. The secretary of state, Oliver Lyttelton, initially rejected his demand for an elected majority in the Legislative Council, but he won his point and at the election of 1955 his alliance took 51 of the 52 elected seats. As chief minister he called for independence by 31 August 1957. On that date British rule in the federation came to an end.[29]

Singapore followed close behind. By 1955 there was an elected majority in the Legislative Council and David Marshall, the leader of the Labour Front, became chief minister with the backing of UMNO/MCA. He failed to agree terms for independence and resigned in 1957. His successor Lim Yew Hock negotiated successfully, but was ousted in the election of May 1959, a triumph for Lee Kuan Yew, whose People's Action Party won 43 of the 51 seats on the council. At midnight on 2/3 June 1959 the colony achieved virtual independence.[30]

The federation became an elective monarchy. The rulers were to choose one of their number to be Yang di-Pertuan Agong for a five-year term. A bicameral legislature was composed of a senate, whose 38 members were to hold their seats for six years, half retiring every three years (22 elected by the 11 states and settlements and 16 by the Agong), and a house of representatives numbering 100 elected from single member constituencies. In Singapore the head of state was the Yang di-Pertuan Negara. A council of ministers was responsible to an elected legislature with 51 members. The vexed question of security became the responsibility of an internal security council on which the chief minister and two of his fellow ministers were joined by the British High Commissioner, two British representatives and a Malayan cabinet minister. Apart from a brief unification between 1963 and 1965 Malaysia and Singapore have remained separate states. They have both prospered greatly.

Although a number of British civil servants continued to serve in the two independent territories, some for a number of years, their presence was the epilogue to a long story. The constant expansion of British responsibilities in Malaya was inevitably matched by a growing administrative structure and the employment of increasing numbers of personnel. The majority of staff was always drawn from a local population that was well able to furnish recruits of the calibre required for the majority of functions. The more senior appointments, and particularly those that called for technical qualifications, were for many years reserved for Europeans. Initially, these officers were nominated by directors of the East India Company and engaged in covenanted service. In 1806 a training programme was introduced at the company's school at Haileybury.

At a council held at Fort Cornwallis on 17 March 1829 Governor Fullerton wrote a minute in which he set up the establishment. In addition to a governor, secretary and head assistant to head the unified administration each settlement would be served by a resident, a deputy or head assistant and one assistant. With three supernumeraries to cover for furloughs this made a total of 15 officers. They supervised a large locally recruited work force. In 1863 Sir Hercules Robinson reported that the Settlements' administration now employed 17 officers and 306 clerical staff.

Following the transfer of the Settlements from the Company to the Colonial Office a new service was established and the first cadets were appointed in 1867. There were no specialized divisions and their duties covered all aspects of government. The formation of the Federated Malay States in 1896 resulted in a theoretically unified service for such expatriate officers. Cadetships were now awarded on the results of competitive examinations and the rate of recruitment rose sharply. In the years 1867 to 1895 the average annual intake was four. By 1904 there were 180 such officers in the Settlements and the Federated Malay States. By 1914 there were 220.

The service remained an elite at the head of the government, providing the senior staff in the administrative and financial divisions. In 1920 it was recognized as such and officially dubbed 'The Malayan Civil Service'. It soon became the practice for its members to place the initials 'MCS' after their names in the manner of an honour or decoration. This no doubt justifiable pride in their achievements and reputation inevitably gave rise to some gentle mockery and the nickname 'the heaven born'.

In practice, a great part of the business of government was carried out by an increasing number of specialized departments whose officers made no claim to celestial origins. The role of such departments extended well beyond the areas of administration then regarded as the proper function of a civil service in most Western countries. The lack of modern private provision of many vital services could only be met by setting up suitable government departments. Thus, long before the inception of the National Health Service in the United Kingdom, the people of Malaya enjoyed the benefit of a medical and health department providing such facilities as hospitals, clinics and travelling dispensaries, paid for from general taxation and staffed at all levels, including consultants, doctors and nurses, by government employees on fixed salary scales. Other departments were concerned with such matters as education, forestry, public works, drainage and irrigation, transport and telecommunications.

The cost of such an extensive administration was met largely from local revenues in a variety of different forms. Central to these was the yield from duties and other imposts on the import, export or manufacture of various products. The collection of these, at first haphazard and inadequately supervised, was gradually brought under the control of a service that was to perform a number of different roles before finally evolving into the two conventional customs and excise departments in Singapore and the Federation of Malaya.[31] The story of their foundation and development is an important element in the history of British Malaya.

Part Two:
The Service

2. Preventive staff (Province Wellesley 1940).

2

A difficult birth

Following his acquisition of Penang, Francis Light faced the problem of financing the little settlement. Initially, its profits proved very disappointing to the directors of the East India Company and it was to be some time before its cost was matched by local revenue. The development of agricultural land proceeded slowly and a land tax contributed little to the accounts. In 1788 Light toyed with the idea of a 6 per cent duty on imported China goods and in 1796 his successor as superintendent, Major MacDonald, displayed an unworldly faith in human nature when he invited a committee of local merchants to discuss with him how revenue should be derived from an imposition on their trade. Thereafter, import duties were gradually abandoned and Penang became, like Singapore, a free port.[1] In both settlements the growing commercial communities were to display a strong antipathy to the imposition of import duties and to the administrative apparatus for their collection. For the present the main source of revenue was to be from 'farming'.[2]

The practice of farming out the collection of revenues to private persons or syndicates has a long history. In Malaya it was in use throughout the nineteenth century. Lacking the resources to operate a tax-collecting organization of its own the administration invited tenders for the right to do so. The contracts for this early example of privatization were usually for three years, during which the government received a fixed sum and the farmer extracted as much as he could from the taxpayers.[3] The farmers were most commonly Chinese. Rivalry was intense and occasionally led to violence.

Farming was briefly applied to the collection of import duties. Following the acquisition of Province Wellesley a duty of 2 per cent was imposed on imports of tin, pepper and betel nuts to Penang and the contract awarded at an auction to Scott & Company, the business of James Scott, second cousin of Sir Walter

Scott and a close associate of Francis Light. The experiment was abandoned after one year. Reluctantly, the Court of Directors came to accept that their most reliable source of revenue was to be found in the farming of alcohol, gambling and opium. In 1800/1 the expenditure of Penang was 184,469 Spanish dollars. Its revenue was still only 53,155 Spanish dollars and of that the three monopolies provided 39,750 Spanish dollars.

Although there were some qualms about this exploitation of human weakness the strongest criticism was directed at the gambling farm.[4] In the first decade of the nineteenth century the issue was raised by a grand jury in Penang and the farm was abolished. From then on gambling was illegal in the settlement.

The foundation of Singapore[5] in 1819 and its establishment as a free port led to another conflict. Sir Stamford Raffles was strongly opposed to the exploitation of vice. When he returned to the colony from Bencoolen before sailing home in 1823, he took the opportunity to override the policy of the resident, Colonel Farquhar, who had instituted farms for liquor, gambling and opium. Indeed, in a flurry of reforms, Raffles abolished slavery and cock fighting and prohibited gambling. Some of the lost revenue was to be replaced by the introduction of licences for pawnbroking and the sale of pork and gunpowder. He lost the battle over opium. It was to remain a primary source of revenue throughout British Malaya for many years as described in Chapters 8 and 9. Although the second resident, John Crawfurd,[6] reinstated the gambling farm in a modified form it did not long survive his departure in 1826. Gaming was henceforth prohibited except for a period of 15 days at Chinese New Year, a concession apparently based on the mistaken belief that it formed a part of Chinese religion. Otherwise, despite occasional attempts to revive it, legalized gambling played no further part in the history of the Straits Settlements.

Malacca, which passed to the East India Company in 1824, was the earliest European colony in Malaya. The previous Dutch administration had followed its own policies in the matter of taxation.[7] Apart from the tithes and tributes levied on local producers, a practice that was to involve their British successors in a foolish war as recorded above, the Dutch also imposed a variety of import duties, which they manipulated to protect their monopoly. In 1699 the duty on European imports was raised to 20 per cent. When this failed to produce the intended reduction in such imports they were, for a while, prohibited. Cloth was subject to import duty but foodstuffs including rice, buffaloes and slaves were exempt if first offered to the company. The competition of Penang was the deathblow to the Dutch monopoly system. Nevertheless, it cannot have been easy for the East India Company's servants to bring Malacca into line with the other two settlements.

Throughout the nineteenth century the commercial communities in Penang and Singapore jealously protected the free port status of the settlements. They rightly feared that the distant court of the company might be tempted to boost its profits by taxing the flourishing ports on the Malacca Straits. In 1836 the merchants of Singapore[8] got wind of such a proposal and wrote to the governor in Penang, Kenneth Murchison, asking for information. In reply, he confirmed that the supreme government had indeed instructed him to prepare legislation to introduce duties on sea exports and imports in all three settlements, ostensibly to meet the expenses of protection against piracy. Following a hastily convened public meeting the merchants dispatched a petition to the governor reminding him that 'the commercial importance of Singapore is entirely owing to its having been continued a Free Port'. They won the argument but cautiously provided for future conflict by the foundation of the Singapore Chamber of Commerce the following year.

In February 1853 the leading English language newspaper, the *Straits Times*,[9] rallied to the defence of Singapore against another challenge to its free port status. An editorial declared

> If the Government of India had succeeded in its endeavours Pinang [*sic*], Singapore and Malacca would long since have ceased to be Free Ports. Scarce a month passes but some new dodge is devised to bring the Straits under the bane of Excise, Customs or other exactions but the amended draft of Act VI of 1852 is one of the most barefaced attempts to injure the freedom of the Straits ports.

Shortly afterwards a public meeting held in Singapore passed a resolution 'that the imposition of tonnage or port dues on shipping is an unwarrantable attack on the freedom of this port, which this meeting views with apprehension and regret as being in direct violation of the principles upon which this Settlement was established'.

Once again the force of local opposition was sufficient to stave off the threat. Four years later the government in India had far more pressing problems to occupy its time.[10] They dealt a severe blow to the confidence of the British government and raised the spectre of similar violence in the company's other possessions. A trade dispute with China was shortly to lead to the second opium war of 1856–60. It became a priority to provide for the defence of Singapore and in 1858 Colonel Collyer of the Madras Engineers arrived there to begin the construction of fortifications. Heavy guns were installed, a naval coaling station was provided and the garrison enlarged. Not surprisingly, the local community began to wonder who would be called on to foot the bill for such heavy military expenditure. In 1862 the new governor Colonel Cavenagh made representations to Bengal on their behalf.[11] He suggested that they might not object to a poll tax. In response, the government of India sent him the draft of a bill to levy port dues. Supported by the chamber of commerce, Cavenagh fought back. The dispute became absorbed into the larger debate on the future of the settlements, resolved finally in 1867 when they were transferred to the crown. Freed at last from the link with India they were to remain free ports. Within eight years, however, they were to be drawn into the affairs of the neighbouring Malay states.

The revenue of the Malay rulers was collected in a variety of ways.[12] During the first millennium they adopted the Indian system of royal trading. They profited from the traffic in such merchandise as gold, silks, ivory and sandalwood, sending their merchant ships on lengthy voyages. Many built large fortunes by this practice. It left no scope for a merchant class and proved all too vulnerable to the competition of the Portuguese and Dutch monopolists. The sultans were forced to turn to other methods. In 1818 the Sultan of Kedah, soon to be deprived of his throne, was in dispute with Penang over the activities of a Straits-born Chinese to whom he had given a five-year contract to farm the revenue from a variety of imports, including opium, cloth and tin. Four years later Selangor helped Perak to eject the Siamese conquerors in return for half the duty collected on her tin. In Kelantan in the early twentieth century the *raja* and his family had a monopoly mint producing a tin coinage. The new British administrators had plenty of strange practices to unravel as they sought to put the state finances on a sound and equitable basis.

In Perak in the 1870s it was the growing Chinese community that played the major part in financing the state.[13] Its members mined the tin and farmed the taxes. After the war that followed the assassination of Birch the local farms were the subject of a power struggle between rival Chinese societies, the Hai San, which enjoyed a virtual monopoly in Larut, the Perak valley and the Kinta valley, and the Ghee Hin, which eventually managed to secure the gambling and pawnbroking farms. Victor Purcell describes the situation: 'Terrorism, blackmail and oppression were the weapons of the gangsters controlling the Triad and Tabut (Malay secret societies). The capitalist farmers who controlled the system mostly lived in Penang. The administration and the police were greatly handicapped in dealing with the abuse since they were only very slowly penetrating the veil of secrecy behind which the societies worked.' In an attempt to rationalize the practice of revenue collection Hugh Low[14] introduced duties on tin, tobacco and spirits, and monopolies for opium, pawnbroking and gambling houses. In the first year these raised a total of S$ 360,000. His reforms were not universally popular. When, in 1879, he visited Larut to allocate tax farms in that area a major riot broke out and his house was surrounded by a mob of about 1500 Chinese coolies demanding an end to all but the duty on tin. Sepoys had to be dispatched to his aid and they opened fire on the protestors, a number of whom were killed.

As the British extended their influence to other states they assumed responsibility for an increasing variety of farms. There were farms for such products as atap, firewood, timber and rattan. In Perak there was even a farm for river turtle eggs. The principal sources of revenue, however, were now becoming well established. The government collected the export duty on tin. The main farms were those controlling the sale of chandu in the coast districts and the collection of import duty on opium in the tin mining areas, the manufacture of spirits and the collection of duties on imported liquors, and the rights to run pawnshops and public gambling houses. Between 1890 and 1894 in the four states soon to be joined in federation, the duty on tin accounted for 33.8 per cent of revenue and the farms for 33 per cent.

The Revenue Farms Enactment,[15] which was revised from time to time, governed the farming system in the Federated Malay States. Farms were granted for a three-year term against tenders, but not necessarily to the highest bidder. Other considerations had to be weighed in choosing the farmer. The contract laid down the monthly rental, defined the farmer's rights and prescribed the rules he must observe. He was required to deposit a substantial security covering approximately three months rental, usually in the form of property deeds. Although the tenders often stemmed from a syndicate, the responsibility for the farm was always imposed upon a single person who signed the contract. There was some subletting, particularly in relation to the 'general farm' under which it was the practice to combine liquor, gambling and pawnbroking. Thus, the farmer had the right to run his own gambling houses or to issue permits to others to do so. These licensees were usually professional gamblers. The main farmer remained responsible for their activities. He was required to report any breaches of the rules and was entitled to the proceeds of the fines imposed on convicted offenders. In practice, however, he might prefer to deal with such problems by extortion. Farmers were often associates of powerful headmen with secret society connections.

The farming system was obviously open to criticism, but it offered many advantages. The administration in the late nineteenth century lacked the resources for more conventional methods of tax collection. The Chinese were a shifting population consisting mainly of temporary immigrants and this was the most effective way to tax them. Moreover, farming was a low cost revenue producer. As the British resident[16] in Perak pointed out in 1894, the current farm revenue of S$ 500,000 a year was equivalent to the yield on an investment of S$ 10,000,000 at 5 per cent. It was also believed that the system attracted Chinese labour to Malaya where it was needed to develop the tin industry. At the time this was still very labour intensive. More workers helped the farmer, who was usually a tin miner, and also contributed to government revenue and general prosperity. In his book *British Malaya*, Sir Frank Swettenham writes 'It was Chinese energy and industry which supplied the funds to begin construction of roads and other public wants, and to pay for all other costs of administration. They were, and still are, the pioneers of mining.' An example of such cooperation occurred in 1897 when the government concluded a contract with a prominent Chinese entrepreneur, Loke Yew,[17] under which he undertook to bear the cost of building a road into the district of Bentong in Pahang to open it up for mining. He was granted a five-year farm monopoly there at a rental of only S$ 500 a year, far more than its immediate value, but likely to become increasingly profitable as the new area was developed.

Tin prices were very volatile and miners could not guarantee a profit every year. The farms offered them a steady income to tide them over hard times. Most tin mines practised 'trucking' and paid their workers in kind through their monopolies.[18] Although it was sometimes argued that the gambling farms were the best way to restrict the vice, in practice it seems likely that the mine owners encouraged it. The general farm was a linked system. A worker might squander his wages at the gaming table, borrow cash from the pawnshop and spend it on liquor. The mine owner profited at each stage. His trucking reduced his cash flow and indebtedness kept his work force in place. The government was also doing well. The rental for the general farm in Selangor was S$ 100,000 in 1886, S$ 250,000 in 1897 and S$ 1,440,000 in 1902. In 1841 the Singapore opium farm was let for S$ 6250 a month. The liquor farm was priced at S$ 3750 a month. In 1903 the combined farms cost the farmer a rental of S$ 470,000 a month.

Two factors contributed towards bringing farming to an end. On one hand there was a growing moral pressure on government to abandon a system that seemed, on balance, to foster vice. Many officials found the practice distasteful and the local Chinese people were voicing their disapproval. In 1905 leaders of the Chinese community in the Federated Malay States submitted a petition asking for gambling farms to be wound up.[19] This was received sympathetically by the under-secretary of state for the colonies, Mr Winston Churchill, who agreed that they should be phased out. In 1908 a pan-Malayan anti-opium conference urged that steps be taken to suppress the use of the drug. As described in Chapter 8 there was growing international criticism of the traffic in opium.

It was also becoming apparent that the system was no longer necessary or helpful to the economic development of the country. The early twentieth century brought hard times for the Chinese tin miners. By 1907/8 many mines were closing. The future of the industry lay with more mechanized methods of extraction, calling for a capital investment for which at this time the mine owners did not have the resources. European joint stock companies moved into Malaya to modernize the mines. At the same time the rapid expansion of rubber plantations was changing the basis of Malaya's wealth. The farmers were no longer able to honour their contracts and the government was forced to renegotiate rentals. In Selangor the general farmer defaulted.

In the FMS there had already been some moves away from the use of farms.[20] Perak began collecting opium import duty directly as early as 1895. Selangor followed suit in 1900 and Negri Sembilan in 1901. In 1908 Selangor separated the pawnbroking farm and in 1910 switched to a licensing system. Although the licensees still had to tender they no longer enjoyed a monopoly. In 1911 the gambling farm was similarly reformed. By 1913 gambling had been made illegal. Thus, although the decision to bring the opium trade under stricter control was undoubtedly the principal reason for winding up the farm system it is also clear that it had outlived its usefulness in all its applications.

In both the settlements and the federated states steps were now taken to set up government departments to replace the farmers as collectors of revenue. In the Straits Settlements there were only two farms, for opium and spirits. It had long been the practice to lease both to the same syndicate in each of the settlements. This arrangement simplified the administration and reduced the costs of the preventive service with which the farmer protected his monopoly. The current contracts were all due to expire on 31 December 1909. So too were those in the mainland states. In its report to the governor, Sir John Anderson, in June 1908 the Straits Settlements and Federated States Opium Commission[21] recommended that they should not be renewed. The commission was clearly aware of the sensitivity of the commercial communities of Penang and Singapore to any suggestion that might threaten the treasured free port status. It expressed the opinion that its proposals

> would not involve any greater restriction or check upon the general trade of the Straits Settlements and Federated Malay States than at present exists. The ports of the Colony of the Straits Settlements are free and the unanimous opinion is that on their freedom depends the prosperity of the Colony. In practice the Commissioners have no desire to advocate the establishment of Customs Houses and cannot accept the view that the existence of a preventive service conducted by Government would of necessity imply the introduction of Customs Houses.

In recommending the formation of the new services they observed:

> It has been contended that the personnel of the Government preventive service would have to be drawn mainly from the same sources and would consist of much the same material as the existent Farm preventive service and that the abuses common to that service would still obtain but there would be this important difference that, if the Commissioners' recommendations be adopted, the Government would

> employ in the Department, to which the control and management of chandu is assigned, a body of European officers, of undoubted integrity, whose sole duty it would be to closely supervise and control the doings of the subordinate staff of the preventive service with a view to checking the abuses which are admittedly existent in the case of the present Farm service.

Although the commission's primary concern was to tackle the evil of drug addiction it had to consider also the loss of revenue its recommendations might entail. The colony was committed to a 'vast cost' of 'extraordinary public works' and the ongoing expense of 'providing for the education of the children, in the upkeep of hospitals [and] in the preservation of the public peace'. Its report briefly reviews alternative forms of taxation. It dismisses the idea of a poll tax as unpopular with the Chinese and likely to discourage immigration to the extent that it would fail to raise the level of revenue required to replace the opium farm. Income tax it suspected would be far too easily evaded. A tax on savings returned to China by immigrants was also rejected as impracticable. Indeed, it was the difficulty of finding a suitable substitute for the revenue derived from opium that was a major factor in the decision against a prohibition of the drug and to recommend instead a government monopoly.

In the Settlements the major task of the new department was to set up an undertaking to import, process and distribute opium. In essence this was a commercial enterprise with monopoly rights protected by a preventive service. In free ports the conventional role of duty collection was of secondary importance. A proposal to establish it as part of the Chinese Protectorate was eventually discarded in favour of an independent department with a name that reflected its priorities and that was clearly calculated to calm the fears of the free trade lobby. This was the 'Government Monopolies Department'.[22] Mr F. M. Baddeley was placed in overall charge and in November 1909 a Mr J. A. Howard began the task of setting up a preventive service to undertake the enforcement of the laws in relation to illegal importation and exportation of dutiable goods, the illicit distillation of liquor and the infringement of the opium monopoly. Legal powers were provided by new legislation, the 1909 Chandu Revenue Ordinance to govern the monopoly and the 1909 Liquors Revenue Ordinance, which imposed duties on spirits and beer.[23] A temporary departmental headquarters was opened in the office of Guthrie & Co. Ltd in Singapore. Legal landing places were designated and in Singapore five examination sheds were acquired.

Staff members were recruited locally. They included Chinese, Malays, Indians, Eurasians and the small number of Europeans required for the senior appointments. The total reported by the end of 1910 was 860 – 520 in Singapore, 282 in Penang and 58 in Malacca. These figures clearly include all employees in the revenue collection branch, the preventive service and the chandu monopoly. The establishment for the preventive service (reproduced in Appendix II) was a maximum of 414. Actual strength was 334 officers and men, organized in divisions, sections and watches. In Penang and Singapore there were separate shore and harbour divisions. European officers, including a Sergeant Murcock in Penang and a Mr Thomazos in Malacca, whose salary was designated in local currency rather than sterling, led the divisions. In Singapore there were three motor launches, *Revenue*, *Excise* and *Scout*. The last was very slow and was replaced in 1911 by *Ferret*. In Penang the service had to depend on a hired vessel.

There was plenty of work for the new service. In 1910 the shipping entered and cleared through the ports of the Straits Settlements amounted to 23,429,495 tons. Imports were valued at £40,343,000 and exports at £35,852,000. The duty collected on liquors was over 1.4 million Straits dollars. The department also supervised over 1800 licensed premises, including opium saloons, liquor shops, distilleries, warehouses, toddy shops, billiard rooms and chemists!

The situation in the Federated Malay States was more complex and the process of reform correspondingly slower. Mainland Malaya was a producer of raw materials and these had long provided a source of revenue. As late as 1908, in Perak, Selangor and Negri Sembilan, there were export duties on dried fish, hides, horns, tin, tin ore and wolfram. In Pahang only tin and tin ore were dutiable. The first three states also levied import duty on opium. The Revenue Farms Enactment No. 11 of 1904 imposed duties on liquor and introduced licensing for the manufacture of chandu and liquor. Farmers were granted exclusive rights for various areas on fixed monthly rentals.

There was no federal customs department. Treasurers at Telok Anson, Taiping and Kuala Lumpur were responsible for revenue collection. At small ports and frontier posts there were customs clerks who reported to the local district officers. In Selangor, the

3. Johore: Customs launch *Rusa* at speed.

protector of Chinese collected the duty on opium. On 1 January 1907 an inspector of trade and customs was appointed to prepare a uniform law. His work was the basis of the Customs Regulation Enactment 1907, which came into force the following 1 January. The inspector became the Commissioner of Trade and Customs but his role was only advisory. Uniform tariffs were now imposed throughout the FMS and price lists were issued for tin and other dutiable commodities. Rules were promulgated designating landing places and collection stations, their opening hours and the overtime rates chargeable for clearance at other times. In April 1908 interstate barriers were abolished and export duties were thereafter collected on removal from the FMS. The opium and liquor farms were wound up in Perak in 1909, in Selangor and Negri Sembilan in 1910 and in Pahang in 1911.

As in the Straits Settlements the FMS had to recruit local staff to serve in the new 'trade and customs' service. A European officer supervised each district. A separate department was set up to administer the chandu monopoly. Two chandu superintendents were appointed, one in Perak and the other to cover the rest of the country. Assistant superintendents looked after the monopoly in each customs district.

In 1910 the rubber industry was growing rapidly[24] and contributed to a great increase in the trade of the Federated Malay States. Total exports that year were worth 102,294,199 Straits dollars, against imports of S$ 50,094,876. Customs revenue was S$ 10,581,354 out of a total of S$ 26,553,018. Some 4500 ships were cleared through the ports of the FMS, representing a total tonnage of 1,750,000.

Thus, by 1910 in both parts of British Malaya there were operational departments, which, however designated, were functioning at least in part as customs services. They were largely locally recruited and remained under the direct supervision of an MCS officer. It would be many years before their role was fully recognized and accepted.

3
Growing up

The new services established in the Straits Settlements and the Federated Malay States were quite separate. It is perhaps significant, however, that Mr W. J. P. Hume, who in 1912 took up the appointment of commissioner in the FMS, was paid on a scale of £1050 to £1200 per annum. In the Straits Settlements Mr G. M. Baddeley was designated 'officer in charge' and paid on the scale £800 to £1000 per annum.[1]

It was the preventive service of the Monopolies Department that was expanding in these early years.[2] The initial establishment is shown in Appendix II. By 1913 its strength had increased to 378 officers and men. In Singapore the European supervisors now numbered seven. In April 1914, however, the preventive service acquired a new head in the person of Chief Detective Inspector W. A. Taylor of the Singapore police. A former officer of the Metropolitan Police, he conducted a thorough reform in the course of which 48 revenue officers were dismissed and a further 37 resigned. The staff now numbered 353. Despite the introduction of import duties on tobacco products in 1916, the preventive service continued to shrink and by 1923 its strength was down to 292, made up of 13 Europeans, 8 assistant supervisors and 271 revenue officers. An increase in the smuggling of opium in Singapore prompted the recruitment of two additional Europeans in 1925 and the doubling of the revenue officer staff in the harbour division. Two new 16 m.p.h. launches were added to the fleet.

As described in Chapter 9, major changes in the organization and staffing of the department accompanied the reform of the opium monopoly in 1928. Perhaps the most significant reform was the introduction of a formal system of recruitment of European officers. From now on these would be appointed by the secretary of state for the colonies and confirmed as permanent officers after completion of a period of probationary service and the passage of examinations in Malay, law and general orders. Mr J. J. Warren, an Assistant Commissioner of police, took charge of the preventive service. Seven locally recruited Europeans were dismissed or resigned. A number of Asian officers were also removed but numbers overall were increased. By 1929 there were 15 European officers, 16 assistant supervisors and 384 revenue officers (including eight in Labuan).

The trade and customs service in the FMS was coping with rather different problems. With the extension of the British Adviser system to the other states of Malaya arrangements were required to manage the passage and taxation of goods across a number of local frontiers. Meanwhile, the federal tariffs were gradually expanding.[3] In 1914 import duties were applied to malt liquors and petroleum and in 1915 to tobacco, including cigars and cigarettes. From then on until 1918 the department collected a range of temporary wartime duties on such imports as matches, motorcars, bicycles and tyres. In 1919 it became responsible for the registration of imports and exports.

In 1920 a Federal Customs Enactment was passed. The Commissioner was now formally in charge of the department and in the following year Deputy Commissioners were allocated to take charge of customs, excise and chandu. As in the Straits Settlements, in the aftermath of the First World War the department was able to recruit a number of ex-service officers and European police inspectors from the Singapore police, whose experience was particularly valuable in the preventive work. One notable recruit in this period was Major Stamford Raffles,[4] a descendant of the founder of Singapore.

In 1922 a rubber restriction system[5] was introduced and its enforcement was added to the responsibilities of trade and customs.[6] Certain preventive officers were given powers to inspect the books of rubber dealers. In attempts to evade the new restrictions on exports there was large-scale smuggling of rubber to the Dutch East Indies, and the department had to muster fresh forces to tackle the illegal traffic. A preventive branch was established with a superintendent in each federal state. Extra staff was recruited, including European launch commanders to conduct sea patrols. In the same year the government took over the licensed toddy shops in Kuala Lumpur and officers were appointed to supervise them.

The year 1923 saw Trade and Customs collect a total of S$ 35,031,168, a record amount. A new customs enactment consolidated and tightened up the law under which the officers were performing their duties. By 1924 it was thought necessary to form a separate excise branch to collect revenue on locally manufactured liquors. Its duties expanded in 1927 when the local production of matches began and an excise duty was imposed. As in the Straits Settlements the reform of the opium monopoly brought changes in the department. Soon the first probationers appointed by the secretary of state began to arrive in the FMS.

In Appendix III I reproduce the authorized establishment of senior officers in the FMS in 1928. All salaries were now designated in local currency. The Commissioner, whose responsibilities also covered the Straits Settlements, was an officer of the Malayan Civil Service. Not until after the Second World War was the head of department to be drawn from its own ranks. Three Deputy Commissioners commanded the three divisions in the FMS – customs, excise and chandu. A chief superintendent led the preventive branch. Then 47 Superintendents and Assistant Superintendents and an unspecified number of probationers completed the structure.

Malaya was hard hit by the worldwide economic recession[7] that followed the stock market collapse of 1929. During the boom years of the immediate postwar period the administrative structure of government had greatly expanded and measures were now taken to reduce costs. In the FMS expenditure was reduced from S$ 109 million in 1928 to S$ 47 million in 1934. In the Straits Settlements the government on 28 September 1931 presented to the Legislative Council a proposal for sharp increases in import duties, effective the same day. These added 35 cents on a gallon of petrol, from 70 cents to S$ 1.60 per pound of tobacco products and between S$ 1.20 and S$ 14 on a gallon of intoxicating liquor. Despite the opposition of all seven unofficial members of the council, the official majority voted through the measure.

The two departments were able to avoid redundancies but all staff had to accept a salary cut of 10 per cent. Nevertheless, the proposals for recruitment of expatriate officers went ahead as planned. Among the first probationers to arrive under the new arrangements was John Lewis[8] who took up his duties in Perak. It was a state with several frontiers, as he explains.

> Parit Buntar and Gemas as well as Tampin were all frontier stations. At Parit Buntar the Malayan Railway and the main road crossed from the FMS northwards into Province Wellesley in the Straits Settlements, which had a different Customs tariff. At Gemas the railway and road crossed southwards into the State of Johore which also had a

different tariff. A branch line extended from Gemas through the jungle to Kelantan. Out Door Officers (local uniformed staff) manned the boundary gates day and night and boarded the trains to collect duty on goods imported by passengers.

Tampin was a border station between Negri Sembilan and Malacca, which again had different tariffs. There was a customs gate on the border, which happened to be in the middle of the town, with most of the shops on the Malacca side. There were another two gates on a road between Tampin and Gemas which dipped in and out of Malacca and yet another at the village of Kendong to cover a minor road which crossed the border. The district to be covered by the Tampin office was about 300 square miles. To deal with the uneconomic gate duties there was a staff of thirty men, including about four plain-clothes preventive officers.

At one gate in the jungle the officers were convinced that their bungalow was haunted by a ghost who walked through their quarters to collect water from a nearby stream. The aborigines who lived in the neighbouring jungle had fixed a wooden musical instrument on top of one of the trees so that when the wind blew it produced haunting music.

The situation described in Perak was typical of the confused pattern of frontiers between the settlements, the federated states and the five still unfederated states, many running through dense jungle, mangrove or paddy fields. Complete control of movement across these borders was clearly impossible and uneconomic. There was no evidence that any large-scale smuggling took place. Nevertheless, there was clearly an argument for some rationalization.

Despite the decentralization policy[9] introduced by Sir Laurence Guillemard in 1925 the customs service in the FMS remained a federal department. Indeed, the Commissioner of Customs and Excise was an official member of the federal council. When Sir Cecil Clementi took over in 1930, however, he favoured a pan-Malayan customs union, which would have included the unfederated states. Both the Straits Settlements and the unfederated states objected strongly to this idea, although for somewhat different reasons. Nevertheless, he was not alone in regarding as absurd a situation in which six separate customs tariffs and administrations were to be found in a territory of 50,900 square miles with a population of 4,345,000. In 1932, therefore, he convened a customs duties committee[10] of the Straits Settlements with a brief to identify new sources of revenue for the settlements and to consider a unified customs system for the whole of Malaya. The Honourable G. E. Cator MCS, Superintendent of Government Monopolies, chaired the committee.

Problems entailed in a customs union were considered to be insuperable. The excise and chandu revenues would still have to be collected on a local basis. Furthermore, it would remain necessary to apportion other revenues between the administrations. Little benefit could be seen in such a union. Interstate trade was very limited and, unlike the Settlements, mainland Malaya had no entrepôt traffic. It was discovered that local steamers carried most goods and that it was rare for road vehicles to pass through more than one customs barrier.

A union would bring together three very different economies. The Settlements were primarily interested in foreign trade. The federated states and Johore were producers of raw materials for export. The other unfederated states were producing for local consumption. Above all, the committee stressed the importance of free movement to the entrepôt trade of the settlement ports. It was noted that between 1926 and 1930 the Settlements' trade with other countries exceeded that with the FMS by some S$ 800 million. Having observed that there was no apparent solution to the problem of export duties, and no identity of economic interest between the FMS and the Settlements, the committee reported its view that a union would not be of benefit to the Straits Settlements.

In view of its role as the manufacturer and distributor of chandu it was suggested that the Monopolies Department might undertake to collect the chandu duty for all states. Frontier checks between states could be abandoned. It was also suggested that Malacca, Province Wellesley and the Dindings might be incorporated into the FMS. This idea was not pursued although the Dindings did revert to Perak in 1935. The proposal for a customs union was dropped.

In Singapore the opportunity was taken to introduce legislation to provide for future changes in the customs tariff. It was clearly desirable that such measures should be imposed without prior warning and the consequent opportunity to anticipate duty increases. A Public Revenue Protection Ordinance[11] gave the governor power to bring in new duties provided the amendments were tabled before the Legislative Council within two weeks. The unofficial members approved this on receiving an assurance that it would not be used to initiate a customs union.

It was in February 1932 that the secretary of state directed the Governor/High Commissioner to introduce the system of imperial preference[12] under which reduced rates of import duty were to be applied to goods originating within the British Empire. Although the FMS quickly complied there was some reluctance in the Settlements, but the unofficial members were not united and the necessary measure was passed. By the end of the year, when the Ottawa agreements took full effect, Johore, Kedah, Kelantan and Trengganu had all introduced appropriate new tariffs. Embarrassingly for Singapore, the preferential rates applied only to direct imports into the FMS.

Despite the maintenance of free port status, the responsibilities of the Monopolies Department were constantly expanding. Since 1916 it had collected import duties on tobacco products. In May 1932 the system of imperial preference was applied to both liquor and tobacco. In July the first local licensed brewery[13] was opened in Singapore. A second began operations the following year. In June 1934 the Rubber Regulation Ordinance[14] came into force and the department assumed responsibility for the control of exports and the collection of cess. Special examination stations and landing places were designated.

Another statute, which took effect that month, was the Importation of Textiles (Quotas) Ordinance (1934).[15] Once again this was an imposition by the home government. On 7 May the president of the Board of Trade invited the governments of colonies and protectorates to regulate by quota the importation of cotton and artificial silk piece goods of foreign origin. Local representatives of Lancashire cotton mills were naturally in favour, but the older trading houses feared the effect on their local trade. They asked for an exemption for Singapore. Local Chinese merchants handled a volume of small re-exports, currently subject only to registration for statistical purposes. Delayed clearance procedures might drive them elsewhere. Once again the seven unofficial members voted against the ordinance and once again it was passed on the votes of the official members. The federated and unfederated states, as well as Sarawak, had all joined the system by July, applying quotas based on the volume of trade in the years 1927 to 1931. In the Settlements the department took over management of public re-export depots and the licensing and control of licensed re-export depots for the storage of regulated textiles. By the end of the year there were two public depots in Singapore and Penang and seven licensed depots in Singapore with a number of harbour godowns nominated for transhipments. Singapore handled the bulk of the trade. In the second half of 1934 the depots there received 38,490,241 yards and delivered 31,404,881 yards of cloth. The equivalent figures in Penang were 1,828,527 and 1,606,453½ yards. As recorded in Chapter 13, the local traders demonstrated great ingenuity in evading the restrictions. In July 1934 the department inherited from the treasury the collection of duties on petroleum products.[16]

From 8 April 1932 the same head of the department and a common senior staff were employed in both the FMS and the Settlements. In April 1935 the Monopolies Department was renamed the Excise Department and in 1938 it finally became the Department of Customs and Excise. Meanwhile, the titles of the senior officers had also been changed. The commissioner became the comptroller; a superintendent was now a senior customs officer and an assistant superintendent a customs officer. These changes, which also applied in the FMS, were much resented by the senior staff of the departments who felt that the new titles did not reflect the responsibilities of their appointments.[17]

During the early 1930s a number of steps were taken to improve the efficiency and conditions of service of local officers. A book of *Working Instructions*[18] was issued to all ranks in 1932 and a museum was set up for training purposes. The first staff quarters, 140 flats, were constructed in Singapore. Others were added the following year. In 1936 the department was able to report that 75 per cent of the revenue officers in Singapore, and a majority in Penang, subscribed to the departmental Cooperative Thrift & Loan Society. All the revenue officers, launch crews and drivers in Singapore were now provided with quarters.[19] The service was finding it easier to attract local recruits and the advertisement of vacancies for revenue officers that year attracted 3000 applicants.

There were now 11 examination stations in Singapore, nine in Penang and Province Wellesley and five in Malacca. Officers made regular visits to aerodromes to inspect baggage. Under the General Passport Regulations they were now empowered to inspect passports. Although the main business of the department was to collect the revenue on legal importations, considerable effort was devoted to the prevention of evasion and the Singapore wharves were under constant surveillance. In the course of checking traffic through the harbour gates in 1936, officers searched 251,235 motor vehicles and 45,886 rickshaws. They examined 4,110,556 packages and checked 109,448 males and 54,749 women and children as they entered the colony. Apart from drugs and dutiable goods, they were looking for prohibited imports of many different kinds.[20] The annual reports record the seizures of firearms, ammunition, counterfeit coins and notes, unstamped letters, animals and birds. In 1937 the department began to collect a new special tax on heavy oil-engined vehicles.[21] In 1938 it took over the management of the chandu factory[22] from the government analyst.

In the FMS the tariff was expanding very rapidly.[23] By 1932 there were 36 items on the import tariff alone. The identification of goods falling within the tariff descriptions and the accurate assessment of value required to calculate *ad valorem* duties led to the introduction of specialist advisers. In 1928 the department acquired its own chemist and laboratory,[24] located initially in the Institute of Medical Research but transferred the following year to the chandu packing plant in Kuala Lumpur. The importance of the textile duties and difficulty of valuation were met by the appointment in 1933 of a technical advisor on piece goods.[25]

Since 1931 the department had been reorganized on a territorial basis.[26] The former branches disappeared and a deputy commissioner took charge of each state. In 1933 it became known as the Customs and Excise Department.

Well-organized customs and excise departments whose role was increasingly the collection of revenue as the chandu monopoly was gradually phased out now served both the Straits Settlements and the FMS. In 1937 import and export duties levied in the FMS totalled S$ 42,339,369.[27] The yield on opium, including fees, was just S$ 7,384,508. Export duties were still a major source contributing S$ 24,415,730 to the total. The bulk of this derived from the levies on tin but their share of the overall revenue was declining. In 1900 they had provided 46 per cent of the income of the FMS. In 1937 they yielded only 24 per cent, little more than the import duties on tobacco, liquor, petroleum and textiles. Rubber export duty accounted for a modest 5.9 per cent (S$ 4,763,000).

The department also provided a customs service for those states that remained outside the federation. Of these, by far the largest was the southern state of Johore. Since its acceptance of a British adviser its revenue had risen from S$ 4,348,642 in 1912 to S$ 20,197,000 in 1937, greater than the other three unfederated states combined. Of this, 37.7 per cent was derived from customs, excise and marine, including import duties on tobacco, liquor and petroleum and export duties on rubber, copra, tin and tin ore. In Kedah, the Muslim year that straddled 1937 and 1938 produced a total revenue of S$ 7,544,682, of which customs duties provided 47.31 per cent. Kelantan was largely a rice growing area; 91 per cent of its population were Malay cultivators and fishermen. Import duties and the opium monopoly accounted for 58.8 per cent of its S$ 3,209,000 revenue. The economy of its neighbour Trengganu was very similar. With a largely rural population of 179,789 it received a revenue of S$ 2,660,399, 77.5 per cent of it from customs duties and opium. Smallest of all was Perlis, a tiny state with just 49,296 inhabitants. To its 1937/8 income of S$ 728,531, import duties contributed 37.6 per cent, export duties 18.2 per cent and opium 21.6 per cent.

In the free ports of the Straits Settlements in 1938 the duties on liquor, tobacco and petroleum amounted to S$ 12,720,459 against a return on opium of S$ 8,450,007.[28] Since its first tentative steps in 1910 the department had grown in size and scope. In Singapore there were now 10 European officers, 14 assistant superintendents and 319 revenue officers. Their transport comprised eight launches, one motor sampan, five lorries, three cars and fifteen bicycles. A new port division building was under construction. In Penang and Province Wellesley two customs officers, four superintendents and 124 revenue officers, with two launches and four vans, supported a senior customs officer. Three assistant superintendents and 42 revenue officers served Malacca. In all three areas there were clerical and administrative staff in support, to which must be added the employees in the opium monopoly.

It is of interest to note that of the 256 permanent revenue officers in Singapore more than half were Chinese. Some 55 officers had been in the service for more than ten years.[29]

Europeans still largely monopolized the senior appointments in both the Settlements and the FMS. Both departments were receiving a regular intake of probationers appointed by the secretary of state. It is to their story that we now turn.

4

The expatriates arrive

In the period between the two world wars the British Empire generated substantial employment for young men whose vision extended beyond the confines of the United Kingdom. The large commercial organizations, trading companies, mining companies, plantations and a variety of other enterprises all required the services of suitable recruits, prepared to make their careers in distant lands and to cope with unfamiliar conditions.

The probationary appointments by the secretary of state for the colonies offered prospects of an interesting, and occasionally adventurous, career in an exotic environment. Those selected were expected to undertake substantial responsibilities at an early stage and to display appropriate judgement and initiative. The first intake was mostly public schoolboys but it was soon found possible to fill vacancies with university graduates.[1]

Malaya in the 1920s was still a comparatively obscure corner of the world and it is not surprising that many of the early recruits were attracted to the country through personal contacts. In the spring of 1928 John Lewis was a trainee with the Eastern Telegraph Company at Hampstead when his elder brother, then an education officer in the Federated Malay States, suggested he might try for an appointment to the customs.[2] Perhaps the word got round. John later discovered that two other successful applicants that year had been working for the same company. John was instructed to sail from Tilbury on board the SS *Naldera* on 13 July 1928. He had to make his own preparations as he recalls.

> I was not offered any training in the UK or any information about Malaya and so I visited the Malayan Information Office in Trafalgar Square for help. The information officer was very helpful and told me what clothes to buy as well as goods such as a cabin trunk, a topee and where to buy them. Little was known about the FMS in those days and

> when I went to a bookshop in London to buy a book on the Malay language, I was sold a book on Malayalam, which I discovered later was only spoken in Southern India.

On board the *Naldera* John shared a cabin with another customs cadet, Dick Darby, whose father was a planter in Perak. He was met at Penang by his brother and travelled with him to Kuala Lumpur the next day in a train that looked to him very top heavy on the narrow metre gauge. There he was allocated accommodation in the Bull's Head bachelor mess.

The recruitment process was generally courteous and considerate. Peter Burgess joined the service in 1934.[3] After a series of interviews he was invited to consider a post in the police or customs in the Straits Settlements and/or the FMS. He was given a small book to read, *Government Services in Malaya and the Straits Settlements*, and was asked to return a week later. As he explains:

> My mother was a little worried at the distance of Malaya and recalled that a friend, Professor Milne who lived in Japan, had said that Singapore was the wickedest city in the world. However, I was very interested and decided I should apply. I duly returned and saw a Major Hutchinson again. I said the post seemed most attractive but my mother was worried about the distance, to which he replied 'Would you like me to see your mother?' That settled it.

In view of the urgent need for additional staff to handle the newly introduced rubber regulations, Peter sailed shortly afterwards with three other cadets. Two disembarked at Penang to serve in the FMS. Peter and Wallace Kemp travelled on to Singapore to disembark in a typical tropical rainstorm. He had been posted to 'the wickedest city in the world'.

The newcomers had arrived on a Friday evening. The following morning they reported to the senior superintendent, J. J. Warren. He was not impressed by Peter's academic qualifications. 'I see you went to a university. I can't say that I think it a good idea to recruit from universities. Men who have experience out of school and college seem to do better. However, if you settle down and pass your exams quickly I may change my mind.' Peter was posted to the preventive service.

It was when watching a cricket match at Tunbridge Wells that Robert McCall's father engaged a fellow spectator in conversation on the problem of finding a career for his son.[4] The stranger, who was distantly related to a Malayan customs officer, Selwyn Buckwell, suggested the Malayan Police. As Robert was then only 18 years of age he was advised to apply again in two years' time. To fill the time he joined the United Africa Company and was eventually posted to its Paris office. It was from there that he sent his application with details of his employment so far. No doubt the Colonial Office took up references. United Africa immediately ordered his recall to London to be sacked. Robert was equal to the crisis, as he recounts:

> I took the precaution of taking M. le Directeur's daughter Renée, who worked in the office, out for a drink or two and then asked her if she could get 'Papa' to give me a reference. I had practically never spoken to him in his exalted position, but I was called to his office and asked what I would like him to write. I suggested he just say I was satisfactory and honest. He said 'Well you write it out in English and tell Renée to put it into French. Her French is better than yours.' I think I had three or four interviews in London later and always on the top of the pile was this letter in French.

It was obviously effective. He was told that in view of his commercial experience he would be more useful in the customs than the police. He arrived in Kuala Lumpur in February 1936 and began preventive work under the wing of Michael Ferrier Mavor who was his senior by just one year.

Jean François Marie (Bicky) Roualle developed an ambition to serve in the East while still at school, when a former pupil described to him the delights of his career with the Hong Kong & Shanghai Bank in Singapore.[5] After two years with a bank in England and the successful passage of various examinations of the Institute of Bankers, Bicky spotted an advertisement for appointments in the Malayan Customs Service and soon found himself before a selection board that seemed more interested in his prowess on the rugby field than in his knowledge of economics.

> In due course I was offered a position as a cadet at a salary of £300 a year and was required to attend a course in the Malay language at the School of Oriental Languages in London. There I found myself one of eleven cadets, six police

> and five customs, all complete strangers and much of an age (20–22) and similar backgrounds. A smartly dressed man in his sixties appeared and indicated he was to be our tutor. He began by giving us a list of books we would have to buy from the nearby Java Head Bookshop, all six written by someone named Winstedt.[6] Our instructor was indeed Sir Richard Winstedt, for many years Director of Education in Malaya. He was reputed to have standardized the Malay language. The resultant quip among the locals was that 'Allah gave us the country but Winstedt gave us the language'. At some stage during the course we were each tested to establish whether our ability to recognize tonal sounds was such that we could be considered for training in a Chinese dialect.

He sailed from Tilbury on 31 December 1937 and was posted to Kuala Lumpur.

Philip Merson was one of the last cadets to join before the outbreak of the Second World War.[7] He was a little reluctant to accept a proffered posting to customs but his father persuaded him to do so. With eight others he was first sent to a three-month course in Malay, taught by Richard Winstedt at Christ College, Cambridge, to which the School of Oriental and African Studies had been evacuated. It was in January 1940 that he sailed to Singapore aboard *The Viceroy of India*, flagship of the P & O[8] and still observing peacetime formalities such as evening dress for dinner. Training was still somewhat sketchy. He tells us:

> I arrived at Singapore at the beginning of February and was sent to Beach Road Customs Station to be taught by Senior Customs Officer Ashley Cooper. The only thing I remember about my training was watching Cooper and Assistant Supervisor Tan Ewe Chee trying out their various conjuring tricks to each other. They were both members of the Magic Circle.

Both commercial companies and government departments provided accommodation for their expatriate staff. Customs officers had to accept frequent transfers, moving from station to station as required by 'the exigencies of the service'. Probationers under training might well be moved around to widen their experience, but a major factor in these changes of residence was the need to replace officers as they went on home leave. After completion of a 'tour', usually four years in the first instance, an officer was required to take an extended leave in a cool climate, necessitating an absence of over six months. A local transferee or a colleague newly returned from his leave would fill his post. In the course of a single tour an officer might expect three or four postings. It was clearly unreasonable to leave expatriates to find their own houses. Most customs officers were therefore accommodated in government bungalows. These were usually simple wooden structures with wide verandas to keep them cool, a purpose also served by the ceiling fans or *punkahs*. The Public Works Department provided very basic furniture but established officers would probably acquire some of their own. Local dealers offered excellent carpets with an agreement to buy them back at the end of the tour at a modest discount. It was a tribute to the 'grapevine' that the dealers always appeared to reclaim the floor coverings just as an officer was packing up to go on leave.

When Stuart Sim brought his bride Katharine back to Malaya they were hoping for a posting to Lumut. To her intense disappointment they were sent instead to Parit Buntar where they found that their allocated bungalow was still occupied by an officer of another department who was preparing to go on home leave. While they waited for his departure she sampled the discomforts of a government rest house. These were simple establishments intended to provide accommodation for travelling government servants. In her book *Malayan Landscape*, Katharine Sim[9] describes her first experience of life in Malaya.

> We lived in the 'Federal Wing' of the Rest House. This sounded palatial, but was in reality only one rather dark room encircled by a very public verandah, across which was a stone bathroom. This bathroom was a revelation to me with its big 'Shanghai jar' full of cold water; the earthenware kept the water deliciously cool; and there was a tin washtub in which hot water was poured by the Boy who quickly appeared bearing the inevitable kerosene tin when one called for a bath. ... The method of bathing was to ladle hot and cold water over one's body from a tin dipper, and then finish with a cool shower. The result was a glorious flood in the bathroom; but it was built for it, the water ran away down a hole in the wall, out into the garden.
>
> The sanitary arrangements were definitely not modern. There were *jambans*, which were attended twice a day by a *jamban* man, a rather furtive-looking, longhaired Tamil

> who padded up the outside stairs with a pail and a large black umbrella. There was only one 'push and pull' in the town and that was at the club.

Happily, the Sims were transferred to Lumut where Katharine was able to accompany her husband on his inspection visits to Pangkor island and to give full rein to her talents as an artist.

In the larger towns probationers, who were almost invariably bachelors, were quartered in 'messes'. In Singapore the department made use of a flat on the roof of Fullerton Building, the General Post Office. Situated on Collyer Quay it provided a fine view of the anchorage and the straits beyond and the opportunity for the residents to keep an eye on the shipping even when off duty. Arriving in December 1934 Kenneth Hellrich[10] was quartered there: Burgess and Kemp, however, were to share a two bedroom semi-detached house in the middle of Singapore. Colleagues had already hired a cook and a houseboy, who were immediately dispatched to buy mattresses, pillows and mosquito nets. They had brought their own sheets from England. Philip Merson shared a rather larger establishment near the docks with three other officers. It could also provide temporary accommodation for others from time to time.

Jim Bailward[11] was another who first arrived in 1940 after a six-week voyage round the Cape of Good Hope in a Blue Funnel freighter.[12] He disembarked at Port Swettenham to be greeted by an officer who dwarfed his 6ft 3ins: Bicky Roualle was a very big man indeed. Jim shared a mess with Bicky and two other officers.

Servants were essential. A bachelor living on his own might manage with a single *amah*, a Chinese woman who would act as his housekeeper, cooking, washing, ironing and cleaning. For these very efficient ladies a single man was the preferred choice. Their sway over household matters was then unchallenged. The arrival of a wife was frequently the occasion for giving notice. Married families, whose houses, though somewhat Spartan, could be quite palatial, would probably require a larger establishment. Most European women were able to take up occupations of their own and were happy to leave the domestic chores to a staff. This might include a cook, an *amah*, a gardener (*kebun*) and, to take care of the children, a nurse. These last were often Malay or Indian and were known as *ayah*s. When Kenneth Hellrich married Conti he moved into a bungalow at Parit Buntar and later into similar accommodation on transfer to Telok Anson. To the two servants who had sufficed in the past they added a *syce* (chauffeur) and a *kebun*. When they started a family they had to employ an *ayah*. Soon both the family and the staff increased further and Kenneth found himself employing a total of six.

Chinese servants were almost invariably members of unofficial associations or *kongsi*s and often cooperated in coping with major social occasions. It was not unusual to find at a neighbour's party that you were eating off your own china.

Freedom from domestic routine was very necessary. Most customs officers, and particularly those who were engaged in preventive duties, were required to be available at all times. It was regular practice for officers to keep their headquarters informed of their whereabouts and by no means unusual to make an abrupt departure from a social occasion to deal with some unexpected development. On occasion, with no other transport home available, a wife would have to accompany her husband on some nocturnal operation, so the malefactors in an illicit opium saloon might be confronted by a raiding party led by a couple in full evening dress. There were no office hours in this sort of work.

The cost of living was not high. In the Singapore mess Peter Burgess recalls that:

> The servants provided meals on contract. We paid S$ 40 a month for cooked breakfast, three course dinner, tea and fresh fruit at dawn and after office at 4.30 p.m. Our colleagues took us to their flat for lunch of toasted cheese, fresh fruit and coffee for which we paid S$ 10 a month. I think we paid S$ 10 a month for laundry, which included a starched white drill suit every day. It worked very well and we managed quite comfortably on our S$ 250 a month.

Clothing was usually purchased locally. On arrival in Singapore Peter Burgess was taken to a tailor to be measured for 12 white drill suits at about nine shillings each. The first two were to be ready the next day! Suitably impressed by the service he took another probationer, a very tall man who arrived a month later, to the same shop. Eighteen years on Peter called there again and reminded the proprietor that he had made his first suits in Malaya. The tailor looked at Peter and asked 'How is your tall friend?'

New recruits were usually given their early experience in large centres where they could acquire specific skills under supervision. As bachelors they were likely to start in the preventive side. In many respects, particularly in the suppression of the illegal drug traffic, this resembled the work of the police. The emphasis was naturally on prior detection of offences rather than subsequent investigation. The purpose was to catch the lawbreakers in the act. The powers of officers were extensive though marginally different in the two jurisdictions. Goods and people arriving from abroad could be detained and searched at random. Ships could be held in port while searches were conducted. At other times officers could stop and search people and vehicles if they had 'reasonable cause to believe' that they were carrying contraband.[13] In the Straits Settlements entry to premises required a search warrant. To provide these some officers were appointed justices of the peace. When Robert McCall returned from leave in 1940 he was posted to Province Wellesley and became a JP. He recalls that:

> The consequence was that I had a constant stream of people wanting this and that witnessed and signed. On one occasion I was rostered to inspect Penang Jail. I had to be there by 6.00 a.m., sample breakfast, inspect this and that and then go through a practice hanging to ensure the trapdoor was working properly. There was a Chinese awaiting execution but the invading Japanese forces came in time to save him from that and me from attending it.

All officers had summary powers of arrest and would take prisoners back to headquarters for questioning.[14] There was seldom any resistance but occasionally a suspect would take flight. Violence against prisoners was, of course, strictly forbidden and would have been a criminal offence. Even the use of handcuffs was regulated. They were never applied at sea. It was forbidden to handcuff women. In a long investigation interrogating officers would see that those detained were provided with food and drink. Unlike the police, customs officers could make use of confessions and admissions as evidence in court. Such statements were carefully recorded by the investigating officer and signed by the accused. They were admissible only if the court was satisfied that they were not the result of any 'threat, promise or inducement'. Those to be prosecuted were escorted to a police station where a formal charge was lodged and bail fixed. The customs had no facilities for prolonged custody.

Goods that were the subject of an offence were seized and produced in court as evidence. If a conviction was obtained the goods were automatically forfeit. A court had no power to restore them. Also liable to forfeiture were the vehicles and small craft in which the contraband had been found. This power extended to vessels up to 100 tons displacement. In 1938 seizures in the Straits Settlements included three lorries, two cars, 118 cycles, one rickshaw, two motor sampans, 28 manual sampans and 14 *koleh*s.[15]

Most prosecutions were heard in magistrates' courts but more serious offences carrying heavier penalties might be tried in district or sessions courts. At both levels it was a customs officer who conducted the case. In Singapore it was the practice to appoint one officer to perform this role but in the FMS and other states such specialization was not possible and it was usually the investigating officer who opened the proceedings by giving his evidence and then stepped back into the body of the court to continue the prosecution. He might well find himself pitted against a qualified lawyer for the defence. This could be an ordeal for an inexperienced officer. In the absence of his mentor, Michael Mavor, Robert McCall conducted his first case just two weeks after his arrival in the country. It concerned an illicit still. 'I had never been in a court in my life before and so didn't know when to stand up or sit down. The main prosecution witness was a non-English-speaking long service Chinese Out Door Officer. The magistrate was Malayan Civil Service and helpful, so we got through somehow. Perhaps the accused pleaded guilty!'

Robert was fortunate. Some magistrates were very difficult to please. Others were eccentric. Early in his career Peter Burgess made a large seizure of prepared opium in various parts of a smallholding outside Singapore. As a leading barrister had been briefed for the defence the district judge, a Mr H. A. Forrer, decided to visit the scene of the crime.

> Many of us were a little frightened by H. A. Forrer. He could be very cutting. I had to go with him to show just where the opium had been found. When I took him to the sheds and pigsties he first went to a hen, sitting on eggs in a basket suspended from a rafter to protect her from rats. He lifted her tail gently and said 'Hello hen, are you sitting on eggs or chandu?' He then went to a pigsty and after staring at the pigs he turned to me and said 'It is a popular fallacy that pigs have curly tails. They don't. They are straight. I made a special study of it when I was in China'. That was our sole conversation!

As recounted elsewhere, Derek Mackay found that H. A. Forrer was still deserving of healthy respect when he appeared before him in Singapore in the early 1950s.

Although the mainstream work of revenue collection might seem rather less glamorous than the pursuit of smugglers it could be varied and demanding. The examination of goods and related documents, the sampling, testing, valuation and classification of dutiable imports and exports were far from routine duties. Officers had to be on their guard constantly to detect attempted evasions and frauds, while bearing in mind the need to avoid unnecessary delay to valuable commerce. Their responsibilities extended to the supervision of bonded warehouses, breweries, distilleries, match factories, playing card factories, petroleum depots and toddy shops. They reported to the Board of Licensing Justices, which issued the licences to wholesalers, retailers and bars. All officers were likely to be involved in the welfare and discipline of junior staff, the inspection of customs posts and examination sheds and the maintenance of vehicles and launches.

Such duties could be shared in the main centres but there were many minor outstations where a single officer might be required to tackle a great variety of tasks, supervising a small port, keeping an eye on the local distillery, managing the chandu monopoly and inspecting licensed premises, while also undertaking the direction of preventive activity in a substantial area of countryside and along a lengthy coast. To many this was the most enjoyable posting, full of interest and largely free of interference from those in authority. An officer in such a station was expected to deal with whatever arose and to solve problems himself, without constant reference to head office for instructions. Conversely, arranging a sudden departure on an extended sea patrol might frustrate tiresome demands for reports and returns.

Such liberties were seldom offered to probationers. Their training was largely confined to on-the-job experience and they carried a further burden. They had exams to pass. There was no formal instruction in law. To master the massive penal and criminal procedure codes,[16] based on the statutes written for India by the great Macaulay, there was little to do but read and learn – so too *General Orders*, the regulations governing all departments. It was not easy to sacrifice a burgeoning social life to sit in the clammy warmth of a Malayan evening wrestling with such weighty books. To learn Malay it was necessary to employ a *munshi*, a local teacher with whom the student could practise conversation, read such classics of local literature as *Pelayaran Abdullah*[17] and struggle to reproduce the beauty of the Jawi script.[18] *Munshi*s needed a great deal of patience.

Initially, Peter Burgess did not enjoy such skilled tuition. A Malay assistant supervisor gave him lessons in the office until the Department of Education appointed a suitable teacher. It was not a satisfactory arrangement.

> Che Sidek was a Java Malay who had a very poor idea of teaching Malay. He set us to read the *Koran* from Arabic script, which is rather more complicated than Jawi. Fortunately our Malay teacher was soon appointed. He was excellent. He was a trained teacher from the largest Malay school in Singapore. He came to our house for an hour, three evenings a week. He had not previously taken expatriate pupils but was well experienced in the oral part of Malay examinations. When our turn came he told us he had coached his successor to speak very clearly and not to go too fast in dictation. Che Wahid was very proud of serving in the Straits Settlements. He always ordered his shoes from Fears of Bristol and when the Silver Jubilee of King George V approached he showed us the *songkok* (cap) which he had ordered. The top was lined with a Union Jack and sides lined with the colours of the Sultan Idris Training College. 'When we give three cheers for His Majesty King George V I shall be waving the Union Jack.'

Peter passed his exam.

John Lewis describes his posting to Port Dickson in 1939.

> I was delighted with this move as I had recently married and Port Dickson was a holiday resort for Europeans. I travelled there by car with my wife, a dog and a cat and stayed in the local Government Rest House for three days. We were then allotted a Government bungalow on a slight hill with a lovely view overlooking the harbour.
>
> Port Dickson was a small town of one street, with the usual native shops, built beside a small natural harbour made by an inlet from the sea. There was a jetty near the entrance to the harbour stretching out to a wharf in deep water on which small ships could unload their cargo. At the town end of the jetty a Customs Office had been built

which overlooked the whole of the harbour. A Malay Assistant District Officer was stationed at Port Dickson together with a European officer in charge of the Police District.

The Customs Department was responsible for revenue activities along the Negri Sembilan coastline from the Selangor border about 15 miles north to the Malacca border about 20 miles south of Port Dickson and inland for about 20 miles. It had a staff of some twenty Out Door Officers, Preventive Officers and clerks. The coastline north of Port Dickson was covered mainly with mangrove and jungle trees but the coast to the south was more densely populated with less mangrove and a few sandy beaches. There was a customs outpost on a local road at its exit into Malacca which was part of the Straits Settlements.

Five miles south of Port Dickson near the coast the Malay Regiment had its headquarters. There was also a European social club nearby where members could sail or play tennis and two or three Government holiday bungalows for senior Government employees. At the eighth mile there was a lovely sandy beach, lined with coconut trees where the European community used to swim. It was protected from sharks by an underwater shoal and was, incidentally, one of the beaches used by Lord Mountbatten's troops when they landed in Malaya after the Japanese surrender.

A Straits Steamship vessel[19] of about 1000 tons burden called at Port Dickson once a week to discharge and load cargo and was small enough to tie up to the wharf at the end of the jetty. The local shipping agent was responsible for producing to customs the ship's manifest of goods landed and for depositing dutiable goods, such as liquor, in a warehouse alongside the Customs Office. Most of the dutiable goods were then sent to Seremban in a sealed railway truck to be dealt with by the customs authorities there. The work affecting the ship was usually finished in a day.

The department had a slow 25-foot single screw motor launch named *Krawei* which was used for sea patrols to deter smugglers, but no arrests were made at sea in my time. The coast to the north was not suitable for smuggling due to the mangrove and to the south was too populated for safety. In 1940 I was delighted to receive a superb new twin-engine motor launch about 35 feet long, the *Brani*. She could travel at over twenty knots – more than a match for

> any smugglers – and was a delight to drive. I had to teach the *serang* how to manoeuvre a twin-screw launch by the proper use of its engines. He had never driven one before.

After his initial training in Singapore Peter Burgess was unexpectedly transferred upcountry to the little town of Kluang in the unfederated state of Johore. As he remarks, life was very different there.

> Kluang was then a small town on the railway which runs from Singapore to Kuala Lumpur and the north of the Malaya peninsula, and on the road which runs from Batu Pahat in the west to Jemaluang and Mersing in the east. The road from Jemaluang to Johore Bahru (the state capital) had only been opened the previous year. There were several rubber estates around Kluang and open cast tin mines around Jemaluang, but about half of the sixty-five miles from Kluang to Mersing was through dense uncleared jungle. I was given three Out Door Officers, one of whom acted as clerk and interpreter.

Preventive work was not easy with such limited resources but the local planters were helpful and welcomed his visits. Theirs was a lonely life.

In small stations it was not unusual for the local customs officer to act in other official capacities. Indeed, the 1926 Dominion and Colonial Office list records that in the unfederated state of Kelantan a Mr C. C. Brown held the appointments of superintendent of marine and customs, acting assistant British adviser, high court judge, and superintendent of posts and telegraphs. While few could match this challenge to Pooh-Bah, the role of harbour master was easily combined with customs work. For discharging this function at Port Dickson John Lewis drew an additional allowance of S$ 25 a month (about £3). Fortunately, during a previous tour of duty in Port Swettenham he had studied coastal navigation under a qualified harbour master, Commander Bucknell RN. Having acquired the necessary tools of his new trade, charts, parallel rulers and hand compasses, he was able to tackle his responsibilities in a professional manner. They proved quite demanding.

> There were two lighthouses to look after. One was a small automatic lighthouse on an island opposite the wharf which

> marked the entrance to the harbour. The other was at Cape Rachado about nine miles south of Port Dickson. This was a lovely old Dutch lighthouse on top of a cliff, manned by a lighthouse keeper and his family. It enabled ships sailing in the Straits of Malacca to plot their position and set their course safely. There were also two leading lights to maintain, one on the wharf and another a mile down the coast, which, when kept in line, directed a ship into the narrow entrance to the harbour.
>
> During 1939 and 1940 the Royal Navy was active in the Malacca Straits with destroyers and submarines carrying out exercises, and the Naval authorities in Singapore discovered that Port Dickson was a pleasant and convenient port for their ships to stay instead of returning to the Singapore Naval Base. I therefore frequently received requests from them for instructions as to where their ships could anchor. The wharf could take two destroyers or submarines abreast and one small ship could anchor in the harbour. The biggest ship to visit was HMS *Cumberland*, a cruiser, which was too big to enter the harbour and had to anchor out at sea. My first job was to pay an official call on the new arrival to meet the Captain of the ship and arrange for his wants and the entertainment of his crew. The British Resident of Negri Sembilan had a Government holiday bungalow on the beach a few miles south of the port and the ship's officers were invited to stay there. The Malay Regiment assisted in the entertainment and I used to arrange soccer matches against the locals which were always popular with the crews.

This increased naval presence was not the only evidence that Britain was now at war. Although there did not appear to be an immediate threat to Malaya the commencement of hostilities in Europe on 3 September 1939 inevitably meant that new demands were made upon the customs service. It was well positioned to play a part in support of the security services and to enforce the various restrictions on international trade imposed by the home government. A series of defeats in Europe served to heighten the danger of a Japanese attack on Britain's eastern territories and measures for the defence of Malaya involved the service in new fields of activity. Both the UK and Malayan governments actively discouraged Europeans from returning home to join the armed

4. Customs Office at Batu Pahat.

forces. The uninterrupted production of tin and rubber was considered a more important contribution to the war effort.

In 1939 the departments began to prepare for wartime duties. They were naturally employed to enforce such emergency measures as exchange control and import and export control, which was now extended to all goods, and to collect new taxes including war duties[20] and entertainment duty. They were also called upon to set up a system of food control. The Comptroller of Customs became the food controller for Malaya. The chandu shops were utilized to introduce a system of registration, as Peter Burgess describes.

> All food retailers had been licensed and it was proposed to register all rice purchasers. Each opium shop was allocated a number of rice retailers – there were three to four thousand in all. The clerks in charge were told to issue to each rice retailer sufficient registration cards for each customer. The dealer was to record in the card the amount of each purchase. The object was that if rationing was necessary each customer would be allowed a fixed percentage of his average purchases. Amazingly the registration scheme worked. For putting this scheme through the opium shop staff received no extra pay. I was told some years later that the rice registration cards survived and were the basis of the issue of identity cards.
>
> After the rice registration scheme got under way I was seconded to the Food Control Department as Food Supply Officer Singapore. I was given a number of tasks – to investigate complaints by rice importers that their trade had been too severely restricted, to investigate the import and sale of live sheep and to consider possible food rationing. Someone thought there should be a five-minute kitchen front broadcast every morning and the job of preparing this was given to me. It was hoped to encourage Europeans to use locally produced foods rather than rely on imported foods which had been readily available in Singapore.
>
> I was Chairman of the Rice Committee composed mostly of leading Chinese rice importers. The Health Department urged the use of unpolished rice and I was asked to mention this at the Rice Committee. I was delighted to be approached by a very dignified Chinese with snow-white hair, the principal of the firm Sin Hua Hup Seng Kee. 'I am very interested in what you say about unpolished rice. I think I would like to try a small consignment.' I thought of a lorry load of about 100 bags and said 'How much?' 'Shall we say 10,000 bags?' was the reply. I put this request to the manager of the Singapore Rice Mill and was told 'Don't be daft. That's impossible. We can't manage more than 200 bags a month. We need the polishings as fuel to operate the mill.' Sin Hua Hup Seng Kee were the principal importers of Saigon rice and by that time the Japanese were in Indo-China.

The service was still engaged in the collection of import and export duties and in 1940 extended this activity under the provisions of the War Taxation Enactment.[21] This was designed to impose a levy in the form of export taxes on rubber and tin, applicable to companies that were not liable to UK income tax.

Philip Merson was soon separated from his conjuring colleagues at Beach Road and transferred to Port Division. He found himself engaged in work arising from the state of hostilities. 'I was sent off in a launch to meet incoming ships and seal up their radio cabins to prevent them transmitting when in port. I met a mixed reception, amounting to a stand up fight aboard a Dutch vessel and being bowed to the radio cabin by the Japanese.'

Individual officers were also becoming involved in activities related to the defence of Malaya. Jim Bailward was still at Port Swettenham.

> All Europeans were required to enlist in and train with the local Defence Volunteer Force and I duly joined the FMSVF and did a full stint of training. We were very much aware of the Japanese threat but thought that come the time the forces gathering in the area would cope, and we drew some comfort from the thought of the supposed impregnability of Singapore. What a gross underestimation it proved to be.

Peter Burgess was already a member of the Singapore Volunteer Corps, but on the outbreak of war found himself in charge of an RNVR detachment guarding an Imperial Airways[22] flying boat.

> I was soon mobilized for active service and after a week's gunnery course in HMS *Terror* and a week in a coal-burning minesweeper I was posted to an armed merchantman HMS *Kampar* (958 tons gross, built in Hong Kong in 1915) as gunnery and signals officer. Ladies recruited as coding clerks had some difficulty in getting used to the naval custom of saying to a yeoman of signals 'make that to Colombo', meaning HMS *Colombo*. A signal intended for HMS *Scarborough* in Penang harbour found its way to Scarborough in Yorkshire and a lonely Pay Lieutenant RNVR had found his way first to Colombo and then to HMS *Terror* in Singapore, instead of HMS *Colombo* in Portsmouth. ... I was disappointed when after three months I was ordered to return to civilian duties.

In fact Peter had already played a part in Malaya's military preparations. From Kluang he had moved into a bungalow on the Mersing rubber estate.

> The manager, Tom Hinde, was convinced that an attack by Japan was inevitable. The only doubt was when and where. He reported any suspicious activities to MI5[23] and together with the Forestry Officers we looked at possible landing beaches. We had three big events – the Coronation celebrations and sea sports, the visit of General Dobbie[24] on a senior staff tactical exercise and then a visit of C Company of the Gordon Highlanders. The staff exercise was most interesting. General Dobbie and Colonel Percival[25] stayed with the Hindes and I put up Orde Dobbie, the ADC. I was surprised to be called in to the plenary session and somewhat nervous when called to sit next to Colonel Percival. The social side was entertaining. Tom Hinde had arranged tennis – Hinde and Burgess against Dobbie and Percival. It rained and we changed to table tennis where I was much more at home. We were winning when General Dobbie fell and had to receive first aid. ... I had to keep a confidential diary and I was briefed by the Staff Intelligence Officer who showed me a map which indicated Japanese establishments at the mouth of every river in Malaya.
>
> We did not have many Japanese ships. An iron ore mine had been opened some way up the next river and we had to meet each ship when it came to load iron ore. Some of the captains were surly but two were charming. One tried to persuade me to visit Japan in cherry blossom time and the other showed me a chart which he had made of the approaches to the Endau River.

Peter enjoyed Mersing and was disappointed when he had to go on leave after only three years three months of his tour. On the night before he left he received an urgent message from army HQ in Singapore that two officers would visit him the next morning. He explained that he was going on leave but was ordered to wait until they arrived. It was a long wait as they were delayed by a motor accident. When they finally turned up they asked Peter if a military landing would be possible during the northeast monsoon. Peter's answer was 'Yes. Coastal steamers work throughout the year.' After the war he met

General Percival at a Malayan reunion and found that he still remembered the table tennis match.

In Port Dickson John Lewis was appointed naval reporting officer, a secret appointment under the senior naval intelligence officer, Singapore.

> I was provided with two codebooks and was required to report by code to Singapore the presence of any foreign warships or unusual vessels passing Port Dickson in the Straits of Malacca. I received various messages from the Naval authorities during the following months regarding British warships and warning messages regarding the crisis in Europe. I was probably the first civilian in Malaya to be told when the war actually broke out.

John was not to remain at Port Dickson. In July 1941 he returned from a leave in Australia and was posted to Penang.

After his brief experience of the navy Peter Burgess was sent to Singapore where he tackled the problems of food control as described above. This was not his only venture beyond the normal field of a customs officer.

> I continued to train RNVR recruits and my only meeting with the Governor was at RNVR headquarters where I was introduced as 'One of the chaps you won't let us have', to which HE[26] replied 'You know Ward you're not the only pebble on the beach.' My other part-time activity was as announcer and newsreader for the Malayan Broadcasting Corporation. On my first night – when slightly nervous – I was greeted by the news editor 'Germany has just attacked Russia. There will be a special 15-minute commentary after the news. I can let you have the first four sheets before the news but you will have to take the last sheet unseen.'

Peter coped but ran into more trouble when he read the ten o'clock news on Friday 5 December 1941. The first item was 'Japanese transports have been sighted steaming northwest into the Gulf of Siam.' After reading it Peter reported to Allington Kennard, the news editor, who informed him that at one minute past ten the press censor had telephoned with instructions to delete the item.

> I said, 'Too late, it's just been read.' However, the censorship was so effective that this report of the first sighting of the invasion fleet does not appear in any official history that I have seen – certainly not in General Percival's despatch. Allington Kennard, then Editor of *The Straits Times*, did mention it once in the 1950s.

Peter read the news again on Sunday 7 December. This time there were mysterious messages to be broadcast, such as 'Cheer up the 3000, you are not forgotten.' He never discovered their significance. At Butterworth Robert McCall was celebrating his first wedding anniversary.

Another officer involved in intelligence work was Cecil Gutteridge, who, for some 12 months, was responsible for maintaining a radio link with Pat Noone, who was operating on the Malayan–Siamese border and was later to disappear during clandestine operations in occupied Malaya. With impeccable mistiming the link was abandoned in late November 1941. In the early hours of 8 December 1941 Japanese forces began to land on the coast of Kelantan.

5
A violent interruption

By 12.25 a.m. on 8 December troops of the Japanese 18th Chrysanthemum Division were ashore near Kota Bahru in the northeast of Malaya.[1] By 1.00 a.m. they had captured the first pillboxes on the beach, killing the men of the 3rd Dogra Regiment who manned them. By 9.00 a.m. the customs service had made its first contribution to the defence of Malaya. Assistant superintendent Tungku Mahmood and revenue officers Syed Mohamed, Engku Yusoff, Jusoh bin Mamat and Mohammed bin Osman captured a Japanese sergeant. He was probably the first Japanese prisoner[2] of the Second World War.

The weight of the attack fell on two Indian Army divisions, the ninth and eleventh. While a brigade of the 9th fought desperately to repel the seaborne landings in Kelantan, the 11th was responsible for the defence of the Siamese frontier. A plan to frustrate a Japanese thrust through Siam by a prior advance into the Kra Isthmus (Operation Matador) was delayed too long for political reasons and was finally cancelled at 1.00 p.m. on 8 December. Instead, the troops were ordered to hold an ill-prepared position at Jitra, north of Alor Star, against an enemy that had landed at Singgora and Pattani and was now marching rapidly through Siam. An attempt to block the road from Pattani by an advance from Kroh to seize a position known as 'the Ledge' was held up by unexpected Siamese resistance. Faced eventually with Japanese forces the column fell back to Kroh. Meanwhile, Japanese aircraft bombed the airfields at Alor Star, Sungei Patani, Butterworth, Kota Bahru, Gong Kedah and Machang.

On 10 December the defenders of Malaya were shocked by the news that HMS *Prince of Wales* and HMS *Repulse* had been sunk by air attack off the east coast. The following day the Jitra position was overrun and Kroh abandoned. The troops who fought so well at Kota Bahru were now struggling to safety along the railway line to Kuala Lipis. The first battles had been lost and the long retreat southwards had begun.

Despite the remarkable achievement of Tungku Mahmood and his men, the customs service as such was not a fighting force. The local staff carried out their duties, but as the invading army forged on down the peninsula they found themselves in occupied territory and faced with the choice of abandoning their posts or staying at work under the conqueror. For the British officers no such choice was on offer. They were fighting for their lives and liberty. Many of them carried an additional responsibility for their families. The wives and children shared their danger.

At Butterworth Robert McCall[3] saw his wife Marye and infant son Andrew onto the train to Kuala Lumpur to stay with her sister there. He then went back to his house and watched a formation of Japanese aircraft bombing the area. Later, two bombers peeled off and attacked the local British fighter force, two unimpressive American aeroplanes known as Brewster Buffaloes. Robert was soon serving on a temporary attachment to an artillery unit, organizing labour to build concrete emplacements for anti-aircraft guns. These were never completed. On 17 December Butterworth airfield was abandoned and was soon in enemy hands. Robert was a jump ahead. He made his way to Ipoh where he was directed to report to Kuala Lumpur.

In Penang John Lewis[4] was working as area supply officer in the food control system. This included a scheme for transporting rice and other foodstuffs by municipal lorries from the harbour godowns in which the reserve stocks were kept. News of the invasion produced immediate problems.

> The local reaction in Penang on 9th December was panic and a rush to buy foodstuffs. The rice permit system was brought into operation by 10th December and confirmation was given to the local inhabitants by radio and newspapers that there were ample stocks of food in Penang and not to panic.
>
> On 11th December at about 9.30 a.m. 27 aeroplanes flew high over Penang town in close formation and unopposed. We thought they were British aeroplanes until the bombs suddenly whistled down upon us killing hundreds of people out on the streets and causing chaos. That afternoon thousands of Penang residents evacuated the town and made their way to nearby villages such as Ayer Hitam,

Pulau Tikus and Jelutong. This exodus continued the following day and by nightfall Penang, a town of some 150,000 people, was empty except for the dead.

The main task now was to feed the dispersed population and it was decided to open food depots at Ayer Hitam, Pulau Tikus and Datoh Kramat village markets. This was a problem, however, because when I telephoned the Municipality on 12th December to order lorries to transport the rice and other foodstuffs from the harbour to the depots I was told that all the native drivers had run away to take care of their families. Luckily the Customs Department had four vans and the Police had a few more. They had to be driven by European Customs and Police Officers as about half the Asian staff in both departments had disappeared. It was dangerous work. Every morning promptly at 9.00 a.m. Japanese aeroplanes flew over Penang town at tree top height to see what we were doing. Any lorries moving about were likely to be shot up and we had no defence against them. As the harbour labourers had also taken leave without permission the officers had to do the loading and unloading. The food was sold at the depots to refugees but given to those who claimed they had no money.

Penang Hill was served by a funicular railway and urgent action had to be taken to supply foodstuffs to those living on the hill before the Japanese destroyed the railway or the power station providing the electricity.

By 14 December the enemy were attacking a position at Gurun on the mainland about thirty miles north of Penang and Butterworth. John Lewis recalls that:

> During the afternoon of 16th December orders were received from the Military authorities that all Europeans had to be evacuated from Penang that night as it was about to be cut off by the Japanese army pushing southwards through Kedah. About 230 people boarded the local ferry boat and sailed for Singapore. This action was looked upon at the time by some people as disgraceful for abandoning the local population to its fate but the fact was that the Japanese attacked Malaya in order to oust the British and had no hostile intentions against the native population.

On his arrival in Singapore John Lewis was able to pass on the benefits of his experience to the local food control, stressing the importance of dispersing the food stocks away from the harbour area.

The war moved on. On 19 December the military evacuated Penang. Just to the south on the mainland was Parit Buntar. Cecil Gutteridge[5] had arrived there on transfer on 1 December and was soon busy explaining to the people in the fishing villages the working of a 'boat denial scheme',[6] the destruction or removal of small craft to prevent their use by the enemy. News of the invasion brought all normal customs work to an end. In his official war report, written on 31 January 1946, Cecil describes what followed.

> About December 12th large numbers of native evacuees, mostly Chinese, started to arrive from Penang by car, lorry, sampan, junk, launch and on foot. From this time, until the evacuation of the Krian District, I assisted Mr Coney (the Senior Customs Officer) in feeding and finding accommodation for these refugees. In this task we were greatly assisted by the local Chinese population, and especially by the Chinese shopkeepers who provided supplies of food for immediate consumption free of charge.

On 17 December aircraft bombed Bagan Serai and Parit Buntar. Cecil called at the rice mill at Bagan Serai, which had been slightly damaged. On return to Parit Buntar he found that his senior customs officer's house had been hit. This was not David Coney's most pressing problem. Orders had arrived to implement the boat denial scheme but as most of the staff was now absent he was not in a position to comply. While he tried to travel to Taiping to explain the situation to the general there, Cecil supervised arrangements for the evacuation of Parit Buntar. The stocks of liquor at the three licensed shops in the area were dumped in the Krian River, with the full cooperation of their owners. Maps, charts and other documents were destroyed and the cash and stocks were collected from the chandu shop.

> At about 3.00 a.m. on December 18th orders were received for all European personnel to evacuate Parit Buntar and to proceed to Taiping. We were instructed to leave in convoy by 4.00 a.m. and take the coast road to Bagan Serai, leaving

the main road clear for military traffic. The enemy were reported to be advancing rapidly on Parit Buntar.

En route the two officers collected cash and chandu from the chandu shop at Kuala Kurau and cash from various customs posts. At Bagan Serai David Coney was mistakenly told to remain, but Cecil Gutteridge pressed on and managed to reach Taiping, where the acting resident confirmed that the boat denial must be carried out. Furnished with full authority to request assistance he made his way back to Bagan Serai but found no help there until he was given temporary use of a platoon of Gurkhas.[7] With their assistance he managed to complete his work at Kuala Kurau. David Coney, with whom Cecil was now reunited, had invited the local customs staff to travel to safety with their families on the department's launch, but they did not appear and their fate is unknown. David and Cecil now boarded a fisheries vessel in which they continued down the coast to Port Weld, destroying and denying as they went. There the Royal Engineers had demolished the godowns and jetty and the stocks of rubber were burning.

At Port Weld David and Cecil transferred to the *Elias bin Ahmad*, a large fisheries boat on which they found a colleague, H. A. Marshall, with a number of staff and their families from Taiping. Accompanied by four smaller launches, including the vessel on which they had arrived, a police launch and an abandoned naval launch, and heavily camouflaged with mud and vegetation, they crept south to Pangkor island, which they reached early in the afternoon of 21 December. On the way they called in at the coastal villages and found the local Chinese population remarkably well organized, with bodies of men to protect them against armed marauders, of whom there were now frequent reports, guards posted on government properties and an apparent determination to hinder the enemy by all means at their power. Craft not already destroyed were immediately rendered unserviceable. Payment for stores supplied was frequently refused. The officers took the opportunity to sell their stocks of chandu to registered smokers in strictly limited quantities and eventually handed over to head office at Kuala Lumpur a cash take of about S$ 40,000.

Stuart and Katharine Sim[8] had been stationed at Lumut since 17 March 1940. It was the posting they had hoped for. His responsibilities included Pangkor island, which he visited at intervals by launch. On about 20 December 1941 orders were received that European women must leave Lumut by car and make their way to Seremban. Katharine travelled in the convoy. It was typical of the confusion of the time that at one stage of their journey they were shown an order that they were all to return to 'set an example'. They pressed ahead. Having reported to the Seremban Club Katharine motored on to stay with friends at Jasin, near the border with Johore. Stuart telephoned her from Kuala Lumpur to say that he was returning to Lumut to supervise the destruction of the jetty, post office, customs office and godown. He made sure that stocks of rice were distributed and then sailed to Port Swettenham in the Straits steamer *Rompin*. Before leaving he visited his house at Lumut and offered the servants a passage. They decided to stay.

Among those fleeing south was schoolgirl Isobel Bruce,[9] the daughter of a tin miner in Perak.

> We had just three hours notice to pack up the mine and the house and leave for the south. My father organized the evacuation of the women and children to the railway station at Taiping. There the platform was covered with stretchers carrying British and Indian soldiers injured in the retreat.
>
> We piled into the train, Dad told us to get away as far as we could travel and left us to join the army. We got into Kuala Lumpur late that night to a scene of total pandemonium. We had one small suitcase each. That night we spent in the servants' quarters of a friend's house; our friends and their servants had already fled.

At Pangkor David Coney and Cecil Gutteridge found that denial had been carried out thoroughly and that Stuart had completed his destruction at Lumut. They were able to report the situation to Kuala Lumpur by telephone before sailing on to Port Swettenham, where they arrived at about 11.00 a.m. on Christmas Eve. There they handed over all five vessels to the senior naval officer and made their way to Kuala Lumpur to report to the deputy comptroller, H. W. Phear.

Port Swettenham was an early target for Japanese bombers. Jim Bailward[10] was still there when the first raids took place.

> There was an airstrip at Port Swettenham where several

> Brewster Buffaloes, an American fighter plane, were stationed. Unfortunately, the propensity of this aeroplane was to flip over on to its nose or even right over on to its back when landing. The result was that there were several 'corpses' littered alongside the runway, which allowed the Japanese Zeros free run to bomb and strafe the Port with absolute impunity from tree top level.

Jim soon left Port Swettenham with the volunteers and found himself driving a Marmon Harrington three-ton truck in which he covered a considerable mileage.

It was now Christmas Day 1941, the eighteenth day of fighting in Malaya. On the west side of the country the enemy had reached the Perak River. On the east coast they were already as far south as Kuala Trengganu. They dominated both sea and air, a commanding situation in a war fought in a narrow peninsula. Nothing had served to stop them. Desperate measures were considered. In his book *Eastern Epic* Compton Mackenzie touches briefly on one such plan.

> In the middle of December Whitehall captivated by tales of the Scorched Earth Policy in Russia ordered unrestricted Scorched Earth for Malaya. It might be rash to claim a record for the ultimate depth of official stupidity, but such an order for a country like Malaya inhabited by people of other races to whom we had guaranteed our protection by treaties would be a powerful competitor. In the end after representing the state of affairs to London the Far East War Council extracted permission to leave the civil population with the food already distributed and not to destroy the water supplies or power plants.

It would indeed have been a criminal folly to do otherwise.

Following a bombing raid on Kuala Lumpur, FMS customs headquarters had moved to the comptroller's house.[11] With so much of the country now in enemy hands an increasing number of British officers were reporting there for orders. There was still plenty to be done. After two days on special duty with the police Cecil Gutteridge went north to Tapah with a colleague, R. S. Clemons, then on to Kampar near the front line where he found a large stock of rice. Since there was no transport to move it he dismissed the store guards and distributed the rice to the military and civilian population. After dealing with the stocks in Tapah he and Clemons returned to Kuala Lumpur. He was sent to Seremban to ferry Public Works Department lorries south to Segamat, a job he shared with Kenneth Hellrich and C. R. Bradley. He eventually drove a load to Singapore where he reported on 11 January. The following day he received permission to join the navy and went aboard HMS *Laburnum* two days later.

Robert McCall[12] was also given a driving job. Oddly enough he was employed to continue deliveries of rice, driving a brand new timber lorry. The situation was somewhat uncertain and he made his last drop at Tanjong Malim just before the Japanese arrived. In early January he joined his colleagues on the route south of Kuala Lumpur and gave up his splendid timber lorry for a ramshackle affair, which only started when two wires were connected. He drove in company with Cecil Gutteridge but had to leave him on the Mantin Pass when Cecil suffered a tyre blowout. At Singapore the Public Works Department knew nothing of the delivery, so he abandoned the vehicle and reported back to the Straits Settlements Volunteer Force. Cecil later told him that he too was unable to find a destination for his load and that when he returned to Singapore in 1945 the lorry still stood where he had left it in 1942!

Isobel Bruce[13] was still in Kuala Lumpur, having joined up with a matron in a local hospital. Her father unexpectedly appeared.

> By now he was in the uniform of a lieutenant in the Royal Engineers. After sinking all his precious dredges he had been moving quickly south, blowing up road and rail bridges behind him.
>
> Just one question 'Why have you got no further than here?' So we lashed a mattress to the roof of matron's car, left him again and motored off towards Singapore ... we weaved our way south using as many side roads as possible and ducking into the rubber trees at every sound of aircraft which were always Japanese.
>
> Our luck still held and we were tipped out at the Oranje Hotel where we grabbed a space for ourselves under the stairs. We spent three weeks trying to get a passage to anywhere and dodging the increasingly frequent air raids. Eventually the shipping agent ... got us and five more women and children into a two berth cabin on a small

> freighter sailing for Perth in Western Australia. By now I had gone down with raging dengue fever, so my memories of the five-day voyage are totally blurred. We docked in Fremantle and I came round in the Deaf and Dumb Hospital in Perth, where we were put up for the first couple of nights.

On Boxing Day Katharine Sim[14] left Jasin and travelled on to Singapore. Stuart was working in food control in Kuala Lumpur but accompanied a naval intelligence mission back to Pangkor, surviving a machine-gun attack on the return journey. From 6 January Katharine was also working in food control in Singapore. Stuart then became involved in the lorry driving activities of the department, travelling between Seremban and Singapore.

On 2 January the Japanese successfully attacked the Kampar position. The British fell back to the Slim River line where the enemy's tanks broke through on the night of 6/7 January. On the 9th FMS customs headquarters was moved south to Seremban. The army began to evacuate Kuala Lumpur the following day. There was now little to stop the Japanese advance and headquarters moved successively to Tampin, to Gemas and then to Singapore. On 31 January the last troops crossed the causeway to the island, the 2nd Argyll and Sutherland Highlanders marching to the sound of their two pipers.

During the 55 days that had elapsed since the Japanese landing in Kelantan the British customs staff in Singapore had not been idle. Peter Burgess[15] was first made aware of the invasion on the morning of 8 December when John Evans, with whom he shared a house, rushed into his room saying 'Peter, this is it. The war has started.' It had indeed. They heard explosions and looking out to sea saw a bomb explode just off one of the islands sending up a great plume of spray. Peter's work soon became very hectic.

> I had for some weeks encouraged employers to lay in reserves of rice, sugar and condensed milk for their staff and now requests for further allocations poured in. Partly through the fortunes of war stocks had accumulated fast and we had easily passed the six months supply target. Stocks were sufficient for over 14 months. On the first day many food shops had closed and the Colonial Secretary

5. Johore Bahru: the causeway to Singapore.

telephoned to say 'You must do something about it'. With the help of colleagues in the Preventive Service all the shops had reopened by the Tuesday afternoon (9th December).

I cannot remember much of the following weeks. Joyce and I took half an hour off to get married and returned to work for the weekend. At first we lived in the house above the opium packing plant with a view out to the western entrance to Keppel Harbour. Houses near the coast were then cleared and we moved to Joyce's uncle's house about four miles from the harbour and town centre. The Food Controller and I had one meeting with Duff Cooper.[16]

The Food Controller said 'I think everyone has enough to eat.' 'Too much' was the reply. Duff Cooper could not offer any advice but said that the Prime Minister had decreed that every rubber tree should be destroyed. 'I understand that for years planters have tried but failed to find an easy and satisfactory way to destroy old rubber trees.'

We kept hoping that the Japanese advance would be halted but I had little confidence that it would. After refugees flooded in and bomb damage increased we opened soup kitchens with advice and help from the Salvation Army. Many Europeans left. Our service was directed to remain to help the civilian population.

Philip Merson[17] was living in the department's bachelor mess at 'Sydenham', a house in Keppel Road opposite the docks. His deputy comptroller was paymaster Lieutenant Commander Leigh, who was not permitted to rejoin the navy and would not allow any of his officers who were not in the Volunteers to do so either. In mid-January 1942 this attitude was finally abandoned. There were now large numbers of officers in Singapore, certainly more than were needed for the current responsibilities of the department. Kenneth Hellrich[18] remembers that the comptroller took a list in order of seniority and drew a line across it. All those above the line would remain to run the food control. Those below the line might do as they pleased. Kenneth was above the line.

Philip Merson was one of 12 officers who joined RNVR the same day.

We had a week's training aboard the depot ship lying at Clifford Pier and another week aboard the *Ping Wo*, a Chinese river boat converted to an Asdic patrol vessel. I was the only one to complete the course and then joined HMS *Circe*, a Straits Steamship being converted into a magnetic

> minesweeper in the Naval Dockyard. We sailed for Batavia (now Jakarta) at the beginning of February, where we were when Singapore fell. ... I was one of the lucky ones. Of the twelve of us who joined at the same time only four got away like me, another four were prisoners of the Japs and four were killed.

Under orders to remain at their posts many married officers now made it a priority to ensure the safety of wives and families by getting them out of Singapore before the trap closed round the port. Katharine Sim was finally allotted a passage on 29 January. Stuart bade her farewell but she did not sail until two days later. She was conscious of the irony that the ship that carried her away from danger was *The Empress of Japan*.

Conti Hellrich had travelled down from Telok Anson with her two small babies, accompanied by her loyal *amah*. She secured a passage in the *Orion* on New Year's Day 1942. The voyage to Perth, Australia, took just five days, and she was able to send Kenneth a telegram to confirm her safe arrival. Despite the situation in which he had been left he had complete faith that he would see his family again. He was quite sure that the Allies would win the war and remarks that many of the local population shared this confidence.

A voyager in the opposite direction was Bicky Roualle.[19] Having served for nearly four years he was given 'home' leave in November 1941. Like many other officers he chose to spend it in Australia and sailed from Singapore about two weeks before the invasion began.

> I landed in Sydney and during the next couple of weeks attended a number of meetings of men on leave from Malaya, including Alex Boyd (the Technical Adviser on Piece Goods), endeavouring without much success to discover what we were supposed to do about returning to Malaya. Eventually I got a passage on the *Aquitania* which was carrying AIF[20] reinforcements. We transhipped to small KPM[21] ships in the Sunda Strait in the shadow of the volcano Krakatoa, where three large Allied cruisers were sunk three weeks later, and landed at Singapore on 28th January, exactly four years to the day since my arrival at Penang in 1938.
>
> I hardly knew Singapore having only spent a couple of

6. Clifford Pier landing stage (Singapore).

weekends there playing in rugby matches. I learnt that there was a large customs bachelors' mess at 'Sydenham', took my luggage there and met up with Ken Hardaker who suggested I report to the Government Offices near the Singapore Cricket Club.

I duly did so and was surprised to find Stanley Jones sitting at a table in a large open-plan office among an assortment of clerks. I had known his daughter when he was British Resident in Selangor in 1938. Until some months previously he had been Officer Administering the Government in the absence of the Governor, Sir Shenton Thomas, on leave. He seemed pleased to see a familiar face. I asked him what was going on. He replied 'I've just been sacked by Duff Cooper' which left me, a somewhat junior officer, non-plussed.

Bicky was soon to find himself an active role. As the Japanese advance rolled irresistibly down the peninsula the military began to make plans for the organization of a continued resistance by forming 'stay behind' parties to harass the occupying forces. It occurred to someone that in the country's prisons there were a number of potential recruits to such units – Chinese communists[22] who had been detained for the last few years. The police special branch had successfully penetrated the Malayan Communist Party and had subverted its Russian trained general secretary, Loi Teck. On 18 December 1941 an agreement was reached at a meeting in Singapore, which was attended by two special branch officers, G. E. Devonshire and Innes Tremlett, and by Freddy Spencer Chapman[23] as representative of the special operations executive. On 31 December John Dalley, head of the counter-espionage department of special branch, accompanied by Chapman, clinched the deal with the communist leaders at Kuala Lumpur. The Chinese had been at war with Japan since 1936. Alone among the Asian population of Malaya they were already hostile to the invaders. The detainees would be released and trained by SOE to wage irregular war.

Shortly after his discouraging visit in search of orders Bicky met an old friend, Douglas Weir, a police officer from Kuala Lumpur.

> He told me of the special unit he was with, made up mostly of government officers who knew the country and the language and who were available to serve as liaison officers with army units or to make up 'behind the lines' sabotage groups. This sounded interesting and Douglas offered to take me along to meet the CO, another police officer by the name of John Dalley. We immediately drove off into South Johore and finished up at the manager's bungalow on a rubber estate near Kulai, some twenty miles north of Johore Bahru where Dalley (now a Lieutenant Colonel) welcomed me into the unit which was known as DALCO. We stayed at the bungalow with about twenty-five assorted policemen, forestry officers, surveyors, ADOs etc. and by 10 p.m. I found myself as a form of sentry in the garden complete with Thomson sub-machine gun. All quiet except for the mosquitoes!
>
> The following day we all moved back to Johore Bahru and occupied for a couple of days the judge's residence. We did some patrols and were bombed a few times, and were then ordered back to Singapore where we were housed in the Belgian Consul's residence overlooking Orchard Road. He was not pleased! We learnt that DALCO was being changed to DALFORCE and our future role was to command Chinese units made up largely of Communists from the gaols where they had been confined following

> prosecutions instigated by John Dalley when in Special Branch. I was collecting stores and equipment for the unit in the Singapore Harbour Board area when I was caught in one of the many pattern-bombing raids. There were a number of killed and wounded around me but my only damage was bomb splinters in my right foot. I could just about hobble to the General Hospital for treatment involving surgery and bed. This must have been about 6th February.

An artillery bombardment of Singapore Island had begun the previous day, with an array of guns that included some very effective 240 mm howitzers. For three days the Japanese aircraft added to the pounding in successive waves of virtually unopposed formations. On 8 February troops of the 5th and 18th Divisions crossed the narrow straits between Singapore and the mainland. The final battle had been joined.[24]

As the fighting extended across the island Peter Burgess found that his house was in the battle area. He and Joyce retreated to the Excise Office to spend the night but returned the following day to collect a few more things.

> The Army was in the house and gave us five minutes. Amongst other things Joyce threw out a mattress and pillows from the upstairs verandah. Work continued during the last week but on the Thursday (12th February) I found time to go to visit some of our soup kitchens and was dismayed to find on my return to Head Office that our local staff had been paid off. Joyce worked in the General Hospital for the last two days but after the ceasefire was advised to return to the office.

Kenneth Hellrich was out with some fellow officers inspecting shops in the countryside when a major in the Gurkhas appeared and intimated that he expected the front line to be in that area within two hours. Kenneth decided that his activities had become irrelevant and withdrew to the custom house in Maxwell Road.

Jim Bailward[25] had driven his lorry all the way to Singapore. He was now plunged into the confusion of the last days of resistance.

> I remember being ordered to go down to the docks to pick

> up survivors from one of the 'Empress' liners, which had been sunk off Singapore and I recall my surprise when, having loaded up with men of the ill-fated 18th British Division, the man sitting next to me in the cab told me that he was the Captain of the ship.
>
> I remember a night spent in a rubber estate listening to the huge artillery bombardment that preceded the Jap assault on the island.
>
> I remember, too, being sent on a mission to the Cathay cinema, Singapore's only multi-storey building. As I arrived a shell exploded in the entrance, killing a child as it lay in the arms of its Chinese mother who was herself unhurt but whose grief was terrible to hear. The cinema seats were occupied by large numbers of Australian military who were said to be suffering from shellshock but whose condition was given another perspective by a young Australian soldier, who stood at the top of the main staircase and, in a lengthy and fluent declamation, castigated his comrades for their cowardly behaviour. It was an astonishing performance.

On 13 February the Japanese attack in the area of Pasir Panjang was threatening to overrun the main ammunition magazine. For two days the 2nd Malay Regiment fought to hold the line until it was almost obliterated. Early on the 14th the municipal water engineer reported that the water supply might give out within 24 hours. Craters wrecked the streets of the city and disrupted the drainage system. Above all, Singapore was packed with non-combatants whose suffering was constantly increasing. General Percival bowed to the situation and at 8.30 p.m. on 15 February the guns fell silent. In little more than ten weeks Malaya had been lost.[26]

Jim Bailward remembers the eerie silence that followed the ceasefire.

> The next morning I ventured forth from our billet and confronted a lone Japanese soldier. We stood and looked at each other, probably both thinking the same thing – 'So this is what the enemy looks like.' I half thought he might stick a bayonet in me but, apparently satisfied that I represented no threat, he turned away to his duties to leave me and my unit to pass into captivity.

Acting Sub-Lieutenant Cecil Gutteridge[27] was at sea in HMS *Giang Bee*, a converted freighter previously used by her owners, the Heap Eng Moh Steamship Company, to carry coal from Singapore to Batavia. Equipped as a patrol ship she had been in action off Singapore, enduring two attacks by dive-bombers and picking up survivors from the *Empress of Asia*. At 9.00 p.m. on 12 February she set sail with about 250 refugees on board, men, women and children. Her complement included three other expatriate customs officers serving in the RNVR, C. R. Bradley, E. J. Evans and E. C. Rowland.

> For the first 60 miles of our voyage we navigated in absolute blackness owing to the extremely heavy blanket of smoke from burning Singapore. Our last view of the Island, as we turned Peak Island, was awe-inspiring; a dark, black pool of water almost completely encircled by roaring flames. The rattle of machine gun and small arms fire, and the metallic clang of bursting shells could be clearly heard.

Throughout Friday 13 February they were under attack by Japanese aircraft. That evening the sight of a number of warships coming over the horizon raised brief hopes that their ordeal might be at an end, but as the distance shortened it became clear that the ships were Japanese. With a single four-inch and two Lewis guns the commander, Lieutenant Lancaster RN, whose skill in handling the old freighter had confined the Japanese aircraft to a single hit, had no option but to strike his colours. While the warships trained their searchlights on the stationary vessel the ship's boats were lowered with as many passengers as they could safely carry. Bomb damage to the falls caused one to break loose, its occupants swept away in the strong tide. There were still about 200 persons on board, passengers and crew, when late that night the Japanese suddenly opened fire. She burst into flames and just after 11.30 p.m. she sank, leaving the survivors to struggle for their lives in the sea.

Cecil Gutteridge writes:

> During the course of the next day I had occasional glimpses of Evans, Bradley and Rowland, but after the second night I did not see any of them again. Once, during the second day, we floated through a Japanese convoy of considerable size, but they made no attempt to pick us up. Each succeeding

> morning saw fewer heads on the surrounding water, until, on the morning of the third day, I found myself with only two companions. We were clinging to a piece of wood about two feet square, which we fondly imagined to be a boat. Towards evening on the fourth day we sighted a Japanese destroyer and cruiser, not far off; we were too weak by then to shout or signal. We saw a boat put off from one of the destroyers, but could not believe they were coming for us; the next thing I remember is waking up on board a destroyer. My two companions were with me, also one European man (an official of the Malayan Broadcasting Corporation) and a Malay woman, both survivors from the *Giang Bee* who had been picked up some time before us. We were the only survivors of those who had taken to the water four days previously.

Cecil was conveyed to Saigon and later transferred to Singapore as a POW.

Of those customs officers who served in the armed forces during the campaign seven had been killed in action and thirty were taken prisoner.[28] These last included Bicky Roualle whose injured foot earned him a lift in an army truck to the POW camp at Fairy Point.

At the time of the ceasefire on 15 February, a total of 52 people were lodging in the customs house in Maxwell Road, including Ethel Phear and Joyce Burgess, and a number of men and women who had been attached to the department to work in food control. Kenneth Hellrich records the events that followed the capitulation.[29]

> The first Japanese troops entered the city at dawn on 16th February and on the following day all European civilians were assembled on the Cricket Club *padang*. They were then moved out to a number of houses in the vicinity of the Sea View Hotel at Katong. In view of the numbers at Maxwell Road it was decided to ignore the instructions to assemble on the *padang* and to stay put in the Custom House. In this respect we were fortunate that the ground floor, as one of the food control measures, had been turned into a store of essential foods.

A curious inactivity resulted. On 18 February a Japanese officer visited the customs house. He was told that the officers there were not prepared to work for the enemy but, in accordance with the governor's orders, would continue to administer the food control system. Although they were issued with passes for this purpose it soon became apparent that the Japanese did not require their services and they withdrew their cooperation. Kenneth Hellrich continues:

> After the initial visit we were left alone until 5th March when we were instructed to join the other Europeans at Katong. We assembled what belongings we had and marched as far as Kallang. There we were met by a Japanese officer who told us to return to Maxwell Road as there was nowhere for us to go. The Europeans whom we were to join had been marched off to Changi that same day. It was not until 22nd April that we too were moved to Changi to join the other Europeans in internment. For over two months, therefore, we were left to our own devices. During that time we gradually made excursions in pairs into town, where those who had any money were able to buy vitamin tablets and books.

Kenneth remembers the sympathy of the local people. The Chinese were not on good terms with the Japanese. Nevertheless 'They need not have been kind to us which they were.'[30]

Peter Burgess remembers that there were seven women at Maxwell Road. The stores included rice, sugar, flour and 15,000 cases of canned pilchards.

> We cooked rice in enormous woks in the yard using wood from nearby bombed buildings. Someone produced an electric cooker and the ladies made scones. One had been brought up in the Australian outback and remembered how they made yeast. I bought hops and someone got some toddy to start the fermentation. In three days we started to make bread.

The march to Changi brought such improvised catering arrangements to an end. From now on the civilian expatriates and their wives were to be interned with other Europeans in secure camps. In addition to the 30 prisoners of war a further 34 officers were classified as internees. The two engineers at the opium plant were compelled to operate it for the occupying power.[31] Some 20 officers were absent from Malaya on leave or already serving in the armed forces. In Appendix IV I list the expatriate staff in December 1941 and their circumstances when the fighting ended.

Most local personnel had little choice but to continue to earn their living in the service of the Japanese administration. It was to be three-and-a-half years before they were reunited with their British colleagues.

6
Back to work

Following the capitulation of 15 February 1942 the government administration of Malaya was re-established under Japanese supervision. In the absence of the expatriate officers most local personnel resumed their employment and continued to carry out their duties in very changed circumstances. In his book *Kempetai Kindness* Tan Thoon Lip records:[1]

> One of the first acts by the Japanese was the recall of certain public and utility services; these functioned under Japanese officers, some of whom were patently incompetent or much too lazy. When the local staff was allowed a certain amount of discretion matters ran smoothly; where the Japanese head tried to introduce reform there was generally chaos. Here and elsewhere a smattering of Japanese was a passport to a comfortable position; here and elsewhere podgy, inexperienced girls were preferred to men who had all their lives been in the clerical service.

On the mainland each state was placed under a military governor.[2] These officials even adopted Malay costume in their attempts to win the sympathy and cooperation of the Malays. But the continuation of the war, the activities of the Malayan People's Anti-Japanese Army in the jungle and the increasing economic distress all contributed to a growing disillusion in the local communities.

For the customs service conditions were peculiarly difficult. The extensive international trade upon which the prosperity of the country was largely dependent abruptly ceased, and with it the revenues whose collection was the principal activity of the departments. For example, in Selangor in 1940 import duties yielded M$ 7,884,489. In 1942 they amounted to just M$ 26,288. The export duties collected fell from M$ 5,998,293 in 1940 to M$ 3131 two years later. The only large-scale trade in dutiable goods was in tobacco. Eventually, the occupying power imposed a duty of 50 per cent *ad valorem* on such imports but this was widely evaded.

Under the Japanese the service was reorganized in two divisions, Marine and Inland. The former was largely engaged in the control of imports and exports. The Inland Division had to cope with the many new distilleries, toddy shops and public houses, for which licences were freely granted. Supervision of the opium monopoly continued but, as described in later chapters, the policy of registration and rationing was not maintained and consumption of the drug was only restricted by the difficulty of obtaining supplies. Additionally, officers were often frustrated in their attempts to enforce the law as their authority was frequently ignored by the military.

In anticipation of their return to Malaya the British were making plans for its future. A Malayan planning unit,[3] controlled and financed by the War Office working with the Colonial Office, was established in July 1943. It was in favour of unification, a policy that was to lead to the short-lived Malayan Union. It also recognized that steps must be taken to provide for an administrative structure in the immediate aftermath of liberation. Since this might have to be achieved by reconquest there would be an initial requirement for a military government, to be replaced as soon as appropriate by the resumption of civil administration.[4]

The unit consisted initially of six officers commanded by Major General H. P. Hone, a colonial civil servant. It expanded rapidly. By November 1944 it comprised 121 officers and 53 other ranks and by April 1945 it had grown still further to a total of 162 officers and 127 other ranks or civilians. It drew up policy directives on some 20 subjects, including finance and opium. The recruitment and training of staff to fill the senior ranks of the government services was also put in hand. The first course was conducted at the Civil Affairs Training School at Wimbledon as early as February 1943. Under Army Council Instruction 1423 of 1944 ten-year contracts were offered for service in Malaya.

In the event the planned invasion of the peninsula was not required and the Japanese forces there obeyed the orders of their government to surrender. On 3 September 1945 an improvised civil affairs detachment was landed at Penang. Although the influence of the Japanese administration naturally declined when it became known that their forces had surrendered they were still able to maintain order in the principal towns. The civil administration, including the customs service, remained in being and was at the disposal of the British Military Administration as it took over the reins of government. It had been the intention only to engage local staff as need arose and then only in the post-operational period, but this policy was now clearly inappropriate. It was therefore decided to re-employ all government and municipal employees immediately. By September 1945, 95 per cent of the local staff of the customs service was back at work.

Few of the permanent expatriate officers of the customs service played any part in the military administration. The majority had endured over three years of captivity as civilian detainees or prisoners of war in the course of which they had suffered severe hardship and much brutal ill treatment.[5] A number of the military prisoners, including Bicky Roualle and Robert McCall, had been transported north to work on the notorious Burma Railway. J. H. S. (John) Jenkins[6] was one of a party sent to labour in Borneo. Until July 1944 Cecil Gutteridge was employed in the Singapore naval base, but was then transferred to a POW camp at Changi where he was reunited with seven other customs officers. The civilian detainees were also imprisoned in the same area and fared no better than their service colleagues. As camp secretary, Clifford Blakstad was one of 19 detainees taken for questioning by the Kempetai on the double tenth, 10 October 1943. He was severely tortured and on his return to the main camp on 12 July 1944 he weighed a mere 61 to 62 pounds. Taken to the camp hospital he immediately organized a game of bridge.

By the time the Japanese capitulated on 14 August 1945 most prisoners had access to news through various channels such as clandestine wireless sets. Indeed, many of them were aware that the war had ended well before their captors. The long delay in the arrival of the British forces was for them a period of great anxiety. In Singapore Cecil Gutteridge and his fellow prisoners were uncertain what attitude the local Japanese commander, General Itagaki, would adopt. In Borneo John Jenkins was particularly unfortunate and suffered a beating from a Japanese guard on the day after the surrender, an injustice that still rankled many years later. In Siam Robert McCall transferred to the Australian army in the hope that he might thus find a way to rejoin his wife Marye who was then in New Zealand. When the liberators finally arrived the surviving civilian expatriates were sent home to be reunited with their families, to rest and recuperate. For some, retirement was already overdue and they never returned to Malaya. The rest made ready to replace the military administration.

One person who did play a part in that administration was Philip Merson.[7] Among the dozen customs officers who were permitted to join the Malayan RNVR he was at sea when Singapore fell and survived to pursue an active career in the navy. On VE Day in 1945 he had just returned to Britain from Murmansk with an Arctic convoy when he was discharged from the navy and transferred to the army for service in the British Military Administration to be deployed in Malaya. As a captain, general service, he sailed to Bombay in early September, crossed India overland and was finally shipped to Singapore. There he found two colleagues, Tony Parker and Kenneth Cantrell, already at work. Taking charge of land division and its local staff who had remained in post during the occupation, he tackled the task of restoring the service and its working efficiency.

Although the budgetary control of expenditure was a stated goal for the military administration this proved impossible to achieve before the return to a civil government.[8] On the mainland, expenditure up to the level of 1941 estimates was given general authority but special permission was required to exceed these limits; in Singapore *ad hoc* authorizations sufficed.

The free port status of Singapore was gradually re-established. Successively, imports were authorized from Rhio and Lingga, Hong Kong and China, and Australia. It proved more difficult to supply exports, but a flow of rubber and tin was developed through the ministry of supply's buying organizations. On 17 December 1945 a handover committee was established to arrange the transfer to the civil administration[9] of 36 government departments, including the customs and excise. The military administration came to an end on 1 April 1946. That day Captain Merson went to his office in Beach Road as plain 'Mr Merson'.

Re-established as a unified department in the Malayan Union the service faced many problems. The total ban on opium[10] introduced in February imposed a major new burden on the preventive branch. It also entailed the redundancy of 400 staff. Those who could not be absorbed into other departments were paid compensation. Control of the Thai border area, where the Malayan People's Anti-Japanese Army was still at large, was a difficult and dangerous task. In all parts of the country the Japanese had authorized excessive numbers of liquor licences. Preventive work was handicapped by the lack of equipment such as launches and motor vehicles. Nevertheless, during 1946 the department initiated 2914 prosecutions and obtained 2664 convictions.

In the course of its brief rule the BMA had been unable to restore the customs and excise revenues to anything like the prewar levels. The export duty on rubber was levied before the end of 1945, but other duties were only reinstated in 1946. As a result the total customs duty collections up to 31 March amounted to just M$ 6,716,876.43. Excise produced only M$ 872,201.84. The restoration of civil government, however, was accompanied by an unexpectedly rapid resumption of trade, both in imports and exports. Estimates of revenue proved wildly inaccurate. Against an expected customs revenue of M$ 38,743,600 in 1946 the department collected M$ 79,267,741. Excise yielded M$ 3,807,427 against an estimate of M$ 2,681,000. The boom continued. In 1947 the value of both imports and exports exceeded £150 million, roughly twice the level of 1939. The following year both topped £200 million.[11]

The government was quick to claim its share of this commercial prosperity. In May 1946 there were sharp increases in import duties.[12] The levy on liquors was doubled. In November an export duty on palm oil was imposed. These were not the only additional responsibilities for the customs service. In July and August the department took over the control of imports and exports and the operation of a system of licensing. Imports were limited and exports managed so as to prevent a loss of essential goods. There were many shortages in the immediately postwar world. Cloth was in great demand and the government made an emergency import of one million yards from India for distribution to the needy.[13] In 1947 it released a further 3½ million yards under this arrangement and 23½ million yards for sale.

The prewar expatriates were now back at work. The 1948 staff list records 64 officers whose first appointment was no later than 1940. Another prewar officer who resumed his duties after the war was Alex Boyd, the technical adviser on piece goods. Their return was well received by the local population who had had more than enough of the 'Greater East Asia Co-prosperity Sphere'.[14]

John Lewis spent nine months on leave in Australia and England, returning to Malaya without his family in July 1946 on the *Mauritania*, which made Singapore in just three weeks.[15] It was not the end of his voyaging. He had been posted to Kelantan in the far northeast of Malaya. The prewar railway to that state was no longer operational because the Japanese had taken the rails for the Burma Railway. He had to travel on a small local Straits steamship. It boasted only two cabins. Most passengers slept on deck and disembarked at various small ports up the east coast while the ship anchored offshore. Kelantan had been an unfederated state and was now a reluctant component of the Malayan Union. On arrival at the capital, Kota Bahru, John was granted audience by the sultan, whose approval of his appointment was a necessary formality. It was also apparently approved by humbler folk.

> At my bungalow early one morning my houseboy told me that some Malays wished to speak to me. I went to the front entrance and found three Malay peasants with a goat. They told me that during the Japanese occupation they had made a vow to Allah in their mosque to make a gift to the British if they returned to Kelantan and ousted the Japanese. As I was the only British government officer they could contact they presented me with a lovely white goat to honour their vow. I accepted the goat with thanks and made an appropriate short speech in my Perak Malay. I was very touched by the gesture, as a goat would have been valuable to a peasant. As government officers were not allowed to receive presents from members of the public I reported the gift to the Resident Adviser. He told me to sell the goat and deposit the proceeds in the Treasury. This I did by buying the goat for my small daughter who named it 'Happy'.

Another arrival in the northern part of the country was Cecil Gutteridge[16] who was located further west in Kedah and Perlis but responsible for preventive work along the whole border with Thailand. This proved a very busy assignment, as he recalls:

> The main road and rail communications between Malaya and Thailand ran through Kedah and Perlis but there were road access points at Betong in Perak and in Kelantan where the railway from Singgora ended opposite the Malayan railhead at Tumpat. My best means of communication with Kelantan was through Thai territory by rail or road via Hat Yai and Singgora; the alternative being by road via Kuala Lumpur, a round trip of nearly 800 miles or an even longer journey by Malayan Railways. Internal air services linking Alor Star in Kedah via Penang and Kuala Lumpur with Kota Bahru did not come into operation until much later. The intervening terrain between Kedah and Kelantan was mountainous jungle and with twenty men and women at my

disposal policing this area was an impossibility. In addition we had over 100 miles of coastline to cope with.

The destruction and desolation engendered by the war in South East Asia resulted, with the return of peace, in an unprecedented demand from the southern areas of Burma, from Thailand, from the Kuomintang controlled regions of Southern China and from what was then Indo-China for manufactured goods and canned foodstuffs of every kind. There was also of course our own Malayan internal demand for the same things. Prices soared and very rich pickings indeed were to be had by those clever enough and able enough to run goods through the various controls to these denuded areas. Because of the prohibition of exports from Malaya almost everything had to be smuggled out and the bullion and other goods used for payment had to be smuggled in, but by about 1948 we had gained control over most of this traffic, even though for those stationed in the area it meant a 20 hour working day and no holidays.

Certain prime facts soon became obvious: first, that the prohibited goods being smuggled out of Malaya were paid for in rubber, gold bullion and opium; rubber because Thai rubber brought into Malaya and incorporated with locally produced rubber avoided the quota restrictions and enjoyed coverage by a local certificate of origin with a consequent lower rate of import duty into the UK under the Commonwealth Preference system; gold bullion as the normal trade methods of payment were subject to the foreign exchange control; and opium as the cessation of the government monopoly left a large unsatisfied demand in Malaya: second, that apart from very small scale petty smuggling, little of this trade went by sea, largely due to the lack of communications between the Thai coastal villages and their hinterland. (The seaward smuggling concerned chiefly the southern areas of Kedah, close to Penang Island, and was more or less confined to the inward smuggling of Sumatran tobacco and matches): thirdly, that in the early days some use was made of jungle tracks. We made a number of seizures of inward contraband on these routes, chiefly Thai leather goods, gold bullion and opium. Control of this means of smuggling was not too difficult in that whatever route was used over the border eventually the goods had to be loaded into road transport and conveyed along one of three main road routes. Roadblocks were mounted on these periodically and appeared to be an adequate control. We were assisted here by the offensive operations in jungle areas of North Kedah and North Perak undertaken by armed Chinese gangs, the remnants of Force 136 and forerunners of the Communist insurrection in Malaya, who plundered the smugglers as they made their way along the tracks. Counter action by police patrols against these armed gangs also helped to keep the smuggling traffic under control.

The outward smuggling of prohibited goods followed the normal procedure of covering such consignments by false documentation and false export permits. Contraband was often concealed in consignments of legitimate goods conveyed by lorry into Thailand. Obviously it was impossible for us to search every package on every lorry, so large quantities of prohibited goods evaded our controls. Seizures, when made, were costly to the evaders as not only were the goods confiscated but so too were any vehicles used in conveying them; the drivers and any others involved were heavily fined and in some cases sent to prison without option of a fine. Nevertheless, despite large seizures and heavy fines the traffic continued, so it must have been extremely profitable.

The outward smuggling by train was a little easier to control, as the fact that only one train per day ran up to the Thai border was itself a limiting factor. This train left Penang in the early morning and ran up though Kedah and Perlis to the border station at Padang Besar, which it reached at about half past two. At four thirty the train returned to Penang along the same single-track route. The last station in Malayan territory accessible by road was some fifteen miles from the border, after which the train trundled on its way through hilly, broken country, covered in scrub and jungle until it reached Padang Besar. Before and immediately after the war this tiny village comprised the railway station, a loco men's running bungalow, a police post, a customs post, two or three shops and a few houses. A year later, that is by September 1946, it had mushroomed into a sizeable village with five or six thousand inhabitants, a 'hotel' or two, many shops and a large number of wood and atap houses. It really did look like a Wild West shantytown in the middle of the gold rush, and the throbbing, pulsating life of the place gave it the same sort of thrusting atmosphere. The difference of course was that this particular community was built on smuggling. Though physically it straddled the border, it was legally within Malayan territory, so goods could be moved in or out without control. Apart from the daily train the only other communications were by walking 20 miles along a track or by rough road through 40 miles of Thai territory.

Export controls were evaded by consigning goods to Padang Besar, where they were unloaded into shops and peddled across the so-called border without hindrance. The traffic reached such proportions by early 1947 that drastic action had to be taken. Borrowing nearly 200 revenue officers from other districts throughout the country I arranged a special train and took them up to Padang Besar, arriving just before dawn. We then swept through all the shops in the village seizing all their stocks of manufactured articles and leaving them only such stocks that we estimated to be adequate for purely local needs. The seized goods were returned to and stored in my headquarters and the owners advised that they would be restored to them when evidence was produced that they were genuinely for local use within the area. It is interesting to note that not a single claim was made. Eventually, through measures such as this and by the decreasing demand for such goods as conditions in Thailand and neighbouring countries returned to normal, the trans-border trade was brought under control, although smuggling of high duty goods of course still continued. By early 1948 the enterprising entrepreneurs had left and life in the village of Padang Besar returned more or less to normal.

The experience of captivity had inevitably left its mark and the resumption of a normal life was not easy. Jim Bailward[17] returned to duty in September 1946 and was posted to Malacca, a delightful town with a lengthy history mirrored in its old buildings. 'I have to say', he writes,

that after the trauma of the war years, I returned to work, perhaps unsurprisingly, in a very unsettled state of mind, quite a bit mitigated though by the fact that I had recently got married and was able to look forward to having my wife by my side when she could obtain a passage. During

> that time the return to regular work had a remarkably beneficial effect and by the time my wife arrived some three months later, having had the experience of flying out in a BOAC Sunderland flying boat on a six day journey, I had, to a large extent, settled down.

The location could hardly have been better chosen. Jim enjoyed the old, largely Chinese town, with its Portuguese and Dutch buildings, and the beautiful surrounding *kampong* countryside. In the course of his preventive duties he was often called to prosecute offenders in the fine old courthouse under the *punkah*s, which were the only means of keeping the temperature bearable. His two children were born in the Malacca General Hospital. He looks back on his three-and-a-half-year posting there as a very happy time.

In Singapore there were problems of a different kind. Philip Merson[18] was a qualified solicitor and bachelor of laws. In the last days before the arrival of the Japanese he had been responsible for the prosecution of customs cases in the Singapore magistrates' and district courts. In 1946 he was to see a different side of the legal system, sitting as a magistrate and second district judge himself in the courts in South Bridge Road. It was several months before the permanent incumbents arrived to replace him and he was able to return to his departmental duties. Not surprisingly, he reverted to his former role of prosecuting officer, conducting cases in the enforcement of food control regulations, which were still the responsibility of the customs department.

Throughout the government services in Malaya there was an urgent need to enlist new recruits to the senior ranks. Wartime casualties, retirements and the cessation of appointments during the occupation had created vacancies in all departments. It was an opportunity to introduce more indigenous staff to the senior ranks. In a report on British Dependencies in the Far East (Cmd. 7709) the Colonial Office records that on 1 July 1941 there were only 48 Asian officers in senior appointments in Malaya. By 1 January 1949 there were 308. Progress was slower in the customs service and vacancies were filled by a new intake of expatriates. Soon after hostilities ended an invitation to commissioned officers to apply for appointments in the colonial service was circulated in the forces. From the resumption of civil government in Malaya there was a steady inflow of new cadets into the customs service, largely demobilized officers of the armed forces. The Malayan Establishment Staff List for 1948 records that there were then three short-term-contract officers in the service, recruited during 1946, and twenty-six cadets who joined at various dates during 1947.

These new appointments by the Secretary of State produced a very different recruit from the prewar intake. Unlike most of their predecessors, the new cadets did not come directly from school or university. They were already accustomed to responsibility and command, but many of them had no experience of civilian life. A number of them were married. Many of them had spent time in the East in such countries as India and Burma. In the event, most of them soon adapted to the requirements of their new careers.

Peter Chattaway's father went to Singapore in 1935 as the airport manager.[19] When the city fell in 1942 he was the officer in charge of the Singapore Volunteer Air Force, which was withdrawn to Java. Peter also became a flyer and spent his war in the Fleet Air Arm. On discharge he stayed with his mother in Durban, South Africa, and there applied to join the colonial customs service, expressing a preference for Malaya. After interview and medical examination in Cape Town he was offered a cadetship in the Malayan customs service and instructed to proceed to Singapore by air. However, when he presented his travel warrants to the Malayan agent in Durban he was told, 'We do not fly customs cadets round the world.' Instead, he sailed for Bombay on a British India Line cargo ship, travelled by rail across the subcontinent to Calcutta and thence by troopship to Singapore where his father greeted him on 22 July 1947.

Peter's first posting was to the inland town of Seremban, the capital of Negri Sembilan. Under the guidance of Arnold Gridley and Selwyn Buckwell he was quickly introduced to all aspects of customs work, revenue collection, licensing and preventive. The last was rendered more difficult by the fact that only one of his preventive ODOs, an Indian, spoke English. 'I remember on one occasion recording a statement from a Chinese accused with the Chinese PODO interpreting into Malay and the Indian into English. The defence lawyer was not impressed but the Magistrate accepted it as it was in question and answer form.' Peter was still studying for his examinations. He found the law syllabus fairly straightforward but, as he records, the Malay language was a different matter.

> There was a shortage of books on Malay customs and history and those lent to me mainly concerned the Malays of the East Coast and were short of information regarding the Malays of Negri Sembilan.[20] Negri Sembilan Malays orig-

> inally came from the Minangkabau area of North Sumatra and their customs were very different from other Malayan groups. Although their religion was Islam they had retained many old Hindu beliefs and customs. The teacher supplied by the government spoke no English and the only books available were Malay primary school readers. The Inspector of Schools, a Mr Lewis, was very helpful and arranged for me to join, on Sundays, a class in the local Malay school. The arrangement worked for a while but it soon became apparent that I was being taught, not the class.

Peter's other problem was money.

> My salary was M$ 300 a month (£35 at the fixed rate of exchange). I messed with the headmaster of the local English school, the King George V School, and naturally, as a senior government officer, he ran an expensive house. I paid him M$ 150 a month as my share of the bills. In addition I had the expense of a Malay servant together with club subscription, transport, etc. It made life very difficult and often I was in the red by pay day. Fortunately on occasions my father came to the rescue and when he retired in 1948 he sold me his car at a cheap price. Until then I had survived by using an ex-Army 15 cwt truck that seemed to lack springs and had a mind of its own! It belonged to the Customs Department.

In April 1948 Peter was transferred to Malacca to take charge of preventive work there. Confirmed as a customs officer he enjoyed an increased salary and the opportunity to go to sea. Both Malacca and Port Dickson had been provided with new 35-foot launches. Although their maximum speed was only about 13 knots they were seaworthy and reliable. Peter got on well with the Malay crews and his command of the language rapidly improved. Their wives provided the food on board and he enjoyed a wide variety of Malay curries, mainly fish and chicken, and the accompanying *sambal*s and sweets.

It took Derek Mackay[21] rather longer to join the service.

> My own unheroic war ended in India where I was serving in a battalion of Burma Rifles quartered at the foot of the Himalayas. A child when the war began, I was of a

generation whose life had exchanged the authority, discipline and given purposes of school for those of the armed forces. Our future was not in our hands. Now, for the first time, we faced the problem of choice. Unlike my older fellow officers who could now return to their families and careers I had to make a belated start in the business of peacetime life.

A circular in the adjutant's office revealed that the Colonial Office was prepared to waive academic qualifications for ex-officers in recruiting for the police and customs services. On application I was scheduled for a first local interview, but a home leave in the spring of 1946 provided an opportunity for a preliminary interview in London. My 'local' examination involved a journey from central Burma to Simla in India. The result was a discouraging request to advise when I had completed my military service.

Returning to England in the summer of 1947 I embarked on a business-training course in Bolton. Fired with ambition to become a tycoon I greeted a summons to London for a final interview at Millbank with little enthusiasm, but I succumbed to the lure of a free trip to the capital where I faced the panel of interrogators with a confidence fostered by an excellent lunch with a former military comrade. The offer of an appointment to the customs service in Singapore arrived on a particularly grey, wet day. England in 1947 was still in the grip of wartime privations. By November I was on my way East.

He found himself sharing quarters with three other bachelors in the mess in Fullerton Building. 'Institutional decor and strictly functional Public Works Department furniture seemed comfort enough to one ex-prisoner of the Japanese and three ex-servicemen. A Chinese servant looked after us but on cadet's pay we lived frugally, taking it in turns to shop at the Chinese Telok Ayer Market for our supplies.'

At customs headquarters Derek was introduced to the mysteries of 'Manifests & Permits', a function that entailed checking huge stock books to trace the movements of dutiable imports.

As a free port Singapore had a very limited customs tariff, imposing duties on tobacco, petroleum and intoxicating liquors. Imported dutiable goods were usually placed in

> bond and liable to duty only on removal for sale or consumption. In addition to the bonded warehouses operated by the department there were private licensed bonds subject to overall supervision and the Shell oil tanks to be checked after a nerve-wracking climb up an external ladder. Officers were expected to make random inspections of security at bonds. One, located in a rough area of Chinatown, was best reached by climbing a wooden ladder from a narrow cul-de-sac to check whether the patrolling Revenue Officer was alert.

His direct responsibility was for the largest liquor bond, 'Bonded D', a vast warehouse stacked with crates and cartons of every kind of alcoholic beverage. Their liability to duty and the rate depended on their strength. Bottled liquors were sampled on first appearance in the colony and thereafter at intervals. Derek's daily journeys between the custom house and Bonded D were made on foot.

> I was often burdened with the day's samples clinking heavily in a bag as I made my way through the hot streets. On more than one occasion I was happy to accept a lift from the chief clerk of the bond, an immaculately dressed Chinese who drove an impressive Rover. It was when I was offered the same service by the head coolie in his car that I decided I had better invest in one of my own. I bought the cheapest I could find, an underpowered, unstable Ford Eight. At speeds over 55 m.p.h. it was almost uncontrollable but at least I had my own transport.

Like Peter Chattaway Derek found his law studies full of interest but for him too the language was more difficult to master.

> My progress in Malay was slow and erratic and my *munshi*, a Malay teacher, was unimpressed by my stumbling conversation and crabbed attempts at writing the beautiful Jawi script. It was, therefore, with little optimism that I took my first Malay examination. Having sweated through the written papers I presented myself for the oral test at the Victoria Memorial Hall in Empress Place and cravenly took my place at the end of the queue waiting to face the formidable Gerald Hawkins, author of numerous books on the country and its language. This only postponed the ordeal and at last

I entered the room. My examiner was in the act of removing his trousers. He explained briefly that he was changing into evening wear and was due shortly at a dinner engagement. The examination too was brief. I was asked to translate into Malay the sentence 'That goat stinks so much I cannot stay in the room.' My *munshi* had not prepared me for this. Hawkins pounced on my clumsy attempt. 'The beauty of Malay is in its rhythm,' he said, speaking rapidly without pause. 'It is in the balance of the words. What's the greatest sentence in the English language?' I pleaded ignorance. 'Consider the lilies of the field, how they grow; they toil not neither do they spin; and yet I say unto you that even Solomon in all his glory was not arrayed like one of these. Listen to the rhythm of that sentence, its perfect balance. How long have you been studying Malay?' I told him one year. 'Oh well, there's plenty of time then.' I was dismissed. I stood disconsolate on the steps of the hall trying to decide in which of the city's many bars I should drown my sorrows. Hawkins appeared beside me adjusting his bow tie. 'Have you seen my car? I told the *syce* to be here by now. I'm running late.' I seized the moment, the great man squeezed himself into the cramped body of my tiny Ford and I followed his directions to his destination. My *munshi* was bewildered and disappointed at such an early end to his employment, but I had no further need of him. I had passed.

In 1947 the department was able to report that its duty collections totalled M$ 137,540,542.[22] Some of the duties on imports (M$ 83,086,542) derived from new levies introduced on the mainland. A 15 per cent *ad valorem* was charged on a range of high value imports, including cameras, binoculars, lighters, electrical household goods, watches, air conditioning and pianos. Patent medicines were subject to 25 per cent. There were new export duties on a variety of local products. In view of these impositions Penang reverted to the Straits tariff but introduced balancing excise levies on items that were dutiable on the mainland. In Singapore import duties were still confined to liquor, tobacco and petroleum products, but entertainment duty introduced as a wartime measure was maintained and collected by the department. There was a relaxation of export controls, but exchange control problems in relation to imports, with heavy drawings on US dollars, led to a review of all import permits. Preventive work was still handicapped by a lack of suitable launches and the continuing violence along the Thai border. An increased use of the postal service to evade duty had been observed.

Since April 1946 Singapore had been a British colony, but Penang and Malacca were now in the Malayan Union. That unpopular constitution was abandoned in 1948 and replaced by the Federation of Malaya, which excluded the colony. The mainland service was now the 'Customs and Excise'. In the colony it was dubbed 'His Majesty's Customs'.

The departmental report for Singapore shows that in 1948 import duties yielded over M$ 49 million.[23] Preventive work continued with 1228 prosecutions instituted during the year. Land transport still consisted of ex-army lorries but there were now 11 launches, including two 72-foot harbour defence motor launches. Air traffic was increasing rapidly. The island's main airport, Kallang, handled 60,000 passengers. A further 15,000 to 16,000 passed through the outlying field at Tengah. The training of staff was now a priority and the report records 15 courses attended by 164 revenue officers.

Outwardly, the future looked bright. The peninsula's trade continued to expand and in 1948 imports and exports were valued at over £200 million. But fresh problems lay ahead. For some time there had been evidence that the largely Chinese communist party was planning violence.[24] Men such as Colonel Dalley pressed the government to take action but such warnings were ignored. The meeting of Asian and Australian communists at Calcutta in February 1948 had set the agenda and on 16 June 1948 the savage murder of three Britons and two Chinese finally forced the high commissioner, Sir Edward Gent, to declare a state of emergency. In the view of the authors of *The First 150 Years of Singapore*:

> His action came months too late, at a time when the Communist Party in Malaya, with the obscene brutality which is an integral part of its philosophy, whatever its particular national or racial guise, was embarking on a murderous campaign which aimed at nothing less than the liquidation of every European planter and tin miner in the Peninsula, every loyal government officer of any consequence, and the reduction of the country to a state of chaotic bestiality and fear.

Three years after the liberation Malaya was once again plunged into conflict.

7
Merdeka

The emergency, as it was officially dubbed, resulted in the deployment of substantial armed forces, police, home guards and a variety of other services to cope with the communist guerrilla warfare and terrorist activities. The measures taken to strangle the insurrection inevitably caused inconvenience to the people of Malaya and outright hardship to some. There were curfews to observe and restrictions on the movement of food. Unfortunate Chinese squatters, who might willingly or unwillingly have provided support to the rebels in the jungle, were forcibly removed to 'new villages' where they could be both watched and protected. The managers of rubber plantations and tin mines fortified their houses, armour plated their cars and went about their business fully armed. Even in the towns some premises were fitted with grilles to defend them against grenades.[1]

The primary responsibility of the customs service was to keep watch on the coasts, frontiers and airports through which supplies and arms might be smuggled to the communists in the jungle. This entailed no major change in the deployment and methods of the service. For some officers, however, there were new activities more specifically directed to the conflict. Peter Chattaway's[2] sudden transfer to Malacca was to replace an officer who had been called up to serve in the Malay Regiment. Once there, Peter was soon required to undertake sea patrols to intercept movements in aid of the communists. His decision to train his crew for this work had unexpected consequences.

> Because of the emergency both the launches were armed with Bren guns and some of the crew were trained in their use. In my time they were never fired in anger, but once we managed to win a few magazines of condemned ammunition and we combined a patrol with a joint practice shoot with the Port Dickson launch. We met at sea off the coast

north of the Linggi River. When we finished shooting in the late afternoon (mercifully having avoided sinking each other) I decided to spend the night in the Linggi River in case any smugglers came that way. It was getting dark as we entered the mouth of the river and our wake stirred up beautiful green phosphorescence. We anchored in mid-stream and waited. About 2.00 a.m. I decided to return to Malacca, as our expected arrival time would coincide with the tide high enough to enter the river. At low tide there was only three feet or so over the bar.

We tied up at the old Custom House and took the gun back to the police station for safekeeping. As I left I met the Officer in Charge who told me that there had been a report of gunfire between two ships out to sea off the Linggi River and later the *kampong* guards had heard a powerful launch come up stream. The guards on both sides of the river then opened fire and the launch retreated. I did not explain the 'sea fight' but suggested that the guards had heard us start the launch before leaving, had panicked and started shooting across the river at each other. In fact we heard nothing above the noise of the engine and I suspected, like ourselves, the shooters were glad of a chance to practise!

One of Derek Mackay's messmates at Fullerton Building, Alan Rodick,[3] was sent to the mainland as a 'resettlement officer' charged with the unpleasant task of transferring Chinese squatters from vulnerable villages to a camp at Bukit Pisang in Johore. He lived there too and, being unarmed, was unable to reply to the shots directed at his hut by the guerrillas firing from concealed positions in the adjacent jungle.

Although hostilities were largely confined to the mainland it was recognized that the waters around Singapore might be used by boats carrying arms or other supplies to the terrorists and the customs were called in to assist in patrolling the area. Derek Mackay writes:[4]

We used the two HDMLs on overlapping patrols of thirteen hours duration, followed by twenty-three hours rest. Thus for those engaged on these duties, including me, day and night patrols alternated. Apart from the crew and some Revenue Officers to conduct searches, I was accompanied by two or three armed police constables and a European auxiliary police officer to share the command. The auxiliaries were usually good company but often remarkably ignorant of local geography. Before my watch below I always briefed them and pointed out the landmarks or, at night, the lights forming the limits of our operational area. On one night patrol I handed over to the auxiliary before taking a watch below. As usual it seemed only minutes before I was shaken awake and made my way to the bridge while the auxiliary snuggled down in his bunk. Automatically I checked the lights to establish where we were but they were totally unfamiliar. The *serang* stood calmly beside me at the wheel. I asked him our position. He replied that we were some distance down the Sunda Strait. We were deep in Indonesian territory in an armed vessel. Visions of an international incident flashed through my mind as I ordered a reversal of course and all possible speed back to Singapore. The *serang*, who seemed remarkably unruffled by the situation, explained that the auxiliary had given him no instruction to alter course and he had assumed it was in order to keep going.

In the course of these lengthy patrols Derek was able to learn a great deal about the tropical seas and those who sailed upon them.

By daylight we spent the time checking every small craft in sight. In those days the variety of local craft in Singapore waters was quite astonishing. Many of them were under sail. From the Celebes came the beautiful pelaris, popularly known as Bugis schooners. With white hulls, green tripod masts, gaffed rigs and twin steering oars manned on outboard galleries they were a fine sight under full sail. Larger, but less pleasing to the eye, were the huge timber ketches, with logs piled so high on their decks that it took about half a dozen men to manhandle the loose footed mainsail across the cargo when tacking. Smaller vessels included the lambok, golekkan, leteh-leteh and Trenggannu penis, a name derived from the European pinnace on which their hulls were modelled. The Chinese too were still using sail for less urgent cargoes carried in *tongkang*s and *twakow*s.

I found the crews of these sailing craft were usually experienced sailors with a profound understanding of the sea and the unlimited patience learned from the unpredict-

> able nature of their voyages. Not so the largely Chinese operators of motor vessels. Many of these were undecked Chinese boats in which an engine of doubtful age and reliability had been inserted, and the crews showed little understanding of their profession. They were often seriously overloaded. I recall seeing motor trucks carried athwart the boat with the wheels overhanging both sides. Since these were not registered ships but operated under licences issued by small ports in the Indonesian Islands their losses at sea would probably have gone unreported.
>
> It was on one of my first patrols that I approached Singapore soon after dawn and met a fleet of *kolehs*, the small canoe-like vessels used by Malays for inshore travel. They were well packed with passengers, men, women and children, dressed in their brightest clothes. They lay alongside the big HDML while I questioned the occupants. They had come from somewhere deep in the Rhio archipelago in Indonesia and crossed into Singapore waters without any form of passport or authority. Indeed, they professed to know nothing of such formalities. After all, as they explained, this was Saturday and they had appointments at the clinic. Apparently, the excellent medical services in the colony were much appreciated beyond its boundaries. Singapore was their nearest city and it seemed to me unreasonable to deny its facilities to people who probably regarded the theory of territorial waters as some obscure European joke. I often exchanged greetings with them on subsequent Saturday mornings.

These additional duties were a makeshift response to a threat for which the government was ill prepared. As reinforcements were drafted into Malaya the anti-terrorist measures became their responsibility and the customs service was able to revert to its normal activities. Despite the problems created by the emergency the two departments in Singapore and the federation were both making good progress in modernization and increasing revenue collections. As described in following chapters they were also coming to grips with the drug problem.

By the end of 1949[5] the department in Singapore had a staff of 582. These included 16 officers of the Malayan customs service, 16 local preventive officers, 44 clerical and administrative employees, 381 revenue officers, eight of them female, and a marine division of 65 *serangs*, engineers and *lascars*. The following year they were responsible for the collection of revenue in excess of M$ 52 million. Preventive staff rummaged 8961 vessels. Their launches steamed 13,890.75 hours. They cleared 7734 aircraft and 105,679 air passengers and rummaged 1463 aircraft during the year. They carried out 1256 raids in search of drugs and 575 inspections of licensed premises. Many of these actions led to arrests and prosecutions. During 1950 these resulted in 408 convictions and fines totalling M$ 218,302.

Released from his maritime duties, Derek Mackay had been transferred to special division and later took over the role of prosecuting officer for the department, a task previously undertaken by the far better qualified Philip Merson. As so often, it was a case of learning on the job.

> I was entitled to take cases before Magistrates and, if more serious, before District Judges. All were salaried members of the Colonial Legal Service and drawn from all communities in the colony, European, Chinese, Malay and Indian. Appeals against their decisions were referred first to a single High Court Judge and from him to a court of three such judges. As an officer of the court I was required to see that 'justice was done' and was subject to the overall supervision of a deputy Public Prosecutor. Minor cases were rarely defended but in many I found myself pitted against professional lawyers. In Singapore there was no distinction between barristers and solicitors. All practised as 'advocates and solicitors'. They too were representative of all races.
>
> The laws of Singapore were all provided by statute, though the courts took cognizance of decisions made in the UK. The majority of my cases were on charges laid under the Customs Ordinance or the Dangerous Drugs Ordinance. We also had to comply with the Penal Code and Criminal Procedure Code, which were modelled on Indian legislation with certain significant differences. Although I was never entitled to be addressed as 'm'learned friend', I was not at a serious disadvantage. Unlike my opponents I only required knowledge of a narrow field of law and could enjoy the benefits of specialization. Nevertheless, when I presented myself on the first morning, attired in the obligatory jacket and tie and clutching a wad of case files, I was in at the deep end with no idea if I would sink or swim.

First business in the courts each morning was to deal with the newly arrested who had probably been held in police custody overnight. The charges were read to the accused and their pleas recorded. In contrast to UK practice their choice was between 'Guilty' and 'Claim Trial',[6] an expression less likely to confuse people unfamiliar with our system of justice. Those pleading guilty on minor charges could often be dealt with immediately. In cases involving drugs the Guilty plea was recorded and sentence postponed pending receipt of a certificate from the Government Chemist confirming the nature of the substance. This was a necessary precaution. At least one accused displayed the greatest anger when acquitted on the ground that the 'opium' for which he had doubtless paid a considerable sum was only a harmless fake.

The acceptance of the certificate was authorized by statute. Unfortunately, in the transfers of power involved in the transitions from the immediately postwar military government to the Malayan Union and then to its successor the Colony of Singapore, the legal drafting went astray. One well-known Singapore lawyer, D. K. Walters, spotted this, challenged a certificate and secured an acquittal. The amendment proved no better and he did it again. After the third revision I tested his sense of humour by telephoning to ask if the statutory instrument was now effective. He passed the test and confirmed that it was.

After the 'first mentions'[7] or subsequent remands had been cleared the court would settle down to the trials scheduled for that day. Proceedings were recorded in English but the witnesses might speak a great variety of languages, Malay, Tamil, Urdu[8] and any number of Chinese dialects. A team of interpreters was therefore employed, one keeping the accused informed of what was going on and others acting between the court and the witnesses. This meant a slow progress, made even slower as the magistrate or judge recorded everything in longhand. There was certainly no opportunity for quickfire cross-examination. A fair proportion of accused changed their pleas to 'Guilty' at the beginning of the trial. This could have been on the advice of counsel or, in the case of professional smugglers, the result of a satisfactory arrangement for compensation. It was known that those who 'took the rap' would be well looked after by their employers.

The percentage of convictions in customs cases was high. The department was not under the moral pressures that drove the police to pursue weak cases against dangerous and anti-social offenders. Our primary task was to maximize the revenue and we had to balance the benefits of a successful prosecution against the cost of time in court, which might have been better spent in the field. Unless there was a good chance of conviction it was more profitable to use our limited resources elsewhere.

The emergency naturally had a far greater impact on the federation customs. Their work inevitably took them into the danger areas and was often handicapped by legal restrictions and considerations of personal safety. Despite these problems the department in 1949 collected federal duties of over M$ 197 million.[9] The preventive service initiated 4638 successful prosecutions for which fines were imposed totalling M$ 732,674. To these must be added the revenue derived from 'compositions'. These usually related to minor offences by the general public, such as inward passengers who failed to declare some dutiable item. A senior officer had powers to offer a 'composition fee' to the offender, on payment of which (plus the duty) his goods were returned and he was free to proceed without a criminal record. As the alternative was a formal prosecution, such offers were almost invariably accepted and in 1949 yielded revenue of nearly M$ 30,000.

Unlike Singapore, the federation imposed duties on a wide range of imported goods, many of which were assessed on an *ad valorem* basis. To ensure accuracy and uniformity of valuation the department in 1952 set up a central assessment office. It inaugurated a price-reporting scheme to provide a centralized record of declared values of goods, which could be disseminated to all stations dealing with such imports. Increases in the duties on petroleum and tobacco in 1953[10] contributed to import duty collections that alone amounted to more than M$ 198 million. Export duties exceeded M$ 112 million. The total money collected by the department that year, including state revenues, was over M$ 395 million.

On the mainland, as in Singapore, air traffic was increasing rapidly. The local airline, Malayan Airways,[11] provided services throughout the peninsula. In 1949 it was operating seven Dakota aircraft. In the ten months to February that year it flew 16,300,000 passenger miles, many of which would have been accumulated on flights between the federation and the colony. Commercial cargoes were still carried largely by sea, rail or motor transport. Following a long established practice the federation customs maintained an office at Singapore railway station. Although it was officially known as the Supervisor of Export Duties Office (SEDO)[12] it dealt also with import duties on goods railed to mainland destinations. It was to this office that Peter Chattaway[13] was posted in January 1949.

Peter's new life was in marked contrast to his previous experience at Malacca. He now worked office hours in a big city. His responsibility was imports and much of his time was spent in the identification of dutiable goods and the valuation of those liable to *ad valorem* duties. Liquor and tobacco from Singapore bonded warehouses set no problems as they had already been checked and classified. Other imports could give rise to difficulties. There were hides from Australia so badly packed that it was hard to reconcile them with their supporting documentation. There were canned goods from China, poorly tinned and crudely sealed with lead solder, which could only be passed after the chemist had checked them for contamination. When an overripe consignment of sharks' fins was in store the warehouse became almost uninhabitable. His decisions occasionally met with disapproval. Head office rejected his classification of gripe water as intoxicating liquor. Although its alcoholic content was 5 per cent it was decreed that it should be treated as medicine. Coping one day with exports in the absence of a fellow officer he valued a baby elephant at M$ 300. Although it was probably worth about M$ 1000 his explanation that 'It was only a baby and I reckoned the poor mite wasn't very healthy and wouldn't live to an old age' was accepted without censure.

SEDO was not unaffected by the emergency and came under increasing stress in 1950 as terrorist ambushes caused shortages of railway wagons and erratic timetables for the goods trains. The restrictions and curfews on the mainland roads also encouraged importers to switch to rail, which added to the pressures on the customs staff. To ensure that no one was able to jump the inevitable queue of merchants demanding clearance Peter introduced a numbering system. This proved effective but he was much relieved when yet another transfer came through and he left Singapore on a posting to Ipoh.

On his return from home leave Derek Mackay[14] had also been transferred and was now in the federation, still in a preventive role at Johore Bahru.

In Johore, the most southerly state, my section had to watch over two extensive coastlines, East and West, the land frontier at the causeway[15] link to Singapore (both road and rail) and the usual internal problems of drug distribution and consumption and illicit distilling. In addition to a small staff of plain clothes officers I boasted some 13 vessels, including a 56-foot ocean-going launch, two high speed 'skimming dishes' for use in the Straits and several outboard motored sampans used to patrol the mangrove swamps. The import duty tariff was extensive and offered corresponding opportunities for evasion by running, false declaration and other ingenious devices. The heavy flow of traffic across the causeway facilitated the smuggling of small high-duty items in passenger vehicles and the coasts were difficult to protect against the running of bulk contraband.

The opium traffic remained a major headache. We were generally aware that there was a movement of the raw drug down from Thailand and that ships and aircraft were used to drop buoyed containers in the South China Sea off our East coast for collection by fishing boats. With a load of fish and ice on top the consignment could be brought into any remote harbour and distributed in smaller loads by road. Without accurate information interception was a matter of luck. It was the sort of luck that evaded me and my occasional voyages in the elderly launch with a maximum speed of about nine knots and the wholly inappropriate name of *Rimau* ('Tiger') were little more than flag displays. Nevertheless, they were enjoyable trips, cruising in tropical seas and usually visiting the tiny, mountainous island of Pemanggil, where we dropped anchor in a bay whose waters were crystal clear six fathoms under our keel, and used the dinghy to land on a sandy beach to sample the headman's hospitality.

The South China Sea was not always calm. Storms could blow up without warning and put small craft in danger. On one occasion I was sailing north in *Rimau* in the hope of intercepting a shipment of opium near Pemanggil. Late in the evening we spotted a local motor vessel lying at anchor in a dead calm, some miles offshore. On inspection we found that it had suffered an irreparable engine failure. Moreover, it had put to sea with no provisions and very little water. Unwilling to give up my mission I put some food and water

> into the vessel and promised to take them in tow when I returned the following day. As darkness fell the wind began to rise and soon we were pushing on through bigger and bigger waves. In such conditions the local craft might drag its anchor. We had no choice but to turn back. I spent an anxious hour or two crouched on the foredeck with the *lascar*s, peering into the blackness ahead as we tried to find the stationary craft. Fortunately, the *serang*'s navigation was dead accurate and the anchor had held. We got a line to them and towed them into the safety of the river at Mersing. Such storms could even threaten *Rimau* and more than once I was grateful for the skills of the crew and the reliability of her single Thorneycroft diesel.

The coast to the north came under the Kelantan office. Immediately after the war John Lewis[16] at Kota Bahru was once again given an additional role as the *shahbandar* or harbour master. The duties were not demanding but he did encounter one mystery when he found stranded on a sandy beach a large empty tank, some 40 feet long, on which was lashed a new motor launch. The boat was the property of the US coast guard. He could only surmise that it had drifted across the South China Sea all the way from the Philippines. Later, Robert McCall inherited these duties and those of naval reporting officer. As such he was called upon to entertain the *Amethyst*[17] when she was sent to Kelantan after her dramatic escape from the Yangtze River. He hosted a cruise down the coast, which ended when he was put ashore at Kuala Trengganu with a severe hangover and a long ride home in a rickety taxi. For his naval duties he was provided with a very imposing special safe. 'Though I examined its contents,' he writes, 'I could find no record of my predecessors ever 'reporting' anything – and neither did I!'

The customs service now had a rival revenue collector. Under pressure from the UK government the two Malayan administrations had introduced income tax,[18] collected by a separate department of Inland Revenue in the federation and an income tax department in Singapore. Direct taxation is always a difficult collection. In Malaya, a country of so many different cultures, languages and methods of accounting the new departments faced a formidable task. When in Singapore, Derek Mackay observed that of all the many rich local merchants he interviewed as prospective bailors for drug carriers, he did not encounter one who had ever paid any income tax. Sterling companies in the UK paid one-third

7. Preventive staff in 1954, Johore Bahru.

of the modest collection of M$ 13 million in the federation in 1948/9. Nevertheless, progress was made. In 1954 federation income tax produced M$ 103 million. Some tax collected on behalf of the federation is included in the Singapore figure of just over M$ 56 million that year.

There is little doubt that the emergency accelerated the pace of progress towards self-government in both territories. In 1955, for the first time, elected members[19] constituted a majority in the Legislative Council of the federation. In government service there was now a pressing need to increase the proportion of indigenous staff in the more senior appointments. It was not easy to attract a suitable calibre of recruit to the less glamorous departments and the process of 'Malayanization' moved slowly in the customs service. The 1955 staff list names 74 officers in the federation. Of these just ten were of local origin, mostly Malay, and almost all were appointed in 1948 and 1949. Such officers were usually promoted from a lower rank such as preventive officer (the equivalent of a police inspector). In both territories there was still a serious shortage in the senior ranks and recruitment of expatriates continued. The same staff list includes 21 who joined the service in the years 1950 to 1954. Despite this the list records that there were 36 vacancies against the establishment.

A new arrival in 1950 was Tony King.[20] Trained as an engineer, Tony joined the Royal Navy in 1948 and learned to fly, but returned to civilian life in 1949 to continue his career as an assistant engineering works manager. The lure of a recruiting advertisement in *The Times* persuaded him to another change of occupation and in February 1950 he sailed to Singapore in the *Willem Ruys*. Tony describes his arrival there as

> In all a good introduction which culminated in an extended tour of Singapore by night and by day before being taken to Johore Bahru to join the Night Mail to travel to my first posting in North Perak. I was taken to the dining car and introduced to three senior *Tuan Besars*[21] who invited me to join them. They explained that the dining car was the only coach that was not likely to be shot up by the communist bandits as we steamed through the jungle. The bandits were bribed by the Chinese head steward of the car and they did not wish to kill the golden goose.
>
> We duly limped into Kuala Lumpur at dawn. The locomotives at the front and the back of the train were wheezing steam like riddled colanders and many coaches had been raked by the bullets, but the dining car was untouched. I said farewells to the senior *Tuan*s who assured me the principal ingredient of their survival through the rigours of the climate, malaria and incarceration by the Japanese was to be found in the bottle or two of Scotch with which we had passed the night. I was greeted by an immaculately dressed representative of the Comptroller of Customs who invited me to join him for a drink in the dining car of the Day Mail, which was to take me to Taiping. He had an orange juice. I stuck to my tipple of the last twelve hours and had a Scotch. Years later I found a signal had been sent to all Senior Customs Officers: 'We have a new cadet, name of King, ex-Navy, drinks Scotch for breakfast'.

Although an inland town, Taiping[22] was a registered point of entry for imports by rail or air. The area included Parit Buntar, which before the war stood on the boundary between Perak, a federated state, and Province Wellesley, an integral part of the Straits Settlements. There were small ports at Port Weld and Kuala Kurau. Stationed there were a modern diesel launch and an impounded Chinese motor *tongkang* used as a 'Q-boat'. Tony collected a brand new 36-foot launch from Singapore to be based at Lumut. He found that his PODOs were all stationed in Taiping where they had established a congenial way of life that produced few cases of any worth. Making use of spare accommodation in the outstation barracks he introduced a revolving rota system that detached the officers from their links with the local community and encouraged them to go after bigger prey. From the subsequent results it appears that it was an effective reform.

While most of this new wave of European recruits were, like their predecessors, newcomers to the country, there were several who joined the service locally. Two had been in government service since 1946 and were transferred from other departments and a third was transferred from the police.[23] Gordon Crocker came to the department from quite another background.[24] His interest in Malaya stemmed from an uncle who had served there in the Department of Education and stayed on the family farm near Dorchester after the war to recuperate from his experiences as a prisoner in Changi. After completing his national service Gordon took a course for ex-officers at the Camborne School of Mines and accepted an appointment as a mining engineer (prospecting) in Malaya. Taking leave of his fiancée Anne, he sailed in November 1950 and arrived in Singapore in the midst of the Maria Hertogh riots.[25] On the night express to Kuala Lumpur he was issued with a rifle and ammunition to help defend the train against a communist ambush. He soon found himself making good use of his military experience, recruiting and training a special constabulary to protect the mines and assist the security forces. It was a dangerous life. Gordon survived two ambushes.

He also learned to like the country and to speak the language. But there were snags. 'I could not see a great deal of future in this particular industry and I wanted to bring Anne to Malaya but not to live behind a barbed wire fence.' Fortunately, he was given an introduction to D. G. (Sam) Hall, the comptroller of customs, who interviewed him at the departmental headquarters in Kuala Lumpur.

> I was offered an appointment in the Malayan Customs Department. The variety of work attracted me and being a rather independent spirit the idea of being given clear terms of reference and allowed to get on with the job suited me well. I raised the question of getting married and bringing my wife-to-be to Malaya. No objections were raised and I booked her passage on the next available ship.

Gordon was posted to Telok Anson to serve under S. H. R. C. (Pat) Paterson.

> Telok Anson was an ideal district in which to start. There was a very wide range of responsibilities, some imports and exports, a match factory, several distilleries, an air strip, outstations at Bagan Datoh and Sabak Bernam, several toddy shops and an active preventive branch which gave rise to a great deal of court work – practically every branch of our department on a small scale.

The temporary transfer of officers from the UK customs service provided further reinforcement. At a time when it was becoming increasingly obvious that Malaya was unlikely to provide a European government officer with a permanent career these three-year appointments served to fill some of the vacancies without calling for a long-term commitment. The first three such officers arrived during 1952. They all had several years experience in the UK service. Although they had to cope with some differences in powers and procedures and a very different environment they adapted quickly. A later secondment in 1955 was that of E. D. N. (Desmond) Kemp[26] who spent his tour in Port Swettenham. He writes:

> Having served in the Royal Navy during the latter part of the war I joined HM Customs & Excise in UK as a Higher Executive Officer. After six years as an Unattached Officer, acting as a relief and covering all aspects of the department's activities I was working in Newhaven when my Senior Executive Officer mentioned that he had just read a novel about Malaya. He commented that as a young man I would have a more exciting time in such a place. Shortly after, the home department indicated that the Malayan Service had three vacancies for unmarried officers on temporary transfer.

Although Desmond was married his application was accepted. With his wife Joan he flew to Singapore in November 1955 and travelled to Port Swettenham.

> My first impressions were very favourable and most of the customs procedures were similar to the UK, duly amended

to cover local circumstances. Two main differences were: no search warrants required and one prosecuted one's own case. As the emergency was still ongoing and although I was used to carrying side arms in the forces it was unusual to be doing so as a Customs Officer when on a raid or patrol. Whilst in Port Swettenham I covered three posts, running the main Customs Godown, the local Investigation Branch and the Port Division. The latter post covered the Customs patrol launch in which I made several long patrols up the north and down the south coast.

In September 1954 the customs duty order imposed a considerably extended import duty tariff in the federation – 28 new items became subject to import duties, mainly *ad valorem*, and another ten items were amended.[27] The initial application of this legislation raised many problems. Apparently simple classifications were found to have a far wider scope than had been foreseen. As an example, the description 'paper products' could be held to cover an extraordinary range of manufactures, including roofing tiles and plastic laminates used in fitted kitchens. Head office had to cope with a flood of requests for decisions and, inevitably, of complaints from importers who challenged the department's interpretations of the new order. Amendments to the *Rulings Book*s held at every collection station were issued almost daily. The valuation office was also kept extremely busy. The new tariff yielded an additional three million Malay dollars in the last quarter of the year. It also required an increase in the staffing of the department but numbers remained well short of establishment.

The following year the federation customs and excise formally adopted the measure of open market valuation[28] in conformity with international practice. The purpose was to assess the price at which the goods would change hands between a willing seller and buyer in a transaction in which price was the only consideration and there was no other relationship between the parties. In practice such transactions were rare. Most imports to Malaya were invoiced between associated parties. Many were shipped by an overseas company to its local branch, or by a principal to an agent whose role might be governed by complex agreements covering such matters as advertising and marketing. It is hardly surprising that the comptroller was led to report that local traders had some difficulty grasping the new concept.

The 1950s were also a period during which, in both territories, there was substantial progress in the training and welfare of local staff.[29] Operating within the confines of a small island the service in Singapore had been able to organize formal training courses since as early as 1948. In the federation there was a clear need for a single centre that could offer the facilities for a structured training programme. This was finally established in 1956. A ten-acre site, four miles outside Malacca, it provided administrative and residential blocks, staff quarters, reading rooms, a library, a museum, recreation rooms and a canteen. It offered a six-week basic course and a four-week refresher course for experienced staff. Teaching aids included films, slides and discussions. During 1957 a total of 299 students passed through the school, 57 probationary and 242 experienced revenue officers. The comptroller reported proposals to introduce courses for senior officers also.

The planning and preparation for the project began in 1954. Stuart Sim went looking for someone to put his ideas into effect and his choice fell upon J. V. (Vincent) Lane.[30] In 1955 Vincent went on leave to the UK with instructions to find out all he could about training methods, systems and equipment that might be relevant to the department's needs.

> At this time, industrial management and training in Europe were enjoying a major renaissance after the doldrums of the Second World War. In the forefront of this movement were gurus such as Douglas McGregor and Peter Drucker, with their emphasis on the 'human side' of management. This new approach gave powerful food for thought to those in charge of industrial training. I was lucky to make useful contacts in this area with the help of the Industrial Society in London, which had excellent relations with the more go-ahead elements in both industry and the trade unions.

Back in Malaya he was soon heavily committed, overseeing and trying to speed up the construction of the school, working on the programmes for the course, selecting staff and developing his own skills as a training manager. This last entailed visits to a number of existing training establishments: the Police Training School at Kuala Kubu Bahru, the Malay Regiment Junior Leaders' School near Malacca and, on the Muar Road, a reform school run by a remarkable former prison officer, Harry Shorters. With Stuart Sim he could now set about planning the first course, which, inevitably, would be for instructors. Meanwhile, the structure was nearing completion.

> The local Agricultural Department had landscaped the site and planted many flowering trees including cassia, acacia, jacaranda and flame trees. Space was set aside for badminton and volleyball. I resisted the temptation to ask for a tennis court!
>
> Exhibits began to arrive from far and wide for the museum. This was to display a collection showing the 'black arts' of the smuggler and in practice was a useful teaching aid for the younger less experienced ROs. British Council and USIS were generous in letting us have a number of general interest films, and training films for the instructors' course were obtained from the Industrial Society in London.

A great deal of the training took the form of practical exercises such as fact-finding excursions, mock trials, liaison with other government departments and a final field day when students were required to track down a gang of 'illicit distillers' in the neighbouring jungle. Apart from the immediate effect upon the efficiency of the service, this opportunity to assess staff in a structured situation could be of great value in selecting individuals for promotion as independence drew near and expatriate officers would have to be replaced.

The construction of staff quarters was another priority.[31] In the larger centres of population entire 'customs villages' were built. In Singapore the policy of providing blocks of flats continued. The colony also boasted a flourishing and active sports club, a canteen and recreation room and a thrift and loan society to assist the staff financially.

There was also substantial reorganization.[32] The division of the preventive service in the federation into units based on each state or settlement was a serious handicap to the exchange of information and coordination of effort. A regional structure had long been advocated and anticipated by individual officers who established unofficial lines of communication with colleagues in other areas. In 1955 such arrangements were followed formally with the appointment of a director of preventive service at head office and three regional assistant comptrollers, north, central and south. The director was also responsible for the operation of the central information office at which the reports received from officers in the field were collected and correlated. The regional structure extended to the whole department. Three senior assistant comptrollers exercised general supervision over all functions in their areas, both revenue and preventive. Within each region were districts of varying size. Rural districts might be grouped under an assistant comptroller. Main entry ports were usually of equivalent status. In some less important locations an officer might still find himself undertaking the full range of customs and excise work. It was, indeed, the policy that all staff should be transferable and familiar with all aspects of the department's responsibilities, although likely to specialize when promoted to senior posts (see Appendix VI).

By 1957 the comptroller was able to describe the price reporting scheme initiated by the central assessment office (renamed the valuations branch) as providing at assessing stations 'a very full and useful guide to values of a wide range of *ad valorem* imports which forms a safeguard against undervaluation of goods which would result in unduly low collections of duty'. The technical adviser on piece goods was now attached to the branch.

A further improvement in efficiency was the mechanization of the accounting systems,[33] adopting methods and equipment recommended after a survey conducted by a firm of private consultants, Urwick Orr, in 1956. In the field of personnel management the introduction of Whitley councils[34] provided the machinery for regular discussion and consultation with representatives of the staff.

In Singapore, a compact island with a limited tariff, there was still some need to adapt to the changing conditions of trade and travel.[35] Four divisions – land, docks, harbour and airports – covered the work of revenue collection and protection. As the city and port spread ever wider the number of rural outstations was reduced and by 1958 there were just four including the major installation at Woodlands at the south end of the causeway to the mainland. There were now just two government bonded warehouses for the storage of dutiable liquor and tobacco. Preventive branch undertook duties of a coastguard nature for the protection of revenue and prevention of imports of illicit drugs and was organized in four divisions, corresponding to those of the revenue branch, commanded by senior customs officers who reported direct to the assistant comptroller preventive. Special branch was concerned with the investigation of revenue evasions and large-scale drug trafficking. In this latter responsibility it worked closely with the narcotics intelligence and liaised with the police, the

Corrupt Practices Investigation Bureau and provost personnel of the services in Singapore. It included a court division, which conducted all prosecutions on behalf of the department.

The Singapore preventive fleet had increased to 17 vessels, including 14 motor launches, two outboard-engined speedboats and a depot ship. All launches were equipped with VHF radio and two with radar. The 15 motor vehicles included a 36-seater bus.

The two departments still collected the bulk of the revenue of their respective territories.[36] In his annual report for the year 1957 J. A. (Tony) Parker was able to record that the service contributed more than two-thirds of the total revenue of the federation. From M$ 137 million in 1947 collections had risen to M$ 533 million in 1957. The import tariff had increased from 30 to 80 items. 'Agency' commitments included the supervision of open general licences on behalf of the Ministry of Commerce and Industry, work on behalf of the marine department, collection of tin buffer stock contributions and the revenue from toddy shops on behalf of Malay states. A new customs station was planned on the causeway at Johore Bahru (it opened in January 1958) to cope with traffic of 1000 lorries and 15,000 passengers a day. Yet staff numbers had fallen to 1914 (against an establishment of 2047).

In Singapore too revenue collections were increasing. In 1957 they topped M$ 100 million for the first time. In the following year they reached M$ 108 million, despite depressed trading conditions, which were blamed for falls in the yields on liquor and tobacco. Petroleum duty was buoyant, its contribution rising from 25 per cent in 1956 to nearly 32 per cent in 1958. The cost of the department remained modest. Over the years it was running at about 3.75 per cent of revenue. Here too there was a shortage of staff. In 1957 the department numbered 675 against an establishment of 746. Proportionally, the deficit was highest among the most senior ranks.

It was proving difficult to recruit indigenous staff to replace the expatriate officers. In the federation a formal process of 'Malayanization'[37] had been initiated but its application to the customs service produced disappointing results. In 1956 the Committee on Malayanization of the Public Service reported that against an establishment of 95 senior officers (Division I), including a training reserve of three, there were 71 expatriates and 21 Malayans. After providing for a 'leave reserve' of 15 expatriates there remained 18 vacancies. Almost all the Malayans had been promoted from Division II.

A particular problem was the 3:1 quota (three Malays to one non-Malay) applied to direct entrants to Divisions I and II. As the report remarks:

> There are many other opportunities for Malay graduates – notably the MCS for Honours graduates and the MAS for pass graduates. Hence it has been difficult to recruit Malays to the Customs Service at Division I or II level. The 18 Malay officers now in Division I are aged between 35 and 40 in most cases. None has more than 8 years' Division I service. The other Malayans are somewhat younger but have less Division I experience. No Malayan is yet of such seniority as to qualify for a super-scale appointment.

As the writer goes on to say 'The work requires integrity, discretion and good judgement, and a great deal of knowledge and skill which can only be gained by relatively long experience.' He sums up: 'In these circumstances, there is little prospect of rapid Malayanization despite the relatively low standard of academic qualifications required.' Clearly, the customs service was not as attractive to the ambitious young Malay as the prospect of a career in the higher echelons of administration in a country that was soon to win its independence.

The race between the two territories was close but it was Chief Minister Tungku Abdul Rahman who won *merdeka* first for the federation, which became a sovereign state on 31 August 1957.[38] The future of all expatriate officers in government service had been discussed at length and presented them with a personal choice. Broadly, they could continue in the service of the new administration with no guarantee of employment beyond five years. They were free to apply for transfer to another territory or to accept a redundancy package that provided a pension wholly commutable into cash by those whose service was less than ten years. Although a number of officers in the customs service were willing to soldier on there was, inevitably, an immediate loss of those who preferred to pursue new careers elsewhere. Their replacements were of local origin and largely by promotion within the department.

The federation staff list for 1958 names 96 officers in the service, 12 short of the establishment. Ten of these were on leave prior to retirement or reversion to the UK service. Of the remainder, 40 were expatriates, including 19 first appointed before the Japanese invasion. The 46 Asian officers included 26 promoted to the scale in 1957. As late as 1961 there were still 16 expatriate officers in post including the comptroller, deputy comptroller and all four senior assistant comptrollers.

Although Singapore was not to achieve self-government until two years later *merdeka* marked the end of the unified service in Malaya. Both administrations were now responsible for their own customs departments. Both territories inherited a service in process of modernization and sufficient experienced staff at all levels to ensure its efficiency. The timing of independence is usually a negotiated compromise and can never be universally appropriate. The transfer of power in Malaya and Singapore was peaceful, orderly and generally amicable. The customs services stepped into the future without a hitch.

Part Three:

The Opium Problem

9. Interior of a government opium saloon (Ipoh 1929).

8
Wholesale monopoly

In 1934 Peter Burgess of the Straits Settlements Government Monopolies Department was interviewing registered opium smokers in Singapore.[1] Their reported occupations covered a wide range and included a Belgian diamond merchant and several 'grasshopper catchers'. Much intrigued by his discovery of insect hunters Peter made enquiries and found that these men did indeed earn their living by providing live grasshoppers to feed caged birds. This, and a wealth of other information collected in the survey, was duly collated in a comprehensive report to provide yet another chapter in the strange story of the opium traffic in Malaya.

Opium has been consumed throughout eastern Asia since time immemorial. Its source, the poppy *papaver somniferum*, has been cultivated in a broad strip of territory stretching from Greece and Asia Minor in the west, and eastward through Egypt, Persia, India and China. The poppies are usually planted in loose, rich soil in November. On a February afternoon the half-ripe heads are wounded with a knife. The following morning the milky sap is scraped off, drained and dried and kneaded into cakes or balls. In this form it is firm and varies in colour from a pale gold to a smoky brown. Among a number of alkaloids its content includes about 6–8 per cent morphine. Widely used in Eastern medicine for the treatment of such ailments as diabetes, diarrhoea and heart disease it is also a highly addictive recreational drug. It was particularly popular among the Chinese who generally consumed it by smoking. For this purpose the raw opium was boiled and filtered, leaving a dark brown substance with the consistency of treacle, which could be packed in individual doses, wrapped in pieces of bamboo leaf. This was commonly called chandu. The smoker would scrape up the chandu with a long steel needle and hold it over a small lamp designed to produce heat rather than light. As the chandu melted and sizzled it was shaped into a little ball by rotating the needle between the fingers, then dabbed on the pinhole in the head of the opium pipe through which the smoker would inhale. The effect was a sense of well-being and, for many addicts, the relief of the pain that had driven them to the drug in the first place.

As the British expanded their territory in India during the eighteenth and nineteenth centuries they found that they had acquired substantial areas of opium cultivation and a profitable export trade. There were mixed feelings about the ethics of such traffic. In 1773 Warren Hastings annexed the opium monopoly for the Indian government.[2] Yet, ten years later, he described opium as 'a pernicious article of luxury', fit only for foreign commerce. In 1839 a House of Commons debate concluded that it was a necessary evil, despite the opposition of such men as Macaulay.[3] That same year Britain was drawn into a war with China,[4] which eventually forced that country to accept the importation of opium from India.

The maritime traffic between the Indian Ocean and the South China Sea passes along the coast of Malaya and its ports must have been involved in the opium trade from very early times. The Dutch governor of Malacca, Balthaser Bort,[5] reported in 1678 that the main merchandise it handled was pepper, opium, cloves, mace, nutmeg and resins. In 1785, following the Dutch acquisition of Rhiau, an island territory to the south of the Malayan peninsula, his successor P. G. de Bruijn,[6] wrote a lengthy memorandum to the governor-general at Batavia, advocating the transfer of Rhiau's trade to his own colony. He was greatly concerned with the traffic in opium of which he wrote:

> Twelve hundred chests of opium a year, perhaps more, could be put up here once the import trade was established as described. Let your Honours allow this Government to buy for the Company as much opium as it can manage to dispose of again within the year, whether by sale to the inhabitants or by disposal to merchants from other parts, provided that none of it shall be shipped to Batavia, the East Coast of Java, or Cheribon. Let your Honours issue authority to the Opium Association, for the purchase and sale of that article here by their agents. The result will be a profit of 50 Spanish dollars per chest, 1200 chests yielding a profit of 60,000 Spanish dollars or 85,000 R (Rix) dollars, which is not to be despised.

It was not indeed. The governor also stressed the attraction to 'the people of Rembau, Selangor and Perak (who, like the remaining natives, cannot live without opium)' who would therefore choose to trade their tin at Malacca. He may well have exaggerated the extent of such addiction but it was inevitable that the drug habit should have been introduced locally, particularly as increasing numbers of Chinese began to settle in the peninsula.

In its settlement of Penang,[7] acquired the following year, the East India Company almost immediately decided to tax vice as a source of much needed revenue. Farming monopolies to the highest bidder did this. In the year 1805/6 the gambling and opium farms yielded S$ 74,640 against a total of S$ 62,072 from all other sources. The Court of Directors was not proud of this, recording that the farms 'appear to give encouragement to the two most dangerous vices of society', but deciding nevertheless that they could only control and confine them to a separate part of the town. At this time the Chinese population of Penang was already about 6000 and the monthly rental of the Georgetown opium farm was S$ 2850. By 1808 the colony was drawing revenue from a number of sources as shown in Appendix I.

Like their Dutch rivals the servants of the East India Company were keen to profit from a general traffic in opium. In a letter to the Court of Directors on 12 November 1805 the governor in Penang outlined the prospects.[8]

> The annual demand for the Malay Market from the best information to be obtained may be estimated at 1000 Chests. Half of this quantity appears to be supplied through the channel of the European and American merchants here, the other half by the first Bengal value of last year. A very large importation of Opium here last year was from 13 to 1400 Spanish Dollars per Chest, yielding a profit of from 56 to 69 per cent on the price at first Bengal value of last year. A very large importation of Opium might not from want of capital meet with a very ready money sale here, but we are of the opinion that there should be no difficulty in disposing of several hundred Chests at the above rates, and we are not aware of any good reason why the Honble Company should not through our means, participate in the large profits the Malay markets afford in the sale of this article.

The temptation is obvious.

In March 1820, Lieutenant-Colonel Farquhar,[9] the resident of

Singapore, suggested that the only revenues in a free port would have to be derived from the establishment of opium, liquor and gambling farms. As recorded above, the objections of Stamford Raffles were ineffective and Singapore followed the examples of Penang and Malacca. That the free trade policy was to be applied to the traffic in opium was made clear in the instructions given to Captain Travers later that same month when he was preparing to take over from Farquhar during his absence on leave. The lieutenant governor at Fort Marlborough wrote:[10]

> Whatever Regulations may be necessary for restricting the indiscriminate vend of Opium & Spirituous Liquors for the consumption of the place, you are to be particularly careful that these in no way interfere with the most perfect freedom of Trade in the former Article. A Certain Number of Houses may be Licensed for the sale of prepared Opium, but Opium in its raw state is to be allowed to be purchased and sold in any quantities however small and to be retained and exported without being in any way subject to the check or License of any Authority.

A Dr Little writing in *Logan's Journal* in 1848 severely criticized the system.[11] He claimed that although the settlement had licensed only 45 opium shops, he had personally visited over 80, ranging from simple atap sheds to solid, two-storeyed, brick buildings. Yet even he felt that farming was the only practical solution to the problem. As the British government took over the East India Company possessions its colonial administrators inherited the system. The Malay states of the mainland successively accepted British advisers or residents and the arrangements for their revenue farms were regularized. In the four states that were to form the FMS in 1896 a standard pattern emerged.[12]

Inland the farms were required to collect an import duty[13] on the opium consumed by Chinese workers in the tin mining areas. In designated coastal districts, which included the area of Negri Sembilan adjacent to Malacca, the farmer held the monopoly of sales of chandu. The coast farms did not make a major contribution to revenue. They were intended to prevent smuggling from the mainland to the Settlements, where the drug was more expensive, and were therefore allotted to farmers in the colony. The Perak coast farmer was based in Penang, the farmers for Selangor and Negri Sembilan in Singapore and Malacca. It was also hoped that the division between coast and inland districts might reduce the power of the secret society monopolists. It is impossible to say whether the system was successful in these terms. There was always a suspicion that the farmers might themselves be the smugglers.

It was also the practice agreed with the government of Johore that its farm be awarded to the Singapore farmer, and with the state of Kedah, even when still under Siamese jurisdiction, that its farmer be the holder of the Penang farm.

Since the inland farms were acting only as collectors of an import duty, it was arguable that the states might be capable of doing the job themselves. In the 1880s Perak, Selangor and Negri Sembilan all experimented with direct collection. They reverted to farming, but in 1894 Selangor again tried its hand at tax collection, relying on the coast farmer to prevent smuggling. The following year it restored the farm, just as Perak opted for direct collection. This time the experiment was successful. Selangor followed suit in 1900 and Negri Sembilan in 1901. In Pahang the import duty was still collected by the opium import duties farmer.

In the Straits Settlements a committee was set up in 1891[14] to consider the possibility of government control of the opium trade, but rejected the proposal. Nevertheless, in 1898 the Legislative Council was again discussing the traffic and received a report from the government analyst, Mr W. N. Bott.[15] He explained the current arrangements for production of the drug.

> Manufacture of chandu ... is carried on by the Singapore Opium Farm at Johore Bahru in two separate buildings about a quarter of a mile distant from one another. Both places are under separate management, employing about 75 and 35 men respectively. India opium is, as far as can be ascertained, used exclusively for the preparation of chandu consumed in the Straits Settlements. In the second establishment 'Patna' opium is worked up into chandu for export to Australia and America. The Johore works formerly supplied all the chandu for Singapore, Penang, Malacca, Rhio and Karimun, but separate works have since been started in these places.

By the late nineteenth century, however, world opinion was beginning to move against the encouragement of opium consumption. In 1895 a royal commission on opium[16] found that smoking was far less harmful than opium eating and cited medical opinion that it had no ill effects when smoked in moderation. Nevertheless, the commission was highly critical of India, 90.5 per cent of whose opium production was currently for export, a practice described as 'unworthy of a great dependency of the British Empire'. In 1900 the government in Singapore took its first step towards a more responsible policy when it introduced controls[17] over the price of chandu and limited the size of a packet to three *hoon*s (0.375 grams). Quality was not specified. Two years later Selangor introduced Enactment No. 20 of 1902,[18] which restricted sales of chandu to licensed premises and provided for their management. The other federated states soon followed suit. In 1903 the Attorney General of the Straits Settlements introduced a bill to the Legislative Council under which all chandu was to be manufactured in a special, government-inspected factory in Singapore. The import of chandu was forbidden and imported raw opium was to be stored in bonded or licensed warehouses. The retail price of chandu was increased from S$ 2.15 to S$ 3.00 per tahil (37 grams). The immediate consequence was a sharp increase in the bids for the farms. They proved ill judged and by 1905 the farmers were in deep trouble and pleaded successfully for rent reductions. In 1906 Straits Settlement Ordinance No. 20 provided regulations on the quality of chandu, the transfer of farms and the powers of government officers.[19] As Margaret Lim observes, the government of the colony, and to a lesser extent that of the FMS, faced a problem of growing expenditure and static revenue, but they had at last taken steps to establish government control and supervision.

In 1906 a general election in Great Britain saw a landslide victory for the Liberal Party and the formation of a government with an extensive programme of reform. In the House of Commons on 30 May[20] a motion introduced by John Morley, Secretary of State for India, that 'Indo-Chinese opium trade is morally indefensible' was carried unanimously. In that same year the Chinese administration made its first moves against the drug in China. It prohibited opium in schools and in the army. It also decreed the registration of addicts and a scheme to ration their supply of chandu on a gradually reducing scale. In Singapore Dr Suat Chuan Yin founded the first opium refuge for addicts.[21]

The following year the issue was again raised in the House of Commons, and the Colonial Secretary wrote to Sir John Anderson in Singapore saying 'I do not see how the introduction of apparently ever increasing quantities of opium into a British Colony and

Protectorate can any longer be defended.'[22] He urged that steps be taken for 'minimizing and eventually eradicating the evil'.

In 1908 Great Britain signed an agreement with China that annual shipments of Indian opium to that country should be progressively reduced to eliminate the traffic by the end of ten years.[23] It was impossible to ascertain if China was also cutting back on local production, but a fresh agreement in 1911 aimed at a cessation of the trade by 1917, provided that China produced satisfactory proof that its own manufacture had ceased.

In Malaya, a Straits Settlements and Federated Malay States anti-opium conference was convened. The majority of the delegates attending were Chinese. At its second session in 1908 it passed a resolution urging the government to take steps to abolish the use of opium. In fact it was already making the first moves.

In 1907 Sir John Anderson, governor of the Straits Settlements, appointed an Opium Commission to investigate and advise on the whole issue of opium consumption in Malaya.[24] It was not an easy task. Even in 1906 more than 50 per cent of the revenue of the Straits Settlements was derived from the opium farms.[25] In the Federated Malay States, which enjoyed the benefit of export duties on tin and tin ore, the proportion was rather less but still a substantial contribution to the budget. The situation varied in other Malay states but most of them operated some form of farm. It was common practice to license the owners of inland tin mines to supply the drug to their employees. In Johore, at that time wholly independent, the *kangchu* (headman) system was applied to the numerous Chinese settlements known as *kangka*s (literally 'river foot').[26] The Chinese headman of each such settlement enjoyed a monopoly of public gaming houses, pawnbroking and the sale of alcohol and chandu. Any interference in the traffic would obviously have serious financial consequences.

Shortly after it began its work the commission was instructed to extend its scope to the Federated States. Its purpose was to report on the prevalence of opium smoking in both territories and the steps to be taken to 'minimize and eventually to eradicate the evils arising' therefrom.

In the course of producing its 1200-page report the commission interviewed 75 witnesses and found that there was still a conflict of view on the effects of opium smoking. A majority of the medical practitioners questioned by the commission asserted that it was not harmful in moderation. Evidence was given that the habit appeared to have only a marginal effect on a smoker's capacity for work, that it did not lead to insanity and produced no observable influence on longevity or heredity. It was further noted that life insurance companies were prepared to accept moderate smokers as a first-class risk. The commission expressed the opinion that 'opium smoking in excess is not indulged in to any considerable extent amongst the communities with which we have had to deal.' The only crime it encouraged was theft. Indeed, one argument against prohibition was that this might drive addicts to consume hard drugs or alcohol with more serious social consequences.

Despite the evidence that many smokers first acquired the habit through taking the drug to ease the pain of various ailments the commission concluded that opium smoking was 'the expression among the Chinese of the universal tendency of human nature to some form of indulgence'. As Victor Purcell sarcastically remarks, 'In other words they did it because they liked it.'[27] The report did, however, draw attention to the deleterious effects of consuming chandu dross.

In considering the possibility of prohibition the commission commented that:

> The well sustained constant increase in the prosperity of the Straits Settlements, as shown by the volume of commerce in and out of the ports of the Colony, and the phenomenal development of the Federated Malay States are in the main due to the energy and business acumen of the Chinese population, and we are unable to accept the somewhat hypothetical view of Antiopiumists that the use of opium by the Chinese has had any noticeable effect in stemming the prosperity of the Colony and the Federated Malay States.

They regarded the difficulties of enforcing prohibitive legislation as insurmountable.

The commission rejected the suggestion of a poll tax to maintain the colony's revenue and also opposed the introduction of import duties on the grounds that they would damage trade. It recommended instead that the farms be abolished and replaced by a government monopoly. Registration of smokers was not favoured since it might interfere with immigration and create a labour shortage. As recorded above the report severely criticized the behaviour of the farm preventive officers (*chinting*s) whom they described as 'usually men of undesirable character' and 'highly corruptible'. They were said to cause annoyance through their highhanded methods of trying to detect smuggled chandu and the commission recommended the appointment of European officers to supervise preventive action.

True to form the commercial community had greeted the appointment of the commission with suspicion. In a leading article published on 20 July 1907 the *Straits Times* made a prediction with the words 'We assume that the Commission is appointed upon instructions from the Colonial Office, and we may be sure the issuance of the Commission's report will be followed by orders from Lord Elgin and his henchman Mr Winston Churchill to suppress the opium traffic.'[28] The writer went on to express the hope that the imperial government would 'replace the balance of revenue over expenditure' and that the colony's military contribution would 'no longer be extorted'. His fears proved groundless. The commission's recommendations were accepted. Nevertheless, the unofficial members of the Legislative Council duly, and ineffectively, opposed the Chandu Revenue Bill introduced to give effect to them.[29]

They were welcomed in the House of Commons where, on 27 July 1909, Colonel Seeley,[30] Winston Churchill's successor as Parliamentary Under Secretary at the Colonial Office, announced that 'The Government is about to set up a State monopoly of opium ... we will not cease to do our best to ... diminish, as far as possible, and as soon as possible, the consumption of opium in all places where the Colonial Office has rule.' In Malaya the farmers, not unreasonably, complained that they faced losses and pleaded for concessions. Very little was done. There was an inevitable decline in revenue.

The current farms were all due to expire on 31 December 1909. On 1 October the newly formed Government Monopolies Department took over the opium factories at Telok Blangah in Singapore and Sungei Penang in Penang to process raw opium, imported from India and Persia, and to pack chandu in small packets, usually with a content of two *hoon*s (approximately a quarter of a gram).[31] The government of the Straits Settlements provided the initial capital for the enterprise. Orders were placed in Britain and China for supplies of paper, pots, bamboo leaves, sealing wax and other materials required for the packing process. A highly reputable local trading house, Guthrie & Company Ltd, was initially employed as the department's agent to purchase the raw opium. This arrangement led to complaints from rivals in business and they too were given the opportunity to tender for import contracts. For the first year of the monopoly, 1910, 3175 chests of opium were imported into Singapore from Persia and Benares and yielded 3,300,000 tahils of chandu (approximately 123 tons). A further 416 chests were delivered to Penang. In Singapore the raw opium was stored at the departmental headquarters. In Penang space was provided in the strongroom of a local bank.

In order that the drug might mature before distribution commenced on 1 January 1910, cooking of government chandu began in November 1909, alongside production by the current farmers. To distinguish the official product from smuggled chandu the senior government chemist added a secret tasteless ingredient. An underestimation of demand and the closure of the Penang factory at the end of April 1910 were met by opening two additional boiling rooms. Eight such rooms were soon in use, each served by a staff of nine. Between 200 and 300 employees worked in the packing plants in Singapore and Penang. Listed among the officials of the Straits Settlements in 1910 are an assistant government analyst and opium inspector and a superintendent of the opium factory (paid on a scale from £450 to £600 per annum).

In a first step towards modernization of the plant it was decided to replace the wood-burning stoves with a Mond gas plant ordered from Britain. Unfortunately, delivery was greatly delayed by labour troubles in England, but when at last installed it proved quite efficient. A new filter system was rejected and dismantled when it turned out to be wholly inadequate for its purpose.

The monopoly was administered as a commercial enterprise. A chartered accountant, Mr H. B. Polglase, was recruited from England to set up appropriate accounting systems. At the end of each year the department published a balance sheet and profit and loss account. In its first year of operation the chandu monopoly repaid the initial loan from government and showed a net profit of 1,792,972.39 Straits dollars.

At midnight on 31 December 1909 the farms were suspended in Penang, Malacca and Singapore. They reopened on 1 January 1910 under the supervision of the department. Sales from the packing plants were confined to licensed operators of smoking saloons or retail shops. The possession of non-government chandu became an offence and a new Deleterious Drugs Ordinance came into force. The new preventive service was soon active in the enforcement of the monopoly.

In the Federated Malay States the process of closing the opium farms was complete by 1 January 1911.[32] Within the new organization of the trade and customs department two chandu superintendents were appointed, and an assistant superintendent was appointed for each district. A separate department to run the chandu monopoly was created within trade and customs in December 1910. Curiously, the uniformed local officers of this department were officially titled 'revenue officers'. Their counterparts in the rest of the service were known as 'outdoor officers'. The Penang opium factory closed in April 1910 and the FMS set up its own packing plant in Kuala Lumpur. By January 1911 this was supplying all the federated states.

Elsewhere the reforms were slower. Kelantan farms were closed on 31 March 1913 and those in Trengganu in early 1917. The *kangchu* system in Johore was not finally abolished until 31 December 1917.

The packing of the chandu was the subject of some discussion. The superintendent favoured the use of sealed tubes, a method already in use in Dutch Java. He agreed, however, that the expense of setting up a suitable packing plant would be prohibitive and it was decided to continue the practice of the farmers wrapping the 'doses' in bamboo leaves and packing them in earthenware pots.[33] These were supplied to the chandu shops in the Straits Settlements and the Malay states. The shops were open to the public and there were no restrictions on consumption.

The pricing of chandu was also a problem, as that of the raw opium was remarkably volatile.[34] The Straits Settlement *Annual Report* for 1910 records that the price in October 1909 was S$ 920 per chest. By August 1910 this had risen to S$ 2325 only to fall to S$ 1800 by the end of the year. Nevertheless, a measure taken to try to control and reduce the consumption of chandu was to increase the retail price.[35] The licensed opium farmers had been selling at a price of S$ 3 per tahil (37 grams) for standard quality and S$ 5 for a more mature product. The price of standard chandu was immediately increased to S$ 4.30 and thereafter by stages to S$ 12.50 by 1919. Whether in consequence or not, between 1911 and 1921 the annual consumption per head of Chinese population in the Federated Malay States fell from 295 grams to 128 grams. In the Straits Settlements it fell from 314 grams to 231 grams.

In the Federated Malay States 1910 saw an increase in the revenue from opium but this was explained by the price increases. Volume was down. The *Annual Report* for 1911 estimated that consumption had fallen by 50 per cent since 1908 and by 30 per cent since 1909. Chandu was now all prepared in the Singapore factory, received in bulk and packed in Kuala Lumpur for Selangor, Negri Sembilan and west Pahang, and in Penang for Perak. Imports of chandu had fallen from 224 tons in 1906 to 91 tons in 1911. By 1912 it was also possible to report a reduction in licensed outlets.[36] Some 284 smoking saloons had been closed since the start of the monopoly and retail outlets were down from 381 to 347.

The deleterious effects of smoking dross were recognized by the administrations in both the settlements and states.[37] Measures were taken to deal with the problem of dross by buying it up. Between 1910 and 1930 some S$ 4 million was spent on such purchases.

In both territories there was preventive action against the illicit traffic.[38] In 1910 there were 66 prosecutions under the Deleterious Drugs Ordinance and an unknown number included in the 634 cases involving either liquor or drugs. Seizures amounted to 418 lbs of raw opium and 1414 lbs of chandu. Other drugs were also confiscated, including 2062 oz cocaine and 366½ oz of morphia. In the Federated Malay States there were only 28 prosecutions under the Dangerous Drugs Enactment in 1912 but 442 the following year. By 1918 prosecutions under the Chandu Enactment totalled 531, giving rise to 445 convictions and fines of S$ 42,886.

Meanwhile, international moves against the traffic continued. The Hague Conference of 1913 appealed for action and in 1917 the Indian government terminated the trade to China.[39] In 1919 the Hague Convention came into effect and the policy in Malaya was reviewed.[40] In both the Straits Settlements and the Federated Malay States supplies to licensed shops were reduced by 10 per cent in an attempt to cut consumption. This inevitably led to hoarding and profiteering and outbreaks of 'rowdyism'. The experiment was abandoned after three months.

In 1919 the factory processed 4044 chests of opium.[41] Sales in the Settlements (including Christmas Island) were 141,727 lbs (63 tons) yielding S$ 17,511,229 of revenue. Exports to the Federated Malay States were 148,050 lbs and to other Malay states 79,208 lbs. The FMS reported sales of 137,577 lbs. Arrangements to repurchase dross had proved disappointing. Licensees of retail outlets were supposed to return 50 per cent of their chandu sales in the form of dross, but had only managed 1797 lbs. It was suggested that about 80 per cent of all chandu was smoked off the licensed premises and the dross was therefore irrecoverable.

In 1924/5 the Geneva opium conferences called for more effective measures to limit production and manufacture of deleterious drugs.[42] This, no doubt, influenced the British Malaya Opium Committee, which in 1924 recommended the replacement of licensed shops by government retail outlets.[43] The committee warned that further restrictions on consumption would be risky. Cheap opium was easily available from China. Instead, it proposed a reduction in the number of retail shops,[44] the packaging of government chandu in metal tubes for easier identification and an increase in the price paid for dross. It still opposed registration.

In the Straits Settlements the number of retail shops fell from 583 at the end of 1923 to just 73 government shops at the end of 1925. In the Federated Malay States the 291 shops licensed in 1919 had fallen to 111 government shops in 1926, private smoking saloons from 25 to 19 and government saloons from 61 to 26. An 'observer system' had also been introduced to identify habitual users. The early 1920s saw an apparently corresponding decline in the imports of opium to supply the government factory.[45] Measured in chests per annum these were:

	Indian	*Persian*	*Total*
1918	3360	351	3711
1921	3001	169	3170
1925	2569	1	2570

Sadly, this trend was not maintained and imports had to be increased to meet a rising demand. Two causes of this unexpected reversal were identified. The fall in consumption had occurred during a period of economic recession and the return of prosperity led to greater indulgence. It was also suggested that the former licensed shops had probably traded in smuggled chandu, a practice less easy in the now universal government shops that were far more strictly supervised. The customers were now forced to buy the government product.

There was also evidence of an increasing illicit traffic, principally from China. In 1921 seizures of smuggled opium and/or chandu were made on 66 ships arriving in Malayan waters, 43 of them from China. In 1924 there were seizures on 360 ships, of which 345 were from China.[46] The total amounts so discovered that year were 1051 lbs of chandu and 7545 lbs of raw opium (3.84 tons). In 1925 the figures were 3055 and 22,924 lbs (11.58 tons). To cope with this problem Singapore recruited two additional European supervisors and a number of local staff and introduced two new 16 m.p.h. customs launches.

These measures appear to have had some effect. To the 11½ tons of smuggled opium and chandu seized that year there were added a further seven tons taken in 1926 and slightly more in 1927. Nevertheless, in that year the superintendent of the preventive service reported that despite a loss to the smugglers estimated at S$ 2 million there had been no perceptible diminution in the traffic.

The apparent failure to control consumption was the subject of increasing criticism. In 1926 the revenue from chandu sales in the Federated Malay States had reached S$ 15,110,897.[47] Matters were brought to a head that same year when the Straits Settlements administration made a large purchase of Persian opium to meet a shortfall in supplies from India. The timing was unfortunate. A League of Nations commission was then in Persia trying to persuade that country to reduce its production. Lord Cecil, who was about to attend a meeting at Geneva, complained that the colonies had done no more than establish a monopoly and that critics in the USA were claiming that the underlying purpose was to maintain the Indian revenue from exports. He chaired an interdepartmental committee of the Foreign and Colonial Offices at which the issues were discussed.[48] It was clear that both Hong Kong and Malaya resented the criticisms of their policies and felt that harsh measures would only lead to corruption of the public services and increased smuggling. In Singapore there was information that a large *kongsi* or syndicate had been formed ready to run opium from Amoy in fast launches. It was also stressed that the Government Monopolies Department was getting better information and making larger seizures of contraband.

The upshot was that on 1 February 1927 the Colonial Secretary, Mr L. S. Amery, wrote to Sir L. N. Guillemard (Governor of the Straits Settlements and high commissioner of the Federated Malay States) urging that steps be taken to introduce registration of smokers.[49] In 1928 a system of voluntary registration was finally initiated. In January 1929 the system became compulsory.[50]

The year 1927 was also the occasion of a major reform in the Government Monopolies Department of the Straits Settlements.[51] Seizures of illicit opium that year amounted to 17 tons and it was feared that the recent loss in the revenue derived from sales of government chandu was caused by increased smuggling. As described above, Mr J. J. Warren carried out a drastic overhaul of the preventive service. In future the European officers of the departments were to be appointed by the secretary of state for the colonies.

In 1928 the first cadets under the new recruitment procedure arrived from Britain. Among them was John Lewis who was posted to Ipoh, the capital of the federated state of Perak. He recalls that the government chandu was delivered from the factory in Singapore, packed in wooden crates in sealed railway trucks.[52]

> The Ipoh office collected the crates at the local railway station and transported them in its own lorry under armed police escort to a concrete strong room at the office. About five Indian labourers were employed in the strong room to pack the blue paper packets into trays for easy transport to the chandu shops.
>
> Each shop held about one month's stock of chandu, which was replenished monthly from Ipoh by the office lorry with one armed policeman. It was my duty to inspect every chandu shop in the state monthly to ensure that the clerk in charge did not 'fiddle the books'. All one had to do was to add up the number of packets of chandu in stock and the cash taken from sales which should tally with the original stock. As Perak is a big state I normally had to stay overnight at one of the government resthouses, which were to be found in every town. One town called Kroh was in the most northern part of Perak and could only be reached through the state of Kedah. It was a very small town in the hills, surrounded by jungle and a very lonely station. It had, however, a European police officer who was always glad to meet visitors. There was another similar town called Grik in north Perak, which was only about fifteen miles from Kroh through the jungle, but about eighty miles by road via Kuala Kangsar.

Purchasers from the shops now had to be registered with the chandu branch and carried cards that established their right to buy. John Lewis remembers that in Ipoh there was still a government smoking saloon, a sort of opium public house, which was, however, closed a year or two later.

A further development was the construction of a modern chandu packing plant at Pasir Panjang in Singapore, completed in 1930 at a cost of nearly S$ 1 million.[53] The contract to build it was given to a British firm. Kenneth Hellrich remarks that:

> The engineer who came out to install the machinery is reputed to have been so frightened of catching malaria that he spent all his time under a mosquito net. The plant was placed under the overall control of a Deputy Commissioner (later an Assistant Comptroller) and two engineers who supervised the operation of the machinery. These two – Wilbraham and Salter – gradually redesigned and replaced the imported machinery with a highly sophisticated system.

The chandu was no longer packed in bamboo leaves or paper but was distributed in small metal tubes, mostly containing the usual two *hoon*s, each bearing a coded identification of the state to which it had been issued and the date. The plant also supplied chandu to the Siamese government in slightly different tubes, easily distinguishable from those used in Malaya and similarly coded. The assistant comptroller and his two engineers were provided with houses on 'Packing Plant Hill' behind the works. The plant began operation on 1 April 1930. In 1931 it produced 66,404,437 standard two-*hoon* tubes and a further 566,400 tubes of two *chi*, ten times as large.

The new metal containers were the basis of a fraud by the clerk in charge of a chandu shop in Perak. They were packed in glass-topped wooden boxes, each holding about 100 tubes. Inspecting the shop John Lewis decided to check the unused stock.[54] He found about half the boxes were empty. The offending clerk, who had presumably pocketed the proceeds of the unrecorded sales, was sentenced to a term of imprisonment.

In November 1931 a League of Nations commission visited the Straits Settlements to check on the current situation. Its report was made available to the department the following year.[55] With the cooperation of officers in the Federated Malay States proposals were submitted to the Malayan opium advisory committee for an improved system of registration to embrace all consumers of chandu. That year the department's annual report was able to claim that the 'cumulative efficiency of the reorganized preventive service is at last making an impression on the illicit traffic'. Deprived of the smuggled product smokers were forced to turn to government chandu.

In implementation of the 'Agreement and Final Act' signed at Bangkok on 27 November 1931 the legislation governing chandu was amended to make it an offence for a non-registered smoker to possess it.[56] To give time for voluntary registration it was decided not to enforce this provision until after 31 December 1933. The Straits Settlements departmental report for that year recorded that its register at 31 July 1933 listed 45,386 names, of which only 10,488 were active. The new register held 23,290 actives.

On 31 December 1934 the registers of smokers were closed to new applicants except on medical grounds.[57] There had obviously been a late surge in requests for registration. The Straits Settlements now listed 55,942 smokers (less 1710 cancellations for various reasons including duplication and death). The annual report noted that only 23 applied for more than the standard maximum ration of four *chi* per day, approximately half an ounce and equivalent to 20 standard two-*hoon* tubes. The aim now was eventual abolition as mortality reduced the numbers on the registers to the comparatively small class of medical cases. The gradual reduction of the size of each smoker's ration would be reflected in the overall figures of production and sale, and improvements in the efficiency of the preventive service should keep the illegal importation of opium in check.

The opportunity was taken to conduct a detailed survey of the smokers on the registers. So it was that Peter Burgess discovered the trade of grasshopper catcher.

9
Retail monopoly

From 1934 onwards the governments in British Malaya were committed to the eradication of opium smoking in the peninsula. Treated at first as a convenient source of revenue the sale of chandu had, since 1910, been brought under control step by step. It was now to be gradually phased out. To balance the consequent shortfall in the accounts an opium revenue replacement fund was set up in 1925 with an initial investment of S$ 10 million, increased over the years ahead by an annual accrual of 15 per cent of the chandu revenue.[1] In the Straits Settlements an increase of 10 per cent in import duties to help the fund was introduced on 24 August 1925. In 1927 the annual increment amounted to S$2,242,500. By 1935 the fund had reached S$ 27,795,853.50. In 1938 it stood at S$ 29,824,097.

In 1910 the Straits Settlements government monopolies department inherited four licensed opium warehouses, 420 smoking saloons and 386 retail shops. By 1930 all such premises had been closed and the department ran all retail outlets.[2] In its struggle against the illegal trade the preventive service had seized nearly 15 tons of raw opium and 38 tons of chandu. It had also confiscated half a ton of cocaine, one-fifth of a ton of morphine and three tons of *bhang*.[3] In 1930 the Chandu Revenue Ordinance was updated to bring it into line with the new approach to the drug problem.

Those responsible for the closure of the register faced a daunting task. They had to cope with large numbers of smokers, many of them illiterate and speaking a variety of Chinese dialects. In December 1934 the senior assistant comptroller of government monopolies reported that by 31 October the Straits Settlement register held 44,616 names, of which 9120 had made no purchases for more than a month and 6040 for more than six months. The closure had been well advertised and there had been publicity in the local Chinese press.[4] Warnings had also been sent to Hong Kong and the British consuls in Amoy, Swatow and Canton. There had already been arrests of unregistered smokers. It was estimated that these were about 10 per cent of the total. In the Federated Malay States the situation was not so satisfactory. The number registered had increased from 16,578 on 1 January to 20,954 on 31 October 1934 but it was believed that some 20 per cent of smokers were unregistered. There had been less publicity in the FMS but its Chinese population was about 349,000 compared with 231,000 in the Settlements. J. J. Warren of Government Monopolies pointed out that the ration of four *chi* (40 *hoons*) per day set on 31 July 1933 was far too generous. The average smoker used only four *hoons*, leaving him 36 *hoons*, nearly half an ounce, to sell on the black market. For a worker living on a remote tin mine it was inconvenient to register and travel to town to buy his ration. It was easier to buy from the surplus.

The registration of smokers was inevitably a slow business. There were many attempted deceptions to be identified and corrected.[5] Some applicants had obtained duplicate cards. Some had given false addresses. It took time to weed out these illegal claims. As the years went by it was also difficult to identify permanent withdrawals from the registers. The Straits Settlements' Excise Department report for 1937 suggests that smokers drawn from the poorer classes might be forced to switch from the government product to smuggled chandu or even dross when times were hard, returning to active membership of the register when their fortunes improved.

A further task for the departments' officers in all territories was to deal with applications to join the registers on medical grounds. There was naturally a constant flow of immigrants who had contracted the smoking habit elsewhere and who were desperate to secure the right to purchase government chandu. No one under 18 years of age was considered but older applicants had to be judged by various yardsticks. The production of a doctor's certificate that they were already smokers and needed the drug for reasons of health might not be conclusive. Blackened or worn front teeth were supporting evidence of long-term consumption. Appearances could, however, be misleading. When John Lewis refused registration to the owner of a fine set of white front teeth the applicant favoured him with a broad grin and extracted his denture for inspection.[6] Peter Burgess in Kluang (Johore) was assigned a doctor to help him in this work.[7] His confidence in professional advice was shaken when the doctor asked him 'How do you tell an opium smoker?' He proved an excessively tender hearted assessor and when Peter rejected an application would occasionally plead 'Oh, let him have some. He seems such a nice old man.'

Major Coles, representing the UK, was soon reporting to the advisory committee on traffic in opium and other dangerous drugs that purchases of chandu in Singapore had fallen to 50 per cent of the norm.[8] The register was therefore briefly reopened and the basic ration was cut from four *chi* to two *chi*. In 1936 it was decided to deregister the 'non-actives' (who had made no purchase for more than six months) and the 'semi-actives' (no purchase for more than one month).[9] This considerably reduced the register. In the Straits Settlements, of 53,150 on the register, 20,152 were non-active and 8239 were semi-active. Under the Chandu Revenue Ordinance the superintendent was given power to cancel all registrations that became semi-active. Only government medical officers had the power to issue certificates to new applicants.

There were still differing views on the way forward. In 1935 a commission of inquiry into the control of opium smoking in the Far East recommended that it be permitted only in public saloons, but at the Bangkok conference Sir Malcolm Delevingne, the British representative, explained that this was not the policy in Malaya.[10] There had been no 'divans' in the Straits Settlements since 1929. In the Federated Malay States there were still 51 in 1930 but the last three were about to be closed. Notices had also been issued in the unfederated states and all would be closed by the end of June 1935. Significantly, the issue was not even mentioned in the final report of the conference.

Sir Malcolm was also briefed on the effects of social developments in Malaya.[11] Considerable effort was being put into encouraging sport. Opening cinemas and amusement parks was also seen as beneficial. Above all, improved roads and greater availability of bicycles and motor transport gave the labourer in a remote location the chance to travel in search of amusement, rather than to find it in solitary opium smoking in his quarters. Finally, the health service had been extended and hospitals were still providing anti-smoking wards. Admission to these was initially on an order signed by the Protector of Chinese. Their success was difficult to measure as undoubtedly many of the applicants for treatment were poor Chinese coolies seeking free board and lodging.

In 1935 the factory and packing plants handled 1289 chests of opium, 253 imported from India, including 24 for Hong Kong, 11 for Sarawak and 1001 from Persia,[12] compared with a reported usage of 330 chests a month in 1926. However, the Persian opium yielded 33 per cent more chandu than the Indian. Output had increased in recent years. In 1935 the plant produced 89,049,642 tubes of two *hoons* and 538,634 of two *chi*. Sales of this larger size, however, had declined rapidly from a peak of over two million packets in 1930. Exports were made to the FMS, Hong Kong, North Borneo, Sarawak, Brunei, Johore, Kelantan, Trengganu, Kedah and Perlis. It was still a flourishing business.

There were now 29 retail shops in Singapore, 17 in Penang, 12 in Malacca and one each in Labuan and Christmas Island. Of the 54,232 registered smokers only 2304 were women.[13] The government spent S$ 137,473.75 on the purchase of dross.

The process of running down the registers to zero would obviously take a long time. One estimate was 30 years. The Japanese conquest of Malaya in 1941/2 brought the experiment to a premature end. Nevertheless, the statistics available for the brief duration of the registration scheme suggest that it was already making good progress. The annual reports of the Government Monopolies and Excise departments record the following figures of sales of chandu in the Straits Settlements (in lbs):

1928	112,025	1932	54,873	1936	42,032
1929	96,016	1933	51,030	1937	46,340
1930	73,515	1934	58,152	1938	42,213
1931	54,797	1935	56,135		

Even more striking is the decline in the number of registered smokers. In the Straits Settlements there were 42,751 on the registers in 1930. By 1938 this number had fallen to 27,441, of whom 24,799 were deemed to be active smokers. An analysis of the nationalities of the smokers in 1936 shows clearly that opium smoking remained largely a Chinese practice. There were then 28,069 Chinese of whom, incidentally, only 1371 were locally born. There were only 2016 women. Non-Chinese registered smokers numbered just 87, including 42 Indians, 31 Malays and one Belgian (perhaps Peter Burgess's diamond merchant).

On 1 May 1938 the department took over the management of the chandu factory from the government analyst.[14] Production was marginally up on 1937 but demand was falling and the output of the packing plant fell by 14,137 lbs. In the factory one boiling room was closed. That year the revenue from chandu sales in the Straits Settlements was S$ 6,433,600.66.

While the legal consumption of government opium was in

decline the problem of illegal smokers persisted and probably worsened. Up to 1929 immigration to Malaya was unrestricted. In that year the Immigration Restriction Ordinance banned direct emigration from China to the Federated Malay States and provided for quotas in immigration to the Settlements.[15] The number of Chinese male labourers entering the colony fell from 195,613 in 1929 to 151,693 the following year and to 49,723 in 1930. By 1933 under the newly enacted Aliens Ordinance the quota had been reduced to 1000 a month. As the country recovered from economic recession it was gradually increased, reaching a peak of 6000 a month in 1937. Subsequent cuts reduced it to 500 a month from April 1938, a level maintained until the Japanese occupation. The quotas excluded immigrants who were able to exchange their landing permits for two-year certificates of admission. It is therefore difficult to find accurate figures of Chinese immigration but it is clear that there was throughout the period 1934 to 1941 a substantial inflow of Chinese, among whom there were bound to be a number who were already addicted to the smoking of opium. In 1936 the Government Monopolies Department reported that the admission of immigrant applicants had resulted in an increase in registered smokers from 26,041 to 28,156. This figure should, however, be set against the estimated population of 1,198,557 of whom 732,843 were Chinese.

It is, of course, impossible to measure the sale and consumption of smuggled opium. Inevitably, many new immigrants refused registration turned to the illicit product. It was the task of the departments' preventive branches to deny them this alternative supply. Importation was generally in the raw form but there was some trade in prepared opium. Peter Burgess remembers imports from Macao under 'Red Lion' brand, packed in attractive brass canisters. His largest seizure on land was 1000 of these (approximately 80 lbs) concealed in various parts of a smallholding in the country outside Singapore.[16] More commonly the raw drug had to be converted to chandu and then sold through illegal suppliers, including clandestine smoking 'saloons'. The responsibilities of the preventive service covered all aspects of the traffic, importation, preparation, sale and consumption. It therefore extended beyond the usual limits of a customs service. The chandu branch in the FMS and the preventive service in the Settlements were effectively an anti-narcotics force. Their powers of search, arrest and seizure were appropriate to that role. Interception at importation was the first aim. Once the drug was ashore it would be broken up into smaller parcels, and seizures would be correspondingly less damaging.[17] The arrest and prosecution of consumers did little harm to the traffickers.

Launch patrols rarely detected smuggling, although they may have had some deterrent effect on the 'running' of contraband in small craft. Most imports would be concealed in ocean-going vessels or in road and rail transport across the land frontier with Siam (Thailand). The first line of defence against the traffic was therefore the staff at ports and frontier posts, employing their routine search procedures or acting on information received.

Even at the larger ports it was not easy to control the landing of goods. At Singapore and Penang ships might lie offshore in the 'roads' and could discharge into lighters. Quite bulky loads might therefore be smuggled ashore. Customs posts on exits from segregated port areas and patrols along the adjacent foreshore provided some protection against this danger but illegal imports were often concealed in apparently innocent consignments. The most effective measure was therefore active ship searching and examination of the contents of cargo containers. The teams of officers employed in this work acquired a knowledge and experience that gave them a remarkable ability to track down contraband, almost amounting to a sixth sense. After his early involvement in market research Peter Burgess was eventually posted to one of the harbour divisions in Singapore and took part in many ship searches. His team was skilled in discovering opium, as he records:

> Our main concern was with ships from China. Many carried large numbers of deck passengers some of whom smuggled small quantities of opium – in wooden clogs, buckets with false bottoms, suitcases with false bottoms. Opium was also concealed in a large range of cargo, such as Chinese teapots or pillows. Early in my service I was shown a load of Chinese black eggs – eggs which are salted and buried for six months. This consignment however comprised false eggs filled with opium and coated with black earth.
>
> On ships our searchers had found life jackets with opium replacing the cork floats and lifebuoys filled with opium. They had also found water tanks in ships' lifeboats filled with opium. Many of our ship searchers had their own special interests. Bugis was the expert on tanks. He often dived into water tanks and was remarkably successful.

> Leong, a very tall Chinese, specialized in coal bunkers. The searchers carried very long steel probes and if these pierced opium they could smell it on the tip. They would then shift several tons of coal. Sometimes we received information but often seizures resulted from careful observation. Tabib usually worked in ships' engine rooms. One day he came to me and asked whether he could take off the cover of the ventilation shaft in the engine room workshop of the ship we were searching. I asked him why and he replied 'There is fresh paint on the heads of the fixing screws.' Concealed in and blocking the shaft he found 40 pounds of raw opium.

On one occasion the search team's reputation may have worked to their disadvantage, as Peter Burgess recalls:

> We received information that there was opium concealed in the Blue Funnel Line cargo ship *Rhexenor*. We searched for ten days but found nothing. Towards the end of our search the engineer said, 'You know, I shouldn't be surprised if the "old man" gave information about opium. Our next port of call is in the United States where there are very heavy fines if opium is found. We know that your men give a very thorough search – better than most – so it is a form of insurance.'

No matter how vigilant the watch on the ports and frontiers some consignments of opium were bound to get through. Seizures of the raw drug in store were not unusual but largely dependant on good information. A more vulnerable stage in the traffic was the process of cooking the opium to convert it into chandu. This was a lengthy process requiring careful supervision. It was common practice to cook at night in a secure building. The problem for the preventive service officers was to gain access and secure the evidence before it could be destroyed. Peter Burgess took part in two such raids in quick succession.

> Our raiding party went late at night to a three-storey house in Chinatown and had no difficulty in getting through to the air well at the back. From there we could watch flames being fanned on a charcoal stove in the first-floor kitchen and we could see the shadow of the cook. We could smell opium. However, access to the upper floor was firmly

> blocked by a large trap door. Eventually one of the officers persuaded someone to open it and the party rushed through to the kitchen only to find the contents of the wok had been poured down the drain. A Revenue Officer turned to me and said 'They have thrown it away.' I could still see something on the floor and said 'Quick. Mop that up.' We collected about half a pint and in due course the Government Chemist reported an appreciable quantity of non-Government opium. A few days later we had a similar case and had to make a forced entry. Again the contents of the pan of opium were poured down the drain but this time one of the Revenue Officers had stayed outside with a bucket at the bottom of the drain pipe!

The annual report of the Straits Settlements Excise Department for 1935 remarks on a decline in offences connected with drugs. Nevertheless, there were 1060 prosecutions for such offences and seizures of 514 lbs of opium, 1665 lbs of chandu, 38 oz of Indian hemp, 871 oz of cocaine, 16 oz of morphine and 2.68 oz of diodide. In the Settlements a further weapon against the traffickers was the use of the Banishment Ordinance. Its provisions gave power to deport undesirable immigrants.[18] The tribunal appointed to consider such cases was entitled to take into consideration indirect evidence of involvement in criminal activities, insufficient perhaps to secure a conviction for a specific offence but leaving no doubt of general guilt. The 1937 annual report records that in the course of that year the department lodged 110 recommendations for banishment on the grounds of illegal trafficking in opium, liquors or tobacco. The preventive service was still busy.

From 1937 onwards there was considerable progress in the compiling of dossiers of vessels, members of crews, agents, dealers and carriers.[19] This was the work of special division, a plain-clothes detective branch of customs in Singapore. In 1938 a similar system was set up in Penang. That year more than 2500 people were convicted of offences relating to opium.[20]

The outbreak of the Second World War in September 1939 did not immediately endanger Malaya and had little effect on the workings of the administration. As described elsewhere, many of the expatriate officers of the customs and excise departments undertook various military and naval duties. Some were actively engaged in intelligence activities. The supervision of the chandu monopoly, however, continued to be a major responsibility of the departments. Philip Merson began his career in Singapore in 1940. After a few months he was posted to special branch where he describes his chief occupation as 'harrying' the unregistered opium smokers. For this activity he employed ten plain-clothes revenue officers, a team of clerks and very little personal enthusiasm for the task.[21] The team used a bus to conduct raids and round up offenders, sometimes as many as 20 at a time.

During Christmas 1939 the criminal fraternity in Perak offered a new challenge to the preventive service. The state chandu store in Ipoh was robbed of its entire stock. Despite intensive investigations by both police and customs the perpetrators were not discovered. Nor did any of the stolen chandu appear on the illegal market until about a year later. When Cecil Gutteridge took over the preventive branch in Ipoh in March 1940 enquiries had been dropped. Security at the chandu store had been increased. The store was an inner brick-built strongroom inside the customs warehouse in the Malayan Railways marshalling yard. The steel grille doors were of the type used in banks and an expanded metal grille across the warehouse, secured by special padlocks, further protected the store. The keys to the warehouse doors were kept in the police guardroom. At night the warehouse was floodlit and patrolled by armed police sentries. Both police and customs duty officers were required to visit the location on surprise inspections.

It was in the early hours of an August morning returning from an evening with friends that Cecil decided to make a spot check on the complex. As he signed the log the Sikh police officers were changing guard. All seemed in order but on his way home Cecil began to feel that things were not as they appeared. He changed into more suitable clothes and walked the mile back to the office by another route. He tells the story:[22]

> I entered the yards at another entrance and made my way behind lines of trucks until I came to the Customs Warehouse when I emerged from cover and was promptly challenged by the sentry who seemed a little nervous but I put that down to my sudden materialization out of the darkness. However, having identified myself I went round the warehouse with the sentry and inspected the doors. They were all in order except for the last set on the side furthest from the guardroom and at these I found the padlocks missing.

So too were the locks on the expanded grille and the inner door. The whole stock of chandu had been removed. Not a single fingerprint, footprint or other clue was found. Since the duty police officer confirmed that the locks were in place when he called in at midnight the robbery had obviously been carried out between then and 3.00 a.m. and must have been the work of a large gang.

Three or four months later Cecil received information that led him to raid the house of a well-known professional Sikh boxer.

> Hidden in various places in the house were several thousand tubes of government chandu. On examination the codings revealed that they were part of the chandu stolen in both the robberies. This was interesting as it was the first seizure made of chandu from the first robbery and indicated that the proceeds of that one had been held hidden for almost a year and had not been put on the market. Questioning the boxer was a long process but from his statement and from scraps of documents found in his house I was led to further searches none of which produced any results until I raided a house in a village some miles from Ipoh where I found several thousand more tubes of chandu, all from the second robbery. This house was occupied by the Chinese mistress of the local police sergeant, who turned out to have been the sergeant in charge of the guard at the time of the second robbery.

The sergeant and the boxer were both given long prison sentences but despite further recoveries from time to time most of the chandu was never found.

But time was running out for the British administration in Malaya and its experiment in the control and reduction of opium smoking. Undoubtedly, it had achieved considerable success. As shown in Appendix X, between 1918 and 1938 the average annual volume of chandu sold in the Straits Settlements had fallen by more than two-thirds. In his *History of Modern Malaya*, K. G. Tregonning sums up the situation as the sale of only 500,000 tahils of expensive opium to perhaps 27,000 middle-aged and elderly people out of an estimated total Chinese population in the Straits of 862,000. Just 51 government chandu shops served them. In 1938 2527 applied to join the register. Only 651 were accepted. As demanded by the British government the system supervised by the two customs and excise departments had certainly 'minimized' and might, given time, have 'eradicated the evil'.[23] The opportunity was denied by the Japanese invasion of December 1941.

Following the British capitulation the Japanese took over the administration and maintained the opium monopoly. The indigenous staff remained at their posts. The chandu shops continued to dispense the products of the Singapore factory and packing plant, and the two British engineers there now found themselves working for the conqueror. A postwar report estimates that at the end of 1941 there were 16,500 active smokers on the register in Singapore. The Japanese chose to abandon the policy of rationing and consumption was only restricted by the availability of supplies of chandu. New cards were issued to smokers and later a licence fee was charged for these. The carefully compiled records of registered smokers covering 15 years were all lost during the occupation.[24]

In the three-and-a-half years that were to pass before their return to Malaya the British had ample time to make plans for the future of the country. It was, in particular, an opportunity once again to review the government's policy on opium. The decisions made were to result in a major change in the work of the customs and excise when the British administration was resumed in 1945.

10
Prohibition

During the three years of the Japanese administration of Malaya the manufacture and supply of government chandu and the operation of the retail shops was continued. The policy of rationing was, however, abandoned. The only restriction on quantity was supply, which became increasingly difficult as the war went on. Thus the great experiment in the controlled reduction of the vice was brought to an end.[1]

It was not to be resumed. The loss of Malaya provided an opportunity to reconsider British policies there. Plans were made for the country's political future and progress towards eventual self-government. The problem of opium inevitably came up for review. The monopoly was the subject of increasing international disapproval. There was growing pressure on both the British and Dutch administrations to prohibit the drug in their Eastern dependencies. The influence of the USA was probably decisive. On 10 November 1943 the British government issued a statement of policy.[2] While acknowledging the success of the monopoly, which, it stressed, was in accordance with the Geneva agreement of 1925, the statement announced that the system would not be re-established on recovery of the occupied territories.

In September 1945 the Japanese occupation of Malaya came to an end and a temporary British Military Administration was put in place. The chandu factory and packing plant in Singapore were closed.[3] So too were the government retail shops throughout the former Straits Settlements and Malay States. In February 1946 a proclamation banned the consumption and possession of opium or chandu and introduced a wide range of criminal offences subject to penalties, including both fines and imprisonment. It offered compensation payments for opium pipes surrendered to the authorities but unsurprisingly there were few acceptors.[4] On 1 March the civilian customs departments resumed their functions. These, however, no longer included the supervision of the chandu monopoly and 400 staff became redundant. Some were transferred to other government departments but the remainder had to be paid off with compensation.

The interception of prohibited drugs on importation is the common task of customs services throughout the world. In Malaya the departments' responsibilities were to be far wider. Their experience of running the monopoly in the past was thought to qualify them to tackle all aspects of the opium traffic, importation, manufacture, distribution and consumption. In effect, they became the anti-narcotics bureau for the territory. It was an ambitious project for a service that had to undertake a wide range of activities with a comparatively small staff and very little equipment. The police were always prepared to deal with any drug offences they encountered but were not required to initiate positive action against the traffic. Information received in the course of their work was passed to the customs for further investigation and action as required. The drug traffic was soon engaging the attention and resources of the preventive staff for much of their time.

Prior to 1942 the traffic in illicit opium had been on a comparatively small scale and the evidence suggested that it was in decline. The abrupt imposition of a total ban on the drug provided the traffickers with a dazzling opportunity to replace the government as suppliers to a large and long-established market. Legislation could do little to reduce the demand. Prohibition could only be made effective by action against the supply.

It is difficult to estimate the size of the market that was thus opened up to profitable exploitation. In Singapore alone there were 16,500 active smokers still on the register at the end of 1941. Although probably limited by the wartime shortage of supplies the numbers had almost certainly increased by 1946. In 1954 the customs and excise reported an estimated 65,000 smokers in the Federation of Malaya. It appears likely therefore that the total market comprised at least 85,000 smokers. Even at the prewar standard government ration of two *chi* per day this represents daily sales of over half a ton of chandu.[5]

The organization of the opium trade differed from any conventional import and distribution business only in its illegality and consequent need for concealment.[6] The passage of the drug from country of origin to the ultimate consumer entailed a similar series of operations and a substantial financial investment. At each stage the appropriate specialist operator would handle it. Dispatched from its country of origin the raw opium would be collected and imported by a 'landing agent'. It might then be stored or immediately broken into smaller parcels for distribution to the manufacturers, who would convert it to chandu and pack it for the retail market. The finished product would then be delivered to the owners of illicit smoking saloons who would keep these outlets supplied with frequent replenishment in small quantities. These establishments provided the pipes, lamps and other equipment required for use by the customers. At each stage the danger of detection increased but the potential loss declined. The interception of a large consignment on arrival would necessarily have a far greater impact on the availability of the drug and the profits of the traders than the seizure of a few dozen packets of chandu in a smoking saloon. But a saloon was easily detected. The smugglers of bulk imports employed great ingenuity and their discovery depended on a combination of good information, diligence and luck.

A serious handicap for the officers engaged in this work was the almost total lack of records in the immediate aftermath of the occupation. There was no central registry to which reference could be made when assessing information or interrogating suspects. Even special division, the plain-clothes section of the preventive branch in Singapore, had very little background information to guide its investigations. Derek Mackay[7] joined the division in 1948 and shared duties with another postwar expatriate officer, Eric Selby.

> One of us concentrated on the direction of the division. The other undertook the specialist task of Court Officer, conducting prosecutions on behalf of all three divisions (Land, Port and Special). Eric and I soon formed a happy partnership and switched duties more than once. Apart from the individual case files the only records were a small card index listing addresses in Singapore at which it was known that opium was smoked. It held close on 2000 locations but nothing to indicate their ownership or sources of supply. Each arrest or seizure was the subject of a separate file. There was nothing to relate these events to an organized traffic. Yet it was obvious that such a large and heavily capitalized trade must be in the hands of substantial organizations. Eric and I spent many evenings tracing links which gradually built up a more coherent picture. We were able to identify individuals, to place them in gangs and to

9. An opium pipe and lamp, Singapore.

add locations, vehicles, fishing boats and other elements in their activities. In later years a Central Registry was established which employed far more sophisticated methods and proved invaluable.

As a European I was unable to play a useful part in the murky world in which my local staff conducted their investigations. I had to devise other methods to seek information and to monitor their work. I soon discovered the value of

> public records, such as the land, vehicle and company registries. These often yielded information which physical observation could never unearth. The plotting of seizures on maps revealed patterns which could lead to further interceptions. I also took a keen interest in the identity of bailors. The police bail required for accused persons awaiting trial was fixed by us. In drug cases it was always substantial and the sureties had to be men of some wealth. There was obviously a better than even chance that such worthy citizens would have more than an altruistic interest in the case and the opportunity to question them and to inspect the evidence they produced to establish their fitness for the role was not to be spurned.

Good prior information, however, was most likely to produce the larger seizures and accompanying arrests. The operations of special division were largely based on such information. The most effective plain-clothes officer was the one with the most knowledgeable informers. These were inevitably very shady characters whose stories had to be carefully checked. They acted for a variety of motives; some sought money alone; some sought revenge; some were acting in the interests of a rival gang; some were using their role to extort money from vulnerable offenders. The department paid cash rewards for successful cases to both the informer and the revenue officer who produced him. There was no fixed tariff but the sums paid related to the importance of the case and the quantity of goods seized.

The best information often came from someone within or closely connected to the traffickers. Such people led a dangerous life. The sudden disappearance of the informer soon after a major case could be because he had gone into hiding. It might have a more sinister explanation. Informers rarely made contact with senior officers, particularly Europeans, and such approaches had to be treated with suspicion. Derek Mackay recalls:

> My own brief contacts with informers proved of no value. I remember a strange American who claimed to have flown with Chennault's 'Flying Tigers'. He slipped the tail I put on him and vanished. I also endured several visits from a plump and voluble Chinese lady, who identified herself as the second wife of an opium dealer, but never produced the information so often promised.

There was little hope of identifying and prosecuting the financiers of the trade. Such people, possibly highly respected members of the community, were careful not to involve themselves in any way that might reveal their role. Funds would be made available for an unspecified investment and the resultant profits absorbed into legitimate businesses. The customs concentrated on the physical operations.

Commercial imports of raw opium were bulky. Consignments might weigh a few hundred pounds or be measured in tons. Inevitably, the majority of imports arrived by sea, mostly in ocean steamers. There were road and rail links across the Thai frontier, but the use of these routes was complicated by the need to arrange passage through that country. Aircraft were rarely involved in any but small imports by individuals.

The shipping routes converged on Singapore from east and west. There was heavy traffic from China, calling at various ports along the way to the colony. The opium imported by this route was generally referred to as 'Yunnan', a term used by traffickers in Malaya to indicate the geographical area encompassing the trans-Salween states of Burma, the southern Yunnan province of China, the independent state of Laos and the northwestern region of Thailand around Chiengmai. From the west came opium originating in India, Iran and Burma. The Indian and Iranian products were of superior quality and fetched a far higher price than Yunnan or Burmese on the Malayan market. At a time when it was reported that Indian opium was selling at S$ 550 to S$ 590 per pound in Singapore, Yunnan was priced at S$ 310 to S$ 325.[8] For a variety of reasons it had become increasingly difficult to smuggle in the western products and the total ban imposed on the cultivation and production of opium in Iran in late 1955 had its effect on the international traffic. Yunnan gradually came to dominate the market. In 1954 it accounted for only 23 per cent of the illicit opium seized by customs against 46.5 per cent from Iran. In 1957 the percentage of seizures from Yunnan was 66.2. Iranian sourced seizures had fallen to 6.1 per cent.

In some ways the simplest use of ocean freighters was to ship the opium disguised as a consignment of innocent goods. This method avoided the involvement of the ship's crew in the concealment of the drug and the employment of persons to smuggle it ashore. Singapore was the destination of choice. It was still a free port in which import duties were levied only on liquors, tobacco and petroleum products. In one of the busiest ports in the world customs examination of non-dutiable goods was comparatively rare and the chance of detection correspondingly the less. The consequences of interception could, however, be serious. If the consignee named on the bill of lading could be traced it would be difficult for him to plead ignorance. What the customs needed was good prior information. In 1950 they received just that.

In Bombay a police investigation into corruption stumbled across evidence of an opium smuggling ring. Documents were found relating to a consignment already on its way to Singapore. Just over 240 lbs of opium had been concealed in a shipment of 22 cases of turmeric, consigned to an Indian business in Singapore acting on behalf of a principal called Rashidbhai Rustumji Irani.[9] The Bombay police immediately tipped off HM Customs Singapore and port division officers watched the consignment being unloaded into a dockside warehouse. They waited for the consignee to collect. Meanwhile, two officers, John Gose of Bombay customs and Inspector Ferrangippe of the anti-corruption branch of the Bombay police, flew to Singapore carrying the documentary evidence. A local flight took them to Colombo where they had to stay the night before picking up an aircraft on its through passage to Singapore. That evening they took the opportunity to see the sights of the Sri Lankan city. On return to the hotel in the early hours they found that their room had been ransacked. Nothing was stolen. If the intruders were hoping to find the vital papers they had underestimated the officers. Inspector Ferrangippe had them well concealed on his person.

Days passed but no one appeared to claim the goods. Losing patience port division raided the Indian company's offices and detained the joint owners of the business. They were searching through files for additional evidence when the telephone rang. An officer picked up the instrument and found himself speaking to Irani. Little expecting the caller to accept he invited him to come to the office. Shortly afterwards Irani walked in. He was an extraordinary character. A former racing cyclist he had later taken up wrestling, a sport for which his vast bulk was now far better suited. He treated the investigation with amused contempt and his arrest as a foolish error. All three suspects were charged, tried and convicted.

The story had a sequel. To give evidence in the parallel proceedings in India the investigating officer, Henry Lewin of port division, was flown to Bombay. On taking the witness stand, Henry, a mild and courteous man, gave his name and address and helpfully spelt them out. The judge paused in his writing and testily informed him that 'in two centuries the British did at least teach us to spell.'

The more common use of sea transport was to enlist the services of crew members to conceal the drug on board. Even a small freighter offers an astonishing number of quite roomy hiding places. There are numerous spaces in the structure of a ship to which access can be obtained by knowledgeable smugglers. Ships' carpenters can use their skills to construct concealed storage. Engineers know how to pack parcels among the machinery. There are coalbunkers in which contraband can be buried. There are water tanks and fuel tanks that can only be searched at the cost of great effort and discomfort. The thorough search of an ocean-going vessel can take many days and much hard work. Many such searches were in pursuit of information received. Others were random in that no tipoff had been given. Nevertheless, it was common sense to concentrate efforts on ships coming from the sources of opium. Those on the regular China run were an obvious target and were repeatedly rummaged, often with positive results. In 1956 alone Singapore customs searched more than 200 ocean-going ships and 2000 small coasting vessels. Harbour division made 26 discoveries of opium totalling 1666 lbs.[10] It was observed that there was an increasing tendency to conceal the contraband in ships' fuel tanks located beneath the cargo holds. The opium was usually packed in airtight tins and secreted far away from manhole covers. The removal of cargo to gain access to tank covers, pumping out fuel tanks and the need to wear gas masks added to the difficulties of ship searching. A variation on this type of smuggling was encountered on an oil tanker from the Persian Gulf, which was escorted to her moorings and searched: 127 lbs of opium were found concealed in the water tanks of the crew's bathroom, packed in rubber bags and ready for dumping in the sea. A speedboat that tried to get close to the ship was driven off by a customs patrol launch. On another occasion the vigilance of a night patrol of revenue officers foiled an attempt to discharge opium in this manner. Spotting a speedboat hovering near a vessel recently arrived from Bangkok the officers boarded and found 305 lbs of opium at the foot of the escape hatch from the propeller shaft tunnel. Packed in four bags and two drums it was lashed up ready for lowering over the ship's side.

To avoid such losses the smugglers often arranged for the contraband to be off-loaded at sea. On the China run a popular practice was to dump the drugs off the east coast of Malaya in watertight containers that could be retrieved by fishing boats operating from the many small ports in the area. Hidden beneath the fish and the ice it would be almost impossible to discover until the cargo was discharged. Later it appears that fast speedboats were preferred. Such small craft were difficult to trace as they came and went about their business. The best chance of detection was to intercept the ocean carrier at the dumping area.

Such an interception was described graphically in an item published in a Singapore English language newspaper in February 1956. Perhaps unwilling to 'name and shame' the ocean steamer the writer christened her *The Pride of Shanghai* and describes how H. G. Boyce-Taylor lay in wait for her with a customs launch 11 miles out in the western approaches.[11]

> At half past one a blip appeared on the radar set. A ship was approaching. The master of the launch focused his powerful glasses in the direction of the oncoming vessel. Twinkling lights soon pointed [out] the mastheads and superstructure. There was no doubt of her identity. Every man in the launch took his action station. The engines were started. At five minutes to two the blacked-out Customs boat was not far from the stern of *The Pride of Shanghai.* Minutes later a light was seen flickering across the sea a few hundred yards from the ship. It evidently came from some tiny boat lying low in the water. The flash was answered by a signal light from the stern of the steamer. The Customs officers saw something thrown overboard from the cargo ship. Within a few minutes they had picked up the first of 17 watertight containers which were tied together with rope. While the Customs officers hauled them in, *The Pride of Shanghai* and the little motor boat of the smugglers sped away into the darkness. On the deck of the launch the oilskin was removed from the packages and inside other wrappings were found 17 parcels of opium.

The consignment weighed 1109 lbs and, as the journalist reported, was worth more than half a million Singapore dollars. There were no arrests but the seizure represented a heavy loss to the traffickers.

In the immediate postwar period the lack of suitable high speed launches handicapped attempts to shadow suspect vessels. In Singapore the two ocean-going customs boats were former harbour defence motor launches (HDML) whose Chrysler engines had been replaced with more economical diesels that could only drive them at 14 knots.[12] A launch would lie ahead of an approaching steamer and follow a parallel course that would keep the target in sight for a limited period as it overtook and left the customs vessel far behind. The HDMLs were not then equipped with radar. Even if they spotted a collection of contraband from a steamer at sea, the smugglers' boats were usually small local craft driven by twin outboard motors and could easily avoid capture.

Ships arriving from the west usually made their first call at Penang at the northern end of the Malacca Straits. The Straits, bordered by Sumatra and the mainland of Malaya, were a favourite dumping area for drugs. If rummaging at Penang proved unsuccessful customs officers might embark on the ship and remain on board as she sailed down the Straits to Singapore where she could be searched again. In 1957 one such ship was searched without result at successive ports of call – Penang, Port Swettenham and Singapore.[13] Speedboats closed her on two occasions in the Straits and again as a customs launch escorted her out of territorial waters. In mid-Pacific the ship's officers finally found 58 lbs of opium.

The acquisition of more powerful pursuit craft equipped with radar gave the customs a much better chance in their duel with the drug smugglers.[14] A night encounter in 1958 proved their value. A patrol boat spotted a twin outboard making her way to the north of Singapore island and gave chase for 20 minutes with both craft attaining speeds of over 30 knots. Finally, the coxswain manoeuvred his boat alongside his opponents and two sailors leapt aboard, overpowered the crew and cut the engines. The cargo was 1180 lbs of raw opium currently valued at about S$ 250,000.

From time to time individuals, passengers or crew imported smaller quantities of opium. It was generally assumed that ships' officers would not engage in such an enterprise but one such case did occur in Singapore.[15] In the course of a routine search of an arrival from China via Bangkok, Preventive Officer Rodriguez, in charge of the squad, got into conversation with the third engineer and detected some nervousness, which appeared to centre on a dynamo. When a parcel of opium was found concealed there the engineer admitted he had put it under the dynamo at the request of the radio operator. The operator confirmed his story but claimed that he had given safe custody to the parcel at the request of a steward who had been helpful to him during his long radio watches. It was only when he discovered its contents that he enlisted the aid of his friend the engineer. Questioned by Rodriguez, the steward denied the story. He could not be convicted on the sole evidence of an accomplice and walked away a free man. The officers paid the penalty.

The overland route for imports was across the Thai frontier by rail, road or jungle track.[16] In 1946 there was general lawlessness in the border zone. The wartime communist resistance, the Malayan People's Anti-Japanese Army, was well established there and used its military power to escort contraband across the border. A further problem was that at this time chandu was still legally on sale in Thailand at a price of only S$ 25 a tahil (1⅓ oz), enough to supply 50 standard two-*hoon* packets. There was a flourishing trade originating in the Thai town of Hat Yai. Women carriers were often used in the hope of avoiding search. One was found to have concealed 1530 tubes around her waist. Another had hidden 458 tubes in soap. A 12-year-old sported specially designed panties carrying 300 tubes.

Cecil Gutteridge was engaged in preventive work on the Thai border for several years in the late 1940s. He learned to suspect even the most innocent looking traveller.

> I was at Padang Besar with one of my female staff, watching passengers embarking on the Malayan train. Amongst them was a party of Chinese women carrying tin washing equipment and to all intents and purposes returning from washing tin in the surrounding hills. Of these a number were apparently fairly well gone in the family way. We looked at them cursorily and the Revenue Officers on duty passed them through the gate. However, my woman officer suddenly turned to me and said she didn't think the pregnant ones were really pregnant. I asked her why and she said they were not walking as pregnant women do. We took the whole party in and searched them. Five of the women were found to have about ten pounds of opium each strapped across their bellies. Of the others, ten or so were wearing special brassières into each cup of which had been sewn forty or more tubes of chandu.

By 1947 the gangs were making more use of vehicles to convey the drug in secret compartments. A false petrol tank detected in one contained 5400 tubes. Raw opium was also smuggled in this way. One motorcar got as far as Ipoh before it was intercepted: 94 lbs were found in a compartment built over the back axle.[17]

The volume of freight carried by rail offered opportunities for large-scale imports of raw opium. One such case in 1955 had a disappointing outcome. At that time Robert McCall was involved in planning an international station on the railway line at Padang Besar, a place he first visited in 1943 as a prisoner of the Japanese.[18] On their way to Thailand and the notorious Burma Railway, he and his comrades were released from a covered goods wagon for the first time since leaving Singapore and permitted to stand under the water supply for the engine. It was there after the war that he was to be involved in a seizure of opium.

> I was rung up by the Out Door Officer in charge and told that opium had been discovered in a goods wagon from Siam. I told him to ensure that the Siamese signed a Release Document and that the truck was shunted to our side of the station. I added: 'Do absolutely nothing else until I get there.' The wagon turned out to be full of onions, consigned to Penang in metal containers. The load had broken the axle on a previous wagon and had been transferred to another with the result that the containers nearest were reloaded into the back of the new wagon and vice versa. Consequently the innocuous containers intended for our inspection were now at the back, and the not so innocuous, and now easily accessible ones in the front. Going through the whole consignment produced just over half a ton of raw opium.

Unfortunately, the Thai customs claimed that they had not cleared the load and after diplomatic exchanges between Kuala Lumpur and Bangkok the wagon and its contents were shunted back.

An example of a smaller-scale enterprise was provided by a police sergeant who was stopped well south of the border on his return from Thailand riding a motorcycle.[19] It was found that the petrol tank had been modified to contain a quantity of raw opium, leaving only a small compartment to receive petrol through the filler. The sergeant maintained that he was unaware of this, having borrowed the machine for the journey. The investigating officer did some calculations and realized that the petrol capacity was insufficient to get so far without topping up the tank. A check back along the route located a filling station whose owner clearly remembered serving the sergeant because it was the only time he had ever been asked to sell half a gallon. A conviction followed.

To reduce the danger of detection large bulk imports of raw opium were quickly broken up and distributed to local wholesalers. Occasionally, a shipment was stored in anticipation of a better market. Concealment was no problem if the drug was hidden in a legitimate cargo, but consignments brought in by other means had to be lodged in secret hiding places. Frequently, these were residential properties. During 1949 the Singapore customs made several seizures of substantial quantities in houses, although these may have been used only briefly while breaking bulk. The largest was a haul of 1109 lbs in a house at Tanjong Rhu, a seaside area often used by smugglers. Some discoveries were made in very respectable districts of Singapore. In 1950, during the communist insurrection in Malaya, police in Singapore stumbled across an elaborate store in the garden of a suburban villa whose flower borders concealed extensive underground chambers. Contrary to their expectation, these were not intended for the concealment of arms: 1095 lbs of raw opium were found in the garage. In May 1953, in the fashionable district of Orchard Road, the Singapore customs made one of its largest finds, 80 sealed metal containers holding 40 lbs of raw opium each, nearly a ton and a half of the drug. A contemporary newspaper report estimated its immediate value at S$ 1,280,000. Sold as chandu it would have fetched S$ 2,240,000. In 1956 in Chiltern Drive, a popular residential area, 308 lbs of raw opium were found stored in a house whose occupant, a woman already known to the department, was convicted and fined.[20]

In Perak Tony King's policy of paying rewards only for information leading to major hauls produced the desired result. In 1951 he supervised a 24-hour raid on the fishing platforms and duck farms of Kuala Kurau.[21]

> We started by unearthing four forty-gallon oil drums each containing about a hundredweight of raw opium. As I sat in the control centre in the principal coffee shop a number of new informants slid in and gave details of more caches of the drug. By nightfall we had made one of the largest seizures ever recorded. I think that from the thirty-odd drums we dug out of the duck ordure there must have been well over a ton of raw and prepared opium recovered.

> There was no way we could realistically apprehend any of the fishermen or farmers who ran these farms as a cooperative venture. However, the total value of the drugs recovered, even at this stage of the supply chain, was estimated to be around seven figures in local currency and there were reports of major losses and large numbers of defaulting bank loans from Penang through to Bangkok.

The inland movement of imports immediately after arrival offered the best chance of large-scale seizures, however, and there were many interceptions at this stage, usually based on prior information. Singapore customs were particularly successful in this type of operation, but it could give rise to problems, as Derek Mackay discovered in his work as prosecuting officer.[22]

> The protection of informers was obviously vital. Whatever their morals or their motives they took great risks and carelessness could place them in serious danger. This was particularly so when the source was an insider. Conversely, we had to plan our operations so that we did not catch them with their partners in crime. Unfortunately, there were times when this was unavoidable. In 1950 one very promising informer was working with a group engaged in receiving and distributing large consignments of opium brought down through Thailand. Contact with him was indirect and we knew him only by a nickname whose meaning, alas, we were unable to translate. He gave prior warning that he was to be one of three in the cab of a truck carrying 1600 lbs of raw opium across the city at night. He told us the route and an ambush was planned at a road junction where our cars could be sited to surround the suspect vehicle. While arresting his two companions the officers would leave him the chance to run off down a conveniently located narrow alley. On the night of the run the cars took up their positions, the truck arrived and was forced to a standstill and three men scrambled out. Two were immediately seized. The meaning of our informer's nickname was now revealed. It was 'limpy'. He was lame. As he hobbled away there was the brief and curious sight of several plain-clothes men apparently running on the spot. It was a pretence that could not be long maintained and, for his own safety, the informer had to be arrested.

> The following morning an embarrassed case officer passed me the papers and admitted that he had been forced to charge his own informer. There was no option but to proceed against all three. To withdraw against the informer would have made his role in the affair all too clear. At best he would have been of no further value as a source. At worst he would be dead. Not for the first time I would have to rely on cross-examination to secure convictions. The defence was bound to be called and it would be my task to discount the explanations offered by the accused. Against the other two I found this easy enough, but the judge was of the view that our man had talked his way out of trouble and, to my relief, acquitted him. I have to admit that in his case my cross-examination did lack penetration.

In 1953 it was again the redoubtable Boyce-Taylor who made the headlines when he drove his car in pursuit of a suspect lorry spotted leaving Tanjong Rhu. Its route took it along a road that crossed the island's main airport, Kallang, and that had to be closed when aircraft were taking off or landing. As the two vehicles approached the perimeter of the airfield the warning lights flashed and the barrier began to fall. The lorry was just in time to beat the boom but it bounced off the back of Boyce-Taylor's car as he kept up the chase and finally forced the smugglers to stop. Some 2000 lbs of opium were stacked in their vehicle. Apart from a tarpaulin thrown across the load there had been little attempt at concealment.[23] This was not always so. One consignment was found in a lorry hidden in baskets of live crabs.[24]

Cars were rarely employed to carry large consignments but in 1956 officers of special division in Singapore received information that such a vehicle would be used to shift a sizeable load and laid an ambush in the area of Lorong N on the outskirts of the city. Forced to stop the driver jumped out and fled but fell into a monsoon drain and broke his leg. In the boot of the car were 12 tins of Yunnan opium weighing 420 lbs. The injured smuggler was sentenced to three years imprisonment. The car was forfeited.[25]

Inland distribution by car was usually in smaller quantities rarely exceeding 50 lbs; accurate information on such movements was not easily obtained. During the 1950s the federation customs had a string of successes intercepting vehicles carrying the drug in false petrol tanks.[26] These operations were disguised as strokes of luck during random checks, a necessary precaution to protect the identity of the informer. He was manufacturing the hiding places. Most traffic into mainland Malaya originated in the ports of Penang and Singapore and had to pass through customs barriers. The distinctive smell of opium was a problem for the smugglers who resorted to various tricks to put searchers off the scent. A load of durians, a popular but evil-smelling local fruit, was so used to conceal a delivery of opium travelling against the usual flow, from the federation into Singapore. The trick did not work. By 1956 Singapore customs were able to enlist the aid of a trained Alsatian dog to discover the hiding places in a suspect car searched at the checkpoint on the causeway to the mainland.[27] It indicated the backrests of the front seats in which 91 lbs of opium were found concealed. The passenger admitted his guilt and was convicted but the driver was acquitted.

Another regular user of the causeway was an affluent Chinese who was arrested when a substantial quantity of opium was found in his car at the checkpoint. At his trial a witness appeared who claimed to be his chauffeur and assured the court that he had concealed the drug in the car without his employer's knowledge. His attempt at smuggling had been frustrated by the employer's decision to drive the car himself. Since his statement in evidence could not be used against him the chauffeur could not be charged. The accused was inevitably acquitted. He offered exactly the same defence when arrested in identical circumstances on two further occasions.[28]

Most such inland movements of opium were deliveries in fulfilment of orders placed by wholesalers and the operators of opium saloons. Occasionally, however, individuals might import or purchase small quantities as a speculation. One such instance was brought to the attention of Peter Chattaway in Seremban.[29]

> The morning started like any other. I checked the Revenue Officers' notebooks and sent them off to gather more information. One of them came back and told me that a woman staying at a local hotel was offering raw opium for sale. The information sounded pretty reliable so I advised Selwyn Buckwell who agreed to come with us. I collected a couple more officers and we went to the hotel where she was living.
>
> It was a typical Chinese hotel, a small bar and desk below with the rooms upstairs. We entered the bedroom, explained to the suspect why we were there and started

> searching. The room was ornately furnished and a double bed took up most of it. There was a dressing table with a large mirror. The suspect, no longer a girl, but still quite pretty, wore a colourful floral baju and sarong. She was quite relaxed and stood by the door joking with Selwyn. I started searching the room without result but realized that the woman kept glancing at the head of the double bed. As I began to search the bed head she became nervous and dashed out of the door with Selwyn in hot pursuit. There was a shriek and Selwyn came back holding her in one hand and her baju in the other!
>
> I examined the thick wooden bed head and found a hidden compartment containing gold jewellery and a small quantity of opium, which I seized with the bed head. A couple of weeks later the case came up in court. She pleaded guilty and was fined M$ 100 or so. The judge returned the jewellery but forfeited the opium and the bed head. As the interpreter explained the sentence to her she threw her hands in the air and started wailing. The judge asked why. The interpreter reported that she worked in the local cabaret as a dance hostess and would be unable to pay the fine without the bed head! The bed head was returned to her and in a week or so the fine was paid.

To establish the guilty knowledge of offenders the prosecution often had to depend on the statements they made at the time of their arrest or in subsequent formal interrogation. Such admissions and confessions, duly proven, were admissible in evidence.[30] However, similar statements made to police officers were barred under the criminal procedure statute. This distinction was to be challenged in court. At Butterworth, the mainland ferry terminal from Penang, officers stopped a car at the Customs barrier and asked the driver to open the boot for inspection. His response was an admission that it contained something illegal. It turned out to be a quantity of opium. Appealing against conviction in a lower court his counsel successfully argued that his admission should not have been accepted as evidence, since the powers of a customs officer were such that in the enforcement of legislation that was no longer concerned with revenue protection he was really a police officer under another name. Had this judgement been allowed to stand the work of the preventive branch would have been crippled. To overturn it a case in Singapore was selected. A Chinese man was the sole occupant and lessee of a room in which opium was concealed. He admitted that he was the owner of the opium and signed a written statement to that effect. In the lower court the newly established precedent was applied, the statement was rejected and the accused acquitted. An appeal was argued before three judges who agreed unanimously that a customs officer and a police officer were two different things, clearly distinguished in the criminal procedure law, and so restored the status quo.

Nevertheless, both in Singapore and the federation, the preventive service was devoting much of its time to duties that, elsewhere, would have been the responsibility of the police. Even in Singapore the resources to tackle the illegal retailing of chandu were totally inadequate. The tasks of dealing with the widespread cooking of opium and the distribution of the prepared product through 'smoking saloons' fell on special division, which could muster just 36 officers and men and which was also engaged in the investigation of offences against the revenue laws.[31] As described elsewhere, chandu factories were difficult to uncover and raids were preceded by long periods of surveillance, waiting for the chance to gain entry to the premises. Smoking saloons set no such problems. Their doors were seldom closed and they were easily taken by surprise. To conduct a raid, however, called for a party of six to eight men and such numbers were rarely available. Infrequent raids were unlikely to put the operators out of business.

Saloons were generally graded by the number of opium pipes they could offer. Four was the number in a small establishment, eight would be found in an average saloon and ten or twelve was generally the maximum. Although the pipes used in such places were cheap to manufacture they matured and grew increasingly valuable through constant use. Most saloon proprietors had spares in reserve and a single raid was seldom more than a tiresome interruption to their business. Hiding places for drugs and apparatus could be most ingenious. The old buildings offered many locations for false compartments in walls, floors and ceilings. Furniture too could be adapted for concealment. Prepared opium was very compact and easily hidden. Pipes and lamps were far more bulky but great skill was used to construct secret storage for them. Special division officers were well practised in identifying hiding places, and once spotted they were quickly opened. Derek Mackay, however, recalls one occasion when they had to admit defeat.

> It was in a small saloon on the outskirts of the city. The dimensions of a handsome cabinet clearly indicated a false back in which pipes could be racked, but all efforts failed to discover the way in. Losing patience I ordered that it be broken open. This was too much for an elderly Chinese who until then had sat watching with ill-concealed glee. With obvious pride he rose and demonstrated the trick required to open the compartment in which nestled four spare pipes. It was, I suppose, a fair cop, but I had not the heart to arrest him.

From time to time the raiding parties found safes in premises that had already yielded seizures of drugs or apparatus. It was obviously desirable that their contents be inspected but, as Derek Mackay explains, this called for expert assistance.

> We always asked the occupants of the premises for the safe keys but they were rarely made available. Indeed, the owner of the safe was unlikely to be present. I would then send for a locksmith. My favourite was an emaciated, elderly Chinese, with steel rimmed spectacles perched on the tip of his nose and a permanently woeful expression. His examination of the lock mechanism was conducted to the accompaniment of a great deal of tutting and repetitive shakes of the head. Assuring me that this would be a particularly difficult operation he would then open the bargaining with an outrageous demand for his fee. The process was purely a formality and honour was usually satisfied when I had driven him down to the regular figure. It rarely took him more than five minutes to open the door.

For the division such raids could be very time-consuming as the premises were ransacked in search of concealed drugs and apparatus. In practice, it appeared that the bulk of such discoveries were made in the first few minutes of a raid. It was decided therefore to try an alternative strategy, a number of brief searches in rapid succession. A period was set aside for the experiment and two raiding parties assembled each day carrying search warrants for up to fifty premises, located in neighbouring pairs. Switching to and fro across the city the raiders were able to achieve surprise. Each address was vacated after a few minutes as the two parties moved on to their next targets. After several days of such intensive raiding there was an observable effect as saloons began to run out of equipment. Cheap, raw pipes and hastily manufactured substitutes for lamps began to appear. Unfortunately, the effort could not be maintained. Other duties took priority. Nevertheless, the experiment showed what could be done if sufficient resources were applied.

The Singapore police frequently came across smoking saloons in the course of their activities in investigating other types of offence. Customs raids often found evidence of such activities as prostitution and gambling. An exchange of information led Derek Mackay to a raid in the heart of old Chinatown.

> In some streets saloons were to be found in almost every building. The omission of an address from my index was therefore ground for suspicion. Was its occupant a lone law-abiding citizen or a saloon keeper under protection? I liaised with the Police Officer responsible for dealing with illegal gambling. He too had an index on which he had noted any signs of opium dealing. Most of his addresses were to be found on my list also, but one in particular caught my attention, the one missing number in my record of the street. The saloon was located on the ground floor behind a shop and was reached by a side passage through which I led my party. I advanced through the room between two lines of wooden platforms on which the customers were busily engaged in smoking. Ahead was a doorway. Concealing it was a furnishing I had seen in many films recording the adventures of Charlie Chan and Dr Fu Manchu but had never met in Singapore – a bead curtain. As I approached it was flung aside and a number of Chinese charged towards me. I stopped, expecting that the sight of me would also bring them to a halt. On the contrary, the leader, a small plump man, hurled himself at me. Somewhat incensed I grabbed him by the arms, picked him up and sat him forcibly on the adjacent platform, explaining meanwhile that it was a serious offence to assault a Customs Officer – or words to that effect. He looked at me in some astonishment and responded 'I'm terribly sorry. I thought you were a policeman!' The whole party dived back through the curtain. By the time I joined them in the back room the game was once more in full swing.

Customers found in smoking saloons in possession of chandu or apparatus for its consumption were arrested as a matter of routine. They usually pleaded guilty and were punished by modest fines. It was rarely possible to take action against those who owned and operated the saloons. Under the Dangerous Drugs Ordinance it was an offence to permit the use of premises for the consumption of opium but this offence was hard to prove. In crowded Singapore property was often let and sublet down a long chain. The rooms in a typical 'shop-house' used for residential purposes were partitioned both vertically and horizontally into tiny cubicles in which an entire family might be accommodated. The occupants paid their rents in cash and the receipts were issued on stock forms with no identifying details. If a saloonkeeper or his manager were present at the time of a raid he would be careful to conceal his role and to excuse his presence with some innocent explanation. The most popular story was that he had just called looking for a friend whose name was, unfortunately, unknown to him.

The disposal of confiscated drugs was another job for the customs. Chandu was destroyed in the local municipal incinerator together with smoking apparatus. A senior officer supervised this operation and remained on site until satisfied that combustion was complete.[32] Raw opium was held in departmental strongrooms and eventually delivered under armed escort to ships with suitable secure storage for carriage to the United Kingdom. There it was used to manufacture medicinal drugs for the National Health Service.

By 1952 it was finally accepted that the suppression of the internal traffic in opium was not an appropriate task for a customs service. In July 1952 the Singapore police took over this work and customs were able to concentrate on the import and export of the drug, a responsibility for which they were better organized, equipped and trained. By the following year this specialization was already producing results: 6479 lbs of opium were seized and there was evidence of scarcity in the rising prices of the drug. The annual report records an increase in the price of Yunnan opium from S$ 350 to S$ 900 a pound. Indian opium rose from S$ 540 to S$ 1160. The market was beginning to feel the pinch.[33]

The retail price of chandu did not directly reflect the fluctuations in the international trade. A stable market suited the saloon keepers and their immediate suppliers and, to absorb short-term changes, they resorted to adulteration at the cooking stage. One ingredient commonly used for this purpose was pig's blood of which there was a plentiful supply.[34]

A factor in the increasing success of the preventive branch was the growing sophistication of the methods and equipment it was able to deploy against the smugglers. By 1954 the federation had set up a central registry to which all the preventive case reports were sent for inclusion in a complex system of cross-referenced files.[35] The registry was soon providing valuable background information to investigating officers. An interception of drugs severs a thread in a smuggling network and exposes it to further damage if the loose ends can be quickly traced, backwards or forwards from the break. Speed is essential. From the information gathered at the point of seizure or arrest the registry might identify a known organization and give a clear direction for further enquiries. Analysis of reports could also provide the basis of successful preventive measures.

Another potent weapon was banishment.[36] Most of the major traffickers came from China. Accumulated evidence of their illegal activities could be presented to a tribunal with powers to send them back to their country of origin. It was a prospect they feared and a procedure that was used more frequently as the records built up.

Singapore took similar measures to improve intelligence on drug smuggling. Following the transfer of inland responsibilities to the police a central narcotics intelligence bureau was established and in January 1955 a special investigation branch of customs was formed, staffed by 32 officers and men.[37] The department's report for that year records that it had 24,000 names on its register and had already secured the deportation of one of the few remaining big traffickers.

There was also a marked improvement in international cooperation. Although regular reports had been sent to the United Nations for many years, that organization gave no practical support to the battle against drugs.[38] The special investigation branch communicated directly with other national agencies, sending bulletins to 90 countries and arranging exchange visits with Manila, Burma, Hong Kong and Sri Lanka. The central narcotics intelligence bureau also issued a quarterly bulletin. Direct exchange of information with other anti-narcotic organizations led to several successes. Between 1955 and 1957 Singapore customs were working with the authorities in Pakistan and the USA to build up a case against a foreign national residing in the colony who was suspected to be the consignee for more than one shipment of opium. Although he could not be charged there was sufficient evidence to ensure his departure on the expiry of his residence permit. Various ships were shadowed on the basis of information received from countries at which they had already called and passed on to the authorities at their subsequent destinations. In 1958 the bureau undertook investigations and reports on behalf of agencies in India, Pakistan, Sri Lanka, Hong Kong, Thailand, Sarawak, Australia, the USA and the international criminal police organization in Paris.[39]

The interception at sea of vessels carrying contraband called for improved equipment. During 1951 some Singapore customs launches were fitted with VHF radio for the first time.[40] By 1956 13 of the fleet of 15 were so equipped and two carried radar. Their performance was now a match for the smugglers' speedboats and ocean-going ships could be shadowed as they came within range. Captured craft were sometimes used for inshore duties but by the end of 1956 delivery had been taken of the first of a new locally built type of 30-knot light craft to replace them. The department was also grateful to receive cooperation from the services. The Royal Navy, the Royal Malayan Navy and the Royal Air Force all worked with the preventive branch in operations at sea.

An unfortunate trend observed from about 1955 onwards was the use of violence by smugglers of all types of contraband.[41] In the past opium traffickers had rarely put up any resistance to arrest or seizure but the preventive service began to encounter men who would use weapons against them. In 1956 an officer guarding a ship from Bangkok opened a steel door at the top of the tunnel escape shaft and came face to face with two Chinese carrying sacks up the ladder. One of the Chinese attempted to stab the officer with a knife. The blow was deflected and both men fled. They left behind them 112 lbs of opium. An even more alarming incident occurred when the elderly HDML *Panah* spotted two speedboats closing on a suspect cargo vessel. She launched her fast interceptor, which eventually overtook the slower of the two craft. As she drew near, the three occupants threatened the customs party with parangs (the local machete) and then threw sticks of dynamite into the water near their boat. As the officers were unarmed and outnumbered they were reluctantly obliged to withdraw.

By 1958 the Comptroller of Customs Singapore was able to

report that the colony was no longer an entrepôt for opium. Moreover, the vigorous campaign waged against the local consumption of the drug, the success of the opium treatment centre since its inception in 1954 and a general improvement in education and living standards had all contributed to the decline of the vice on the island.[42] Seizures that year were little over half the total in 1957 at 1995 lbs. The new administration inherited a situation very different from the formidable difficulties that faced the customs in 1946.

Part Four:
The Course of Duty

10. Inner tubes filled with samsu for concealment by women in Singapore.

11
The demon drink

The principal tasks of a customs service are to collect and protect the revenue derived from import, export and excise duties. In Malaya, as in most countries, there were also fees for licences, rental for storage in bonded warehouses and charges for services such as surveys, weighing and the destruction of unwanted goods. The different dutiable commodities required different methods of identification and assessment, of measurement and classification and, therefore, corresponding differences in preventive measures. As described above in Chapter 2, the customs services in Malaya were established to take over the revenue farms from which the governments had previously derived the bulk of their income, including the opium monopoly. This last remained a state monopoly but the other farms were abolished or replaced by more modern methods of duty collection. In the Malay states export duties on such commodities as tin and rubber made a substantial contribution to the revenue. Over the years import duties were levied on an ever-widening range of goods. In the Straits Settlements, and later Singapore, however, the free port policy was incompatible with such extensive tariffs. There were no export duties and those on imports were confined to the broad categories of intoxicating liquors, tobacco and petroleum. Since these were also dutiable in the other territories it will be convenient to consider them separately.

As recorded above there were liquor farms in all jurisdictions from the very beginnings of the British administrations in Malaya. In the Settlements the 1909 Liquors Revenue Ordinance imposed import duties on spirits and beer.[1] In the FMS the liquor farms had all been wound up by 1911.[2] Thereafter, in both territories, the import duties on liquors were collected by the customs services on scales that were gradually extended to cover and distinguish all types of alcoholic beverages.

Alcoholic liquors were defined as those whose alcohol content exceeded 2 per cent by weight. This definition could lead to some unexpected applications. As we have already seen Peter Chattaway's discovery that it brought gripe water within scope met with disapproval at federal headquarters. In Singapore, however, a popular hangover cure was tested, found to have a very high alcohol content and ruled to be an intoxicating liquor, a seeming vindication of the claimed value of the 'hair of the dog'. A Sykes hydrometer[3] could provide a fairly accurate test but the final proof of liability to duty was a certificate from the government chemist. To incur duty the liquid had to be potable. Denatured spirit[4] was checked on import to ensure that it had been rendered effectively and permanently unfit for human consumption before release without payment of duty. Measurement of strength for the purpose of classification was calculated in terms of 'proof',[5] a figure expressed as a percentage but somewhat confusingly unrelated to weight or volume. Different rates of duty applied to the various types of alcoholic beverages, such as spirits, wines or beers. Most were imported in bottles and, once classified, subject only to occasional checks. Bulk shipments in casks or barrels were always sampled and only released after certification by the government chemist. In the warehouse at Kuala Lumpur Bicky Roualle encountered occasional shipments of Chinese rice wine, which arrived in earthenware jars with earthenware tops, holding approximately seven gallons each. The jars had to be opened and the contents measured in a calibrated metal drum. Apparently, this did not impair the quality of the wine.

The process of examination and analysis might also involve confirmation that the imported liquors conformed to regulations governing their specific description. Thus, the government chemist would check brandies to measure their ester content. Scotch whiskies were only released for distribution if covered by an official certificate that they had indeed been distilled in Scotland and had been aged in the wood for a minimum of three years. Both were to be between 75 and 81 per cent proof, although liqueur brandies were permitted to fall below the minimum.

On arrival liquors were first stored in bonded warehouses.[6] These were usually government bonds, staffed and protected by the customs service. Major importers operated private bonds under licence and overall customs supervision. Duty was only levied when goods were removed from the bond. Most importers requested a survey on arrival so that breakages or other losses in transit could be agreed. Goods removed from bond for export were not liable to duty. The government bonds were intended as short-term transit stores and a system of 'rack renting' discouraged longer storage. After a brief free period importers were charged a rental per case in bond at rates that were continually increased. Such charges could quickly swallow up the profit on the shipment.

In 1945, believing that the traditional European sources for wines and spirits would be unable to satisfy local demand, a number of Singapore importers decided to speculate in the importation of liquors from other countries.[7] In the event, French wines and brandies were soon back on the market in great quantity and the bonds were full of rival products for which there was no demand. Eventually, the burden of increasing rental became too great and the importers were forced to ask for destruction in bond. Derek Mackay spent many hours supervising the disposal of a shipment of South African crème de menthe and found that for days thereafter it seemed that everything he ate or drank tasted only of peppermint.

It was in the same warehouse, Bonded 'D', that Derek regularly sampled the shipments of draught beer imported for HM forces. Draught beer was a rarity in Singapore at that time. The popular drink was cold bottled lager.

> The deliveries were supervised by an elderly Englishman with the appropriate name of Gill. He held a Malay knighthood and was therefore a Dato. Sampling was a ritual carried out in my presence after the casks had had time to settle and recover from handling. The Dato would draw a sample into a jug from which he would fill two small bottles, one for me to seal and pass to the Government Chemist and the other for his check sample. This invariably left the jug half full. Having accepted his apologies for overestimation I would then produce two glasses with which we could share the task of destroying the surplus. Since the beer was exempt from duty the chemist was only required to confirm that it was fit for consumption.[8] On one occasion, when he was away giving evidence in a court case in Borneo, it was his assistant and wife who undertook the examination and sent me an adverse report to the effect that the beer 'contained foreign matter'. A very angry Dato Gill appeared at my desk: What the lady had discovered was that this beer, like any other 'live ale', contained hops!

Immediately before and after the Japanese occupation the

presence of large numbers of servicemen in Malaya led to a substantial increase in the releases of duty-free liquor for their consumption. Between 1936 and 1938 such releases of beer in the Straits Settlements doubled to over 350,000 gallons in a year. Together with the exemptions on wines and spirits this represented a waiver of some S$ 530,000 at a time when the total import duty collected on liquor was less than S$ 4 million. There was little evidence of any large-scale malpractice and the customs service did not begrudge the troops their privilege.

Since the Malays are Muslims, the Chinese provided the biggest market for imported liquors and had developed a taste for French brandy. This carried a heavy rate of duty. High duties encourage smuggling. The source of contraband was the entrepôt trade of Singapore and Penang. European goods, such as brandy, were re-exported to neighbouring territories without incurring duty. Running them back was a profitable business. Sumatra and the Rhio archipelago are only short voyages from Malaya and high-speed craft could make frequent trips with small cargoes. Such expeditions were seldom intercepted and, prior to the Second World War were probably of little consequence. In its report for 1938 the Straits Settlements' customs and excise claimed there was little evidence of organized smuggling. After the war, however, the incidence of such smuggling increased. To identify illicit importations all exporters were required to stamp the words 'EXPORT ONLY' or 'SINGAPORE DUTY NOT PAID' on the label of every bottle. In the late 1940s brandy so marked was frequently discovered back in Singapore. Some went further afield. On sea patrol off Malacca Peter Chattaway[9] spotted a motor *tongkang* near Pulau Besar, which turned and made off towards Sumatra. 'We gave chase and after about two hours we caught up and boarded. The boat was laden with cases of Cyprus brandy marked SINGAPORE DUTY NOT PAID. By the time we arrested the boat we were well on the way to Sumatra and were probably outside territorial waters.' The haul was about 100 cases and a lawyer appeared from Singapore to conduct the defence. Fortunately, Peter was able to satisfy the court that the smugglers' vessel was first sighted within territorial waters and a conviction was secured. The normal practice of selling off seized goods by auction was not followed, for the marked bottles could not be allowed on the local market. So Peter had the task of pouring the contents down the drain, an unpleasant experience. 'The brandy was lousy and the smell seemed to hang around for days.'

In Singapore 1956 seems to have seen the peak of this type of smuggling. By this time the department there was well equipped to intercept at sea, with a fleet of fast launches using VHF radios, some with radar. Special division was receiving good intelligence, which led to some very satisfactory results. In January, 197½ quarts of the popular Hennessey brandy were found on a motor vessel arriving from an Indonesian port. The annual report describes a successful ambush laid at Tanah Merah Besar near Changi.

> A speedboat approached and was signalled by a party of smugglers on shore. The speedboat's cargo was unloaded and while the smuggling party was taking it up the cliff the Customs party intercepted and arrested them. 408 quarts of brandy, 60 quarts of gin, 125 lbs of cigarettes and 170 lbs of leaf tobacco were seized. One of the smuggling party was arrested as he reached the top of the cliff laden with bottles of brandy. The second member fled down the cliff but was caught before he could escape to the motorboat. The third member, who was stranded on the beach, plunged into the sea and tried to swim away but was pursued and captured in the water. The three men subsequently were sentenced to terms of imprisonment ranging from three to six months.[10]

Other seizures were made when huts near the sea were raided and searched.

Interceptions at sea were the business of the Preventive Branch and revealed a new taste in contraband, Benedictine liqueur. On patrol one night a customs' launch picked up a craft closing the beach at Katong on his radar. The annual report tells us:

> The Customs launch increased speed and illuminated the speedboat with its searchlight. The order to stop was ignored but fortunately one of the fugitive's outboard engines stalled and the *Pengejar* rapidly closed and prepared to board, whereupon the two occupants of the speedboat dived overboard. Their craft was found to contain 383 lbs of cigarettes and five cases of DOM liqueur with a customs duty potential of S$ 3126. The two smugglers were rescued and subsequently charged in court and were sentenced to one year's rigorous imprisonment. The speedboat, after repair, has been turned to good account for preventive patrols.

A police launch made a very similar capture of an outboard-engined speedboat carrying a mixed cargo of cigarettes, tobacco and DOM liqueur.

It was unusual for the public to undertake preventive work, but the inhabitants of one west-coast village decided to tackle some smugglers without any assistance from the customs or the police.

> Early one morning, when two fishermen were returning home, they observed an unfamiliar sampan approaching the mouth of their river. They immediately reported the incident to their Headman who promptly ordered three friends to investigate. As they approached the suspect craft the occupants threatened to shoot them and, when this had no effect, began bombarding them with bottles of DOM liqueur. The villagers, however, pressed on and as they ran alongside the sampan the two occupants dived overboard and made good their escape in the darkness; 250 lbs of cigarettes and five bottles of liqueur, the unexpended portion of the smugglers' ammunition, were recovered. The Headman guarded the contraband against possible retaliation by the smugglers and then handed it over to the Department. His good work and that of his aides was suitably rewarded.

By 1958 the department was able to report a decline in this method of smuggling liquor, of whatever description. The writer comments, 'There was a sharp fall from 571 gallons of contraband liquor seized in 1957 to 148 gallons in 1958. This was mainly due to competition from the illicit trade in cigarettes, which attracted larger profits and enjoyed better channels of distribution. Most of the liquor seized was intercepted while being smuggled ashore from shipping in the port.'[11]

It does appear that liquor was never smuggled on the scale of cigarettes and tobacco. There was, however, another form of duty evasion, which, over many years, engaged the attention of the preventive service and whose suppression called for a great deal of physical effort on the part of its officers. This was the illicit manufacture of liquor to avoid the payment of excise duty.

In the Federated Malay States the Revenue Farms Enactment of 1904 introduced the licensing of liquor manufacture.[12] In practice, the licensees were largely Chinese distilleries producing peculiarly Chinese spirits, such as Ngo Kah Pee and Boon Quee Loh. In 1910 there were already four distilleries in the Straits Settlements contributing to a total of S$ 6,316,433 'miscellaneous revenue'.[13] In 1935 the service in the Settlements was actually renamed the 'Excise Department'. Nevertheless, the number of distilleries was never large and in 1949 the comptroller in Singapore reported that there were only two operating there. In the mainland states there were a number of distilleries of varying size and efficiency. In the FMS alone there were six in 1938. During the occupation the Japanese permitted a great increase and the Malayan Union inherited the responsibility for a total of 97 distilleries.[14] The temptation to malpractices and the difficulties of control required a rapid reduction. By 1947 there were only 17 licences on issue.[15]

Even these few survivors were fairly primitive installations. The sophisticated plant of a modern whisky manufacturer was not to be seen in these traditional Chinese liquor producers. Peter Chattaway[16] describes the licensed distillery at Seremban in 1947.

> The Distillery (Ban Joo Lee) was an interesting relic from the past. There were two or three old-fashioned pot stills, the condensers of which consisted of straight pipes running through long water troughs. The ends of the pipes protruded over earthenware pots, which received the liquor as it dripped from the pipes. At the end of the day the Revenue Officer on duty placed the day's collection into the bonded store. When the proprietors wanted to remove liquor from bond a senior officer attended, took samples and measured the strength of the liquor with a Sykes Hydrometer. The samples were then sent to the chemist to determine the correct strength. Provisional duty was paid on the hydrometer reading and although this was usually below that of the chemist, it was a black mark if the variation was too great!
>
> The products made at that time were a rice *samsu* and medicated *samsu* (Ngo Kah Pee) and because rice was in short supply the distillery sometimes produced a liquor made mainly from sugar. The sugar *samsu* and the medicated brands were, in my view, the best tasting. However, my opinion of the medicated brew changed dramatically when I found out that the *samsu* was medicated by steeping a variety of reptiles, insects and fruits in the liquor!

The old-fashioned premises were often very uncomfortable places to work. In 1940 Philip Merson[17] spent a time supervising the Ming Huat distillery in Singapore. His 'office' was a wire cage in the roof and when the stills were unloaded off the steam mash on the floor below he got a good steaming too.

The control of such manufacturers in the more remote parts of Malaya was a difficult and delicate task. Malays were forbidden alcohol by their religion, but leading figures in the community might have financial interests in local industrial enterprises, including distilleries. Although it was never suggested that such prominent persons might be aware of malpractices the responsible customs officer had to conduct his investigations with great care. Robert McCall[18] was convinced that the very modern distillery in Kota Bahru was recording an output that was far too small, an anomaly that might explain the increasing quantity of high-quality Chinese liquors on sale in licensed shops as far away as Penang and Kuala Lumpur at prices that did not cover the duty payable on them. Tony King[19] was invited from Taiping to conduct an investigation. The building had been designed with advice from UK customs and the local contractors had followed their recommendations for its security. It was found, however, that they had added an additional feature by the provision of external access doors, well hidden by the secondary vegetation in the surrounding fields. After the official closure each evening, and the departure of the supervisory customs staff, the distillery was accustomed to admit a 'night shift' whose production was removed before the legal operation was resumed the following day. During his enquiries Tony was lodged at the elderly town rest house, which he describes as a wooden and atap structure with creaking floorboards and creeper covered walls.

> We had accumulated a large quantity of Chinese books of account covering the illegal operations with a skilled searcher, a senior Chinese ODO from Malacca known as 'Dustbin Fong'. These valuable documents were stored in steel cases and kept under my bed in the Rest House, as we worked day and night to close this investigation. The local ladies of the town were renowned for their beauty and their skilful attractions. When at last I got to bed the boards in the corridor creaked and seductive offers were made both through and under my bedroom door. As this failed the next I heard was heavy rustling in the creeper outside my bedroom window. As the shadowy figures mounted the branches below the window I was able to push them down

> with my charm-endowed walking stick, a bamboo called 'Semambu', which the Malays believed would cripple any joint it touched with permanent arthritis. I had bought this cane from a Sakai in the jungle below Grik; I still have it!

The distillery was closed until further notice.

The high rate of excise duty on spirits provided an opportunity to market illegally distilled *samsu* at much lower prices than the duty-paid product. There was a ready market for this 'moonshine' among the poorer Chinese, particularly in rural areas and the operations could easily be concealed in the extensive areas of jungle, scrub and swamp. The consequence was an ongoing 'guerrilla war' between the illicit distillers and the preventive officers, in which both sides demonstrated much ingenuity and, not infrequently, considerable physical endurance.

The method of distillation of rice liquors used was extremely simple and the illegal apparatus was constructed from everyday articles easily obtained and, when dismantled, apparently for wholly innocent employment. The fermented rice was loaded into a suitable container, most commonly a 44-gallon oil drum, standing on a simple fireplace. The open top of the drum was then closed with a *kuali*, a shallow conical metal dish, filled with constantly replenished cold water. As the rice boiled the rising steam condensed on the cold underside of the *kuali* and ran down to the tip of the cone, its lowest point, where it dripped into a small pan and down a pipe inserted in a hole in the side of the drum, to be collected in a jar. Once the operation was complete the components of the still were separated. Only the *kuali* bore telltale signs of its illicit employment, the underside clean and bright within the circumference of the drum, but blackened with smoke beyond that limit. A sceptical magistrate was unlikely to accept this as sufficient evidence of an offence. To secure a conviction the distillers must be caught in the act.

Despite these difficulties the departments made frequent seizures of illicit stills,[20] *samsu* and rice mash. Even in the limited area of the Straits Settlements several hundred stills were forfeited each year. In 1933 the figure reached 917 stills, along with over 3000 gallons of liquor. Large quantities of mash were also destroyed, in 1938 over 30,000 gallons. In that same year 786 stills were confiscated in the FMS.[21] Immediately after the Second World War the pursuit of distillers was fraught with danger and difficulty, but the 1946 Malayan Union report records the seizures of 225 stills. The

11. Singapore: a typical 44-gallon still in action.

following year the figure had increased to 454. In 1956 Singapore customs seized 258 stills, 2054 gallons of illicitly manufactured *samsu* and 59,953 gallons of rice mash. In 1957, the year of *merdeka*, the federal customs tracked down 212 illicit stills.

For the moonshiners the distillation was their most vulnerable time. Their apparatus was assembled and identifiable and required constant attention. The cooking fires gave off smoke that might be seen or smelt at a distance. In addition to concealment they took elaborate precautions to guard against surprise, including the posting of sentries, guard dogs and trip wires concealed on the approaches to the still. To catch them the preventive men needed sound information and the skill to get near without detection. As the operators usually did their work in the small hours the raiding parties had to make an early start and often trek considerable distances through sometimes very difficult country.

John Lewis[22] was regularly in pursuit of illicit distillers and found it necessary to acquire suitable clothing for the work.

> To push one's way through the jungle undergrowth (known locally as *blukar*) and through swamps, and even on raids in towns, the preventive officers had to be suitably clothed. The Asian officers were provided with khaki uniforms

> although most of them wore old clothes of their own so as not to be conspicuous. I designed for myself a special suit for raiding purposes which was made of khaki drill cloth with long trousers and a jacket with long sleeves with cuffs which could be buttoned back. When travelling at night in the jungle the cuffs could be turned down to cover the hands against mosquito bites and scratches from unseen thorns. I had a pair of boots made for me with canvas tops and leather soles. Tin miners wore these as they enabled the wearer to walk through mud and water without losing them and the water drained through the canvas.

His face smeared with insect repellent John still had to cope with the problem of leeches. They could work their way through clothing and suck their victim's blood without his knowledge.

> The practice amongst people who were used to travelling in the jungle was to stop every half an hour or so for a leech check. As leeches could go through socks and woven clothing it was necessary to strip down to the skin to find them. Leeches should not be pulled off the skin as they leave their heads behind, which could become septic. The usual method of removing them was to burn their tails with a match or lighted cigarette which caused them to let go and fall off complete with their heads.

When the officers got close to the distillery they had to take great care to avoid detection. On one occasion Peter Burgess[23] reached a position from which he could establish the location of an illicit still at the top of a half-mile long ravine.

> We could see the smoke from the fire and could also see a sentry on the hillside about a quarter of a mile from the still. My Chinese assistant said, 'I will deal with him.' We kept out of sight while he stalked and eventually gagged the sentry. We then made our way under cover of the scrub, achieving complete surprise.

In the mid-1930s John Lewis[24] was able to outwit some illicit distillers in the Port Swettenham area by rising even earlier than they did. Setting out at 4.00 a.m. he drove with his raiding party to the edge of the jungle.

> The informer, who was with us, then led the party into the jungle which was so dark that we could not see each other. We all had torches which had to be used with care so as not to advertise our presence but the informer somehow found his way to the distillery. The rest of us followed him in single file, each of us holding on to the man in front.

Lying in ambush the officers watched the arrival of two Chinese who lit the fire and set the apparatus going. On John's signal the party closed in and made the arrests.

In August 1947 Bicky Roualle[25] was responsible for what the *Malay Mail* described as the largest ever seizure of illicit distilling apparatus and liquor in Malaya.

> 'On information received', accompanied by a newly arrived Customs Cadet and half a dozen Out Door Officers, I left Kuala Lumpur before 4.00 a.m. and travelled by road to Sungei Rayong in Pudu Ulu, five miles south of KL, an area with a somewhat insalubrious reputation, as it was known to have the hideouts of various gangs of Chinese who had been carrying out robberies in and around KL. After about half an hour on foot from the road in the dark, through an overgrown rubber estate and secondary jungle, we were approaching the site when we saw two rows of lights coming towards us along a nearby ravine. We closed in on the lights and secured half a dozen or so Chinese including a couple of women. Several others got away in the dark. When dawn came it enabled us to check on the area. We found a couple of large sheds beside a small stream, a large stack of firewood, two tons of sugar, 130 gallons of rice wine and over 1000 gallons of fermented rice mash in large earthenware jars and wooden vats. There were two large stills, each with a diameter of some four feet, set on brick and cement bases in which fires could be lit to boil the mash. These stills were connected to the nearby stream by bamboo pipes, ensuring an ample supply of cold water to facilitate the distillation process. We had handcuffed our prisoners to trees and I sent a couple of Out Door Officers back to KL for reinforcements and for an official photographer. These duly arrived after we had completed a detailed survey of the whole set-up and taken samples of and measured the gallonage of the mash on the site. We were photographed

> smashing up and destroying the huts, sugar and mash, resulting in a quagmire of mash and sugar. We carted back pieces of the stills and all the liquor to Kuala Lumpur. These were duly produced in court when four various prisoners were convicted and gaoled for their involvement in illicit distilling. I have a couple of photographs of the operation and on close examination note that I have the butt of a revolver protruding from my trouser pocket.

Bicky was wise to go armed. Until the late 1950s it was rare for offenders to offer any violent resistance to arrest, but illicit distillers were always the exception to this rule. Usually apprehended in remote and hidden places they were often equipped with parangs and other implements that could be employed as offensive weapons. Some of them were prepared to attack officers in defence of their apparatus and its products. Chasing a Chinese whom he had surprised in the act of distilling John Lewis[26] overtook his quarry, who turned in his tracks and threatened John with a parang. On the sight of John's revolver he dropped his weapon and submitted to arrest. It was therefore a prudent precaution for the officer in charge of the raiding party to carry a firearm with which he could defend them.

On one such occasion the practice proved counter-productive. In Singapore Derek Mackay[27] made his largest seizure in what was then an area of scrub near Braddell Road.

> The location was betrayed by two men who had been severely beaten by the owners of the stills. As usual, the raid meant an early start, as illicit distillation was best done under the cover of darkness. My party reached the area soon after dawn. In case of trouble I had stuffed a .32 Colt automatic in the pocket of my shorts. I was bringing up the rear of the column when I glanced over an adjacent hedge and saw two stills in operation a few yards away. As I scrambled through the prickly obstacle a small Chinese fled from the scene. I followed him at full speed as he dodged through what proved to be swampy ground. I seemed to be holding my own, or even gaining, but the heavy pistol was beating a tattoo on my thigh and I decided it would be more comfortable to remove it from my pocket. The fugitive looked back over his shoulder in time to see me draw the gun. He responded with a turn of speed which left me out

12. Pudu Ulu: Bicky Roualle with his record-breaking illicit distillery.

> of the race. Fear was obviously an effective accelerator. I returned somewhat breathless to the rest of the party. We had a fine array of stills, pottery jars and inner tubes,[28] but, alas, no arrests.

The inner tubes were one solution to the distillers' problem of delivery. The liquor produced by their illegal operations would have to be conveyed to the market, another vulnerable stage in their activities. A common method was to pour the *samsu* into inner tubes, which were then sealed at both ends and concealed beneath the clothing of women carriers. Bicycle inner tubes could be wound round their bodies, while larger tubes were sometimes strapped in place to produce an appearance of pregnancy.

Distillers often conducted their operations on or near rubber plantations and planters sometimes tipped off the customs about these activities. Others preferred to deal with such matters themselves. When Peter Burgess[29] was stationed in Kluang he asked the local planters if they had any trouble with illicit liquor.

> The reply I received from one of the largest estates was 'Don't worry about that. If we suspect any trouble we

> round up all the squatters on the edge of the estate, break up any stills we find and kick the offenders out. But don't let that stop you from visiting us. We are delighted to see you any time.'

Planters were notoriously hospitable and Peter sometimes found it very difficult to get away!

In those days Peter came across some very small stills making use of the standard four-gallon kerosene tin. Such cans were adapted to a wide variety of uses. With a wooden handle fixed across the top they were a convenient water carrier. Cut diagonally they could be affixed to a long pole to make a back-saving dustpan plied with a long-handled coconut broom. Stills for a commercial output were generally larger. In 1956 the Singapore customs found an unattended still of 80 gallons capacity, with 352 gallons of mash and 138 gallons of *samsu* ready for transport in the one-gallon lubricating oil tins found nearby.[30] A much more elaborate apparatus was discovered in 1947. The still was equipped with charcoal filters, cooling jackets and a coil condenser. Sugar cane was crushed in a small mill operated by a jacked-up motorcycle. The proud owner demonstrated his equipment and was then arrested.

The outdoor officers of the FMS customs were worthy opponents of the wily distillers.[31] One officer disguised himself as a Tamil labourer and picked up a still concealed in the *blukar*. Carrying it he deliberately walked past the house of the suspected distiller who rushed out to catch the thief who was stealing his valuable property. It was he who was arrested. On another raid an outdoor officer and his informant had to carry two seized 64-gallon drums slung on a pole between them as they made their way 300 yards along a pipeline without handrails above a sheer drop 30 feet to the rocks beneath.

The communist insurrection of 1948 made it dangerous to penetrate the jungle in search of distillers. The Raub area was much affected and Johnny Johnson,[32] with just one Chinese preventive officer and a .38 pistol, was in no position to tackle the moonshiners. Like most terrorists the communists were not averse to drawing a profit from commercial crime and probably involved themselves in the activities of the distillers.[33] In 1949 a Chinese woman was convicted of obstruction and destroying illegal *samsu*. Later, among papers discovered at a 'bandit' hideout, the security forces found a report of the case lamenting the loss of profit to the communist cause.

By 1956 Singapore customs were reporting a new development in the moonshiners' technique. In a Chinese cemetery they came across a still in operation fired by a blowlamp with three burners.[34] This cooking equipment did not produce the smoke that could attract the curiosity of members of the public who might be tempted to turn informer. It probably shortened the time in which the still was in operation and therefore reduced the danger of detection. It was in that same year that a glider pilot attached to the royal naval air station reported to customs his suspicions regarding a clearing on a hilltop.[35] Following the compass bearing he indicated, an officer discovered an illicit distillery and 132 gallons of mash. Delighted by this success the officer accompanied the pilot on an air reconnaissance of the Mandai forest reserve and spotted a distillery deep in the jungle. In 1958 aircraft were employed to locate three large distilleries in the Seletar and Senoko river areas.[36] Reporting this the comptroller goes on to say that there was, nevertheless, 'little evidence that moonshiners experienced even mild slump conditions during the year'. Although the two licensed Singapore distilleries enjoyed buoyant production and sales during 1958 it is apparent that the war against illicit distilling was still far from won.

An alternative licensed production of intoxicating liquor was the brewing of beer. This was confined to Singapore where the first such enterprise, Malayan Breweries Limited, was opened in 1932. In 1933 the same owners started a second plant, the ABC Brewery.[37] These were best known for their excellent lagers, Tiger and Anchor. As their output was confined to bottled beers the collection of excise duty was a simple matter. The levy was charged on removals from bond. Both breweries collaborated fully with the revenue collectors. After the liberation they were soon re-established and they built up a substantial export trade. In 1949 releases from bond totalled 3,230,000 gallons of beer and 2,228,000 gallons of stout.[38] More than half of this was for export.

Illegal production of beer was hardly likely to yield the profits to justify the risks, yet in 1957 the federation customs discovered several unlicensed breweries in Kuala Lumpur and Malacca where large quantities of stout were adulterated for sale as genuine branded products.[39] In general, however, the protection of the revenues on 'beer, ale, stout and porter' did not require the attention of the preventive service.

The sale of intoxicating liquor was also subject to a system of licensing. Distributors held wholesale licences. Retailers were of several types – public houses, retail shops (off-licences) and Chinese liquor shops. Boards of licensing justices, which met at regular intervals to consider grants and renewals, approved the licences.[40] Senior officers of the department had a right to attend and were required to assist the boards in their decisions. It was departmental policy to restrict the numbers of retailers and thus reduce the danger that competition might lead to malpractices, such as the purchase of smuggled liquors or sales outside the permitted hours. This, however, inevitably drove some shops and restaurants to make unlicensed sales. In Singapore there were occasional prosecutions of such offenders. Nevertheless, the controls worked fairly well and numbers of licensees were kept within reasonable limits.[41] In the Straits Settlements the number of public houses rose only from 83 in 1910 to 136 in 1938. Retailers actually decreased from 702 in 1910 to 463 in 1938. Premises were subject to surprise inspections, a task that fell to Derek Mackay[42] during his time in special division, Singapore. He found stock checking in Chinese shops was hampered by the fact that they were permitted to keep their books in Chinese. However, he managed to master the Chinese characters for various types of local spirits and contrived to bluff his way through.

One curious relic of the liquor monopoly lingered on. Toddy[43] was a very popular drink among the Indian manual workers. It is a natural product obtained by tapping the toddy palm but has to be drunk within a short time before uncontrolled fermentation makes its condition unacceptable. The only methods of preserving it, once used by unscrupulous suppliers, were by additives that were often toxic. In the interests of public health and safety the trade had to be regulated. The objective was to ensure that only pure fresh toddy was sold to the consumer.

Contractors were licensed to supply the product of designated tapping areas in which a senior officer of customs approved and registered the numbers of trees tapped and labourers employed. Fresh toddy was delivered daily to shops where it was sold to the customers for consumption then and there. It was an offence to possess toddy anywhere else. Large estates employed their own tappers and supplied their own shops from trees on the estate. Initially, the licensing board licensed all public shops, but in 1922 the FMS government began to take over the shops, beginning in the Kuala Lumpur area.[44] By 1934 two-thirds of all shops were being run by the customs service. In the Straits Settlements there

13. Raub: Johnny Johnson's alcoholic bullock.

were still 165 licensed toddy shops in 1930, but all had been closed by 1935, leaving 40 estate shops in Malacca and 28 in Penang, which included ten in the Dindings. Off the estates, 20 government shops in Penang and Province Wellesley, ten in Singapore and just one in Malacca handled sales. The system survived the Japanese occupation and in 1947 the Malayan Union received M$ 1,418,043 revenue from a total of 86 shops of various kinds.[45]

Even the government shops were not designed for customer comfort. Peter Chattaway[46] was given the task of inspecting the shops in Seremban. 'Toddy was mainly drunk by Indians, mostly labourers and rubber tappers, and on occasions they became rowdy and violent. In consequence the manager and his staff served the toddy in tin mugs from behind a wire barricade. Our visits were to check the sales and purchases and to see that only fresh liquor was sold.' In Raub Johnny Johnson[47] suspected that there might be some illicit drinking at the local shop.

> I was told that the ox who pulled the cart on which were the jars of toddy to be taken to the shop would not move unless he had his own drink of toddy. I thought this might be an excuse to hide a bit of illicit drinking so I went to see for myself. Sure enough, the animal would not move until it had its drink.

Aware that no one was likely to believe such a tale Johnny took back a photograph as evidence.

An apparent anachronism, the toddy monopoly continued to contribute a small revenue to both Singapore and the federation. In 1957 federation customs collected over M$ 7.5 million on behalf of the member states. In Singapore, now largely urban, the yield was only just over M$ 0.5 million.[48] The system's justification was health rather than wealth.

12
Up in smoke

Unlike intoxicating liquor, tobacco was never traded through a revenue farm. Indeed, the decision to impose import duties on tobacco products, including cigars, cigarettes and pipe tobacco, was taken during the First World War, at a time when a number of wartime taxes were imposed. The Federated Malay States introduced such a duty on 18 March 1915.[1] During that year it produced a yield of S$ 0.75 million. The Settlements, where there was always a reluctance to deviate from free port policy, were slower to approve a similar tax; but it finally came into force on 16 June 1916. By 1919 it was contributing S$ 1,550,135 to the Straits government's coffers and in both territories was accepted as a valuable source of revenue.[2] In the 1930s its yield surpassed that on liquors and continued to do so thereafter.

Importers were subject to a system of licensing.[3] Initially, there were large numbers of small businesses engaged in the trade. In the Straits Settlements alone there were 268 licensed importers in 1920, but these numbers fell over the years to come and in 1933 there were only 123. Many of these handled only tobacco originating in neighbouring countries. European style cigarettes and cigars were concentrated in the hands of the manufacturers' local subsidiaries or representatives, of which by far the largest was Malayan Tobacco Distributors, which conducted the operations of Imperial Tobacco in the area. Like liquor, imports were unloaded into bonded warehouses and became subject to duty on removal from bond.[4] There were a few private bonds for the larger importers. Most tobacco products were in retail packs and ready for sale to the public. A substantial proportion of imports were, however, of leaf tobacco for delivery to local manufacturers. These too were licensed and once again their numbers were whittled down over the years. In the Settlements they fell from 49 in 1920 to 19 in 1933.

All tobacco products were dutiable at flat rates per lb. Leaf tobacco was therefore weighed in bond. Cigarettes were test weighed to establish standard weights per pack. Weighing was usually done in Singapore and the results accepted throughout both territories. Cigarettes were by far the largest class of imports. In 1935 releases from bond in the Straits Settlements weighed 3,276,195 lbs. This compares with 592,045 lbs of manufactured tobacco and 17,988 lbs of cigars. A total of 784,667 lbs of unmanufactured tobacco left bond for delivery to the licensed factories.

The introductory rates of duty were quite low and there was very little incentive to smuggle. The Straits Settlements' report for 1919 records, nevertheless, that the Government Monopolies Department seized 6735 lbs of contraband.[5] After the First World War and the cessation of the special wartime taxes it proved necessary to make substantial increases in duty rates. From 9 August 1921 all rates were raised by 50 per cent[6] with the inevitable result that smuggling rose too. In the years 1927 to 1930 seizures in the Settlements amounted to 54,000 lbs.[7]

A particular problem was that quite substantial quantities of tobacco were grown in Malaya and were not subject to duty. In 1935 the Straits Settlements Excise Department reported that 370,000 lbs of tobacco were delivered 'ex-plantation'.[8] Such tobacco was used in the local factories. Its appearance was identical to the products of neighbouring territories, which, therefore, once smuggled into the Settlements, could be passed off as local leaf and processed in local factories. As early as 1932 anxiety was expressed in the department's annual report about the increase in the quantity of Malayan tobacco believed to be smuggled in from Johore and Negri Sembilan.[9] The governor had set up a committee to consider the imposition of an excise duty. There was also a problem with smuggling leaf from the Dutch islands. There had been 317 prosecutions. The following year there were 241 prosecutions for offences involving tobacco and 20,277 lbs were seized.[10]

The late 1930s saw a decline in local tobacco production in the Straits Settlements, particularly Singapore where there was an increasing demand for land for other purposes.[11] Imports of tobacco products from countries such as Java, Siam and China also fell in the face of competition from cheap UK cigarettes. Revenue meanwhile increased and in 1938 it exceeded S$ 5 million. Only 83 people were charged with tobacco-related offences.

As recorded above the Japanese administration during the occupation identified tobacco as a source of revenue and imposed a 50 per cent *ad valorem* duty, a great encouragement to the daring smuggler. The returning British administration reinstated the prewar arrangements and in 1946 the Malayan Union collected over M$ 18 million in tobacco duties.[12] Once again there were far too many licensed importers and their numbers in Singapore were cut from 122 in 1947 to 76 in 1949.[13] The newly designated colony was still performing its role as an entrepôt, redistributing imports to adjacent territories. There was a large re-export of tobacco products. In 1949 some 6,408,715 lbs were released from bond for export,[14] the vast majority in the form of cigarettes; by comparison, releases, duty-paid, for consumption in Singapore amounted to 4,448,733 lbs. Although the bulk of such exports were probably legitimate, suspiciously large quantities were dispatched to such destinations as Rhio, from which it was easy to smuggle them back into Singapore. The practice of marketing different brands of cigarettes in different countries greatly facilitated identification of such illegal imports. Revenue officers checking tobacco shops and street vendors in the city could easily spot such exotic trade names as Pirate and Singing Birds, which, as they could testify in court, had never been the subject of duty payments in the colony.

Nevertheless, for some years it was the illegal importation of leaf tobacco that challenged the preventive service. Interceptions were made from time to time but the traffic continued to flourish, running in consignments across the Malacca and Singapore Straits and over the frontier with Thailand. In 1947 Bicky Roualle[15] was involved in the seizure of five tons, which had arrived by the overland route. A Chinese admitted ownership but was unable to produce evidence that he had paid duty on it.

> I was subsequently able to produce statistical evidence in court to the effect that less than fifty pounds of Siamese tobacco had been imported, duty paid, during the previous two years. The owner of the tobacco was convicted and gaoled for twelve months. I had personal knowledge of the type of Siamese tobacco we had seized. It was identical to the tobacco purchased during the war by allied prisoners of war working on the Burma/Siam railway. It was very strong, black as night and, in polite circles, was referred to as 'Sikh's beard'. In order to make it smokeable the POWs washed it in several buckets of water, sprinkled it with some cane sugar syrup and then dried it in the sun.

> A sequel to the prosecution was the disposal of the five tons of tobacco, which the court had ordered to be confiscated by the Customs Department. The normal practice was for us to auction off confiscated goods, provided that a bid in excess of the import duty on the goods was received. In this case the import duty payable was in excess of M$ 35,000 for very poor quality tobacco. A Chinese associate of the convicted man came to my office several times after the court hearing and asked what was to happen to the tobacco. I told him about the auction and that the date would be advertised. He asked what the price would be. I explained that it was to be a sale by auction and about the minimum price. After two or three visits it was obvious that he was endeavouring to negotiate a deal involving some form of bribery. I duly reported the matter to the Comptroller of Customs and to the Police. Some days passed. I was then given a message to the effect that the Chinese 'businessman' would be calling to see me at my quarters at lunchtime that day. I hurriedly contacted the appropriate senior Police Officer who arrived at my house, followed a few minutes later by the Chinese. The Police Officer had ensconced himself in one of the bedrooms in my wooden bungalow and heard the Chinese make me repeated offers of M$ 12,000 for the tobacco and M$ 5000 for me personally. He emerged from the bedroom and arrested the Chinese who was gaoled for twelve months for 'corruptly offering a gift to a public servant'. After the case I remember the Chinese court interpreter saying to me 'You're a very hard man. It's an old Chinese custom.' I indicated that it was high time that the custom was discontinued.

The laws protecting government revenues are designed to discourage a highly profitable crime and provide heavy financial penalties. In Malaya the various statutes imposed minimum fines on conviction, usually three times the duty evaded, and imprisonment for default. Enforcement set Tony King a problem in Kelantan.[16]

> The magistrates in the Kelantan courts were all Malays and all the proceedings were conducted in the unique Kelantan dialect using the Kelantan enactments. My first prosecution was to proceed against a lusty Malay fisherman who had brought in a sizeable shipment of tobacco to Pantai Chinta

> Berahi, a local leisure beach translating as the 'Beach of Passionate Love', where road access was easy. The magistrate, the officers of the court, the defendant and the audience packed into the body of the court were pleased to assume that even if I could understand, let alone speak Malay, I would not understand a word of the interchange which was to take place in the local patois.
>
> The evidence for the prosecution was given and the magistrate advised the accused to change his plea to 'guilty' as there was no way he could find him other than guilty. This, he explained, would enable him to give him a short prison sentence without the further penalty of a fine. The accused demurred and explained that he expected to be released, as he had no claim over the tobacco, which, after some months in a dry Customs warehouse, was of no further value. The magistrate told him it was either a large fine based on the quantity of tobacco seized or the option he was offering of a short sentence. There followed loud shouts of advice from the audience to take the magistrate's offer and go to the comfortable 'holiday camp', their description of the model jail, and to enjoy the food and recreation there.

At this stage Tony intervened to offer the magistrate a copy of the statute and to draw attention to the minimum sentence. The magistrate reluctantly agreed that the accused would have to accept a longer stay in the 'holiday camp'.

H. G. Boyce-Taylor[17] laid a successful ambush for tobacco smugglers on the east coast of Singapore. Under cover of darkness he took a party to the place named by the informant and concealed them close to the beach.

> After several hours a boat came and anchored and started to unload. A man waded ashore carrying a large sack, which he dumped almost on my head. He returned for another load and as he was preparing to drop this in the same place I grabbed his ankle and gave the pre-arranged signal for the rest of the party to move in.

When he realized Boyce-Taylor's identity the captured smuggler was surprisingly relieved. As he explained, 'Tuan, I thought you were a ghost.'

At Christmas 1953 a stroke of luck and some good police work offered a breakthrough in the efforts of the federation preventive service to stem the flow of smuggled leaf tobacco into local manufacturing industry.[18] The west coast of Johore was almost entirely mangrove swamp, a maze of mud banks crowned with thick bushes, intersected by numerous narrow channels in which small craft could be well concealed. An excellent motor road ran parallel to the coast a short distance inland, crossing a succession of creeks and inlets. This was a paradise for tobacco smugglers. It was a profitable business to bring Sumatran tobacco across the Malacca Straits and through the mangrove to be collected by motor vehicles and passed off as locally grown. Just before Christmas a police car patrolling the coast road turned off towards the sea down a track leading to an Indian village a few miles south of the little port of Muar. There they met a Land Rover travelling in the opposite direction. It was the property of a major tobacco manufacturer in Kuala Lumpur. On the front seat sat two employees of that business and a third who worked for their branch in Singapore. In the back was an unwrapped bale of leaf tobacco. Detaining the vehicle the policemen conducted a search at the village. On a pier they found torn matting of the kind used to wrap tobacco bales. Nearby in the bushes they discovered a sampan loaded with leaf tobacco in matting bales. A powerful outboard motor concealed nearby matched the impressions on the stern of the sampan. It was not hard to frame a theory to fit the facts and the case was handed over to the local customs officer, Leslie Hewitt, recently seconded from the UK service.

At this time Derek Mackay was in charge of preventive operations in south Johore. Although Muar was outside his jurisdiction it was agreed that he should conduct the prosecution.

> When the case came up for trial in the following year I was due to transfer to Kuala Lumpur and was in the process of handing over duties in Johore and packing my belongings. I travelled up to Muar and stayed with Leslie and his wife Muriel. Defence counsel was David Marshall, a Singapore lawyer who had established a formidable reputation following two sensational victories against the Police (he was later to be Chief Minister of Singapore). I had crossed swords with David several times and knew him well enough to enjoy his hospitality. I was therefore unwisely irritated when, on the eve of the trial, the officer in charge of the

14. Singapore: officers with their haul of smuggled leaf tobacco.

Muar Police assured me that I was bound to lose the case, and stung into a rash response. The prosecution took two and a half days to present. The magistrate, Jimmy Kirby, was, like Leslie, a new arrival in the country. The European community in Muar was small and, as usual in such stations, centred on the club. There, throughout the trial there might be seen each evening the magistrate, prosecutor, defence counsel and senior prosecution witness, drinking and chatting together. Our business in court was never mentioned.

I closed my case late on the third morning. To my surprise Marshall rose to submit that there was no case to answer as I had not proved that the tobacco was 'uncustomed'. This was a groundless argument since the point was covered by a presumption in the Enactment. Jimmy decided to adjourn for lunch and I appeared on resumption ready to answer the defence submission. To my further astonishment the magistrate announced that he accepted it and acquitted all three accused. It was then that he saw my face and realized that he had not given me the right to reply. As the accused had been acquitted in open court there was now no point in responding but I indicated that I would seek an appeal.

In a very angry mood I set off to motor back to Johore Bahru. I was driving a small sports car and making good progress when I ran into a heavy rainstorm. At this time the 'emergency' was still in progress and there was a curfew under which all traffic was forbidden at night. Mistakenly I thought this was now imminent and pressed on too fast. Coming round a blind bend I found myself skating on a sea of mud washed down across the road by the heavy rain. Out of control the car rolled into a ditch, from which it would not budge. Within minutes a British Police Lieutenant appeared and took me to his quarters for a drink while he called up an armoured car to tow me out. Despite a deal of damage the car was driveable and I continued on my journey home, now furnished with a curfew pass. Arriving at Johore Bahru I found that Marshall on his way back to Singapore had seen my car in the ditch. As I was absent he assumed the worst and assured my Assistant Comptroller that I was either in hospital or a morgue.

The process of appeal took its usual slow course and brought an order that the magistrate should resume the trial and call the defence. I was now at work in Kuala Lumpur. By coincidence, so too was Jimmy Kirby. As two of the three accused also lived there, and for Marshall it would be a much easier journey by train or plane, we all agreed to continue the proceedings in the Federal capital. I entertained David to dinner at the Selangor Club the night before and was joined in court the next day by Leslie Hewitt who had travelled up from Muar to share the work. During his investigation he had recorded statements from all three Tamil-speaking accused, using two Indian Out Door Officers as interpreters. It was crucial to the defence that some innocent explanation of the facts be given. Since the accused naturally denied all knowledge of the discoveries in the village, and swore that the tobacco in the Land Rover was from their employer's stock in Kuala Lumpur, they had to offer a reason for their visit to the Indian village. To Leslie all three stated that they had driven down the track in the hope of selling their load there. This was a thin story. Prospective purchasers of leaf tobacco would almost certainly be known and unlikely to be found in a mangrove swamp. In court the first accused elected to give evidence on oath and it soon became clear he and his associates had decided to improve their tale. He now claimed they had driven down the track to see a famous Indian temple located in the village. So far the statements taken by Leslie had not been tendered in evidence but they could now be used to rebut the defence. To do this, I would have to prove them, calling as witnesses Leslie and his interpreters, both of whom had recently left Muar on transfer. As I began my cross-examination Leslie was on the phone trying to find them. Luck was with us. The interpreter for the first accused was on duty at Kuala Lumpur Airport. He was immediately dispatched to court. My application to prove the statement was accepted and Leslie gave evidence that he had recorded it. Marshall was content with his admission that he could not speak Tamil. The interpreter then took the stand and proved an excellent witness. His English was perfect. As Tamil was his native tongue there was no problem in proving the statement. Armed with this I found no difficulty in breaking the accused's story. Applying for an adjournment David asked me if I would show him the statements made by his other two clients. After reading them through he changed tactics. The second and third accused made statements from the dock. Not surprisingly Jimmy Kirby found all three guilty. It had been a long haul and I was relieved that I was not called to prove the other two statements. Their interpreter was beyond recall in Kelantan, the most remote part of Malaya.

The duty evasions practised by dishonest manufacturers were now all too obvious. On 1 November 1956 the federation introduced an excise duty on locally grown tobacco.[19]

In Singapore it was cigarette smuggling that was imposing an increasing burden on the preventive service. In 1952 the rate of duty on cigarettes was M$ 6.70 per lb (M$ 6.20 preferential), which gave scope to make a substantial profit on uncustomed goods.[20] Total revenue from tobacco products was M$ 33.7 million: 96.5 per cent of this was from cigarettes. In 1956 the comptroller reported that a further increase in the rates of duty had given rise to attempts to smuggle cigarettes from Hong Kong, which had a duty differential of M$ 5.65 per lb. An officer examining cargo in the docks noted two consignments each of three or four cases of vermicelli on a ship's manifest. Knowing from experience that this commodity was normally imported in much larger shipments he ordered a thorough examination, which revealed 400 lbs of cigarettes concealed between layers of the pasta. A further nine cases were due on another vessel.[21] These concealed a further 600 lbs of cigarettes. No one claimed the cargoes.

There were several seizures of cigarettes in small, motorized craft, often carrying liquor as well. Shore watches could yield good results. In the Kallang River an outboard-engined *koleh* was spotted entering from the sea. A search along the banks stumbled on five Chinese who fled, leaving 250 lbs of cigarettes and two cars, all of which were confiscated. Police radio patrol cars also had their successes, intercepting vehicles carrying contraband cigarettes. This sometimes entailed high-speed chases in which the drivers of the suspect cars were often unable to match the skills of their police pursuers. One fugitive lost control of his vehicle and hit a stationary car and then a wall. Another encountered a traffic light at red and simply drove into it. A particularly unfortunate driver hit a telegraph pole in the early hours of the morning immediately outside the house of a police inspector. Meanwhile, acting on information, officers of the preventive branch made several successful raids on premises on the island. More than one seizure was made from atap huts on Pulau Minyak near the Kallang River.

Despite these achievements the smuggling persisted and the comptroller's report in 1957 makes clear the problems his department faced.[22]

> [Tobacco smuggling] presented quite the most formidable problem of recent years, as the revenue from the largest single item on the tariff was threatened and immediate counter-measures had to be taken. Cigarette smuggling received its impetus in November 1956 when the import duty was raised by M$ 2 a lb to M$ 8.60 [full rate] and to M$ 8.10 [preferential rate]. This offered large profits to persons aiming to exploit the proximity of the tariff-free islands of the Rhio Archipelago to which, under Singapore law, dutiable goods may be exported from bond without payment of duty. As the distance to the nearest island is barely ten miles, financiers of the traffic, many of them Singapore based, organized fleets of light hulls powered with twin and sometimes triple outboard engines of 35 h.p. capable of speeds exceeding 25 knots, to run 500 lb cargoes twice or thrice nightly to Singapore. Exports of cigarettes

> rose from 158,000 lbs in October 1956 to about 233,000 lbs in September 1957 and by the close of the year average monthly exports totalled 211,000 lbs with reports of several million cigarettes awaiting dispatch from Pulau Samboe and Pulau Blakang Padang to Singapore. This development was nevertheless not unexpected in that during 1957 Singapore merchants had been supplying over four-and-a-half times the quantity of cigarettes than could reasonably have been consumed by the population of the Archipelago.
>
> The Department's preventive resources were inadequate, at the time, to counter a revenue loss conservatively estimated at $3 million per annum, but it had fortunately received into commission in December 1956, the first of several 30-knot light craft to be built locally for interception duties. Captures came slowly at first, but eventually a small force of forfeited smugglers' craft was brought into service pending the arrival of new vessels. Volunteers from the Department manned these very flimsy and unstable craft against determined and aggressive opposition and by their tenacity and courage regained the initiative.

The measures described brought their reward. Nearly 28 tons of cigarettes and tobacco were captured that year together with 39 hulls and 49 outboard engines and 209 persons were convicted of tobacco smuggling offences. Despite these losses the traffic continued and in 1958 the comptroller was still moved to report a very worrying situation.[23]

> The prevailing high duties on tobacco resulted in intensive smuggling activity not only from the nearby Customs free Indonesia but also, on occasion, from Hong Kong where the duty differential was such that smuggling of duty-paid cigarettes into Singapore showed a handsome profit. In the case of the Rhio Archipelago, tobacco, especially cigarettes, was exported from Singapore bonds duty-free to ports in the area and, often in a matter of hours, was loaded into fast smuggling craft to run the few miles, usually under cover of darkness, to Singapore beaches. Better and faster interceptor craft, coupled with a high degree of training and the use wherever possible of intelligence reports, enabling patrols to be in the right place at the right time, took a heavy toll and nearly 23 tons of cigarettes and tobacco, together with 23

> smugglers' speedboats were captured during the year, often after tenacious and exciting sea chases.
>
> The leading organizer in Singapore of the traffic from Rhio was arrested and banished during the year. This had a pronounced dampening effect for several months on the activities of his fellow smugglers.

A most undesirable development was the increasing use of violence to resist arrest and the seizure of contraband.[24] There is an impression that the large profits to be made from the traffic had attracted a new breed of smugglers, gangsters who would stop at nothing to achieve their ends. In one case a smuggler's speedboat, powered by three outboard engines, ignored signals to stop and had to be brought to bay after a stern chase. The smugglers then rammed the customs craft, leapt overboard and swam away. Some 750 lbs of cigarettes were recovered, liable to a duty of M$ 6000. Another speedboat was chased to the shore but was prevented from beaching by a customs patrol. The occupants managed to escape under cover of a gang of about 50 hooligans armed with sticks and bars. The arrival of other patrol boats and warning shots from firearms prevented the gang from securing the cargo, which consisted of 600 lbs of uncustomed cigarettes on which duty of M$ 4800 was leviable. Another suspect speedboat was chased by a patrol craft and eventually forced to run for the beach. There the smugglers emptied the contents of their petrol tanks over the vessel and set it on fire while a crowd of gangsters began removing the cargo. By this time a second patrol boat had arrived on the scene and landed a small party who put the fire out while the gangsters were held off at gunpoint. Some 535 lbs of cigarettes, dutiable at over M$ 4000, were recovered. The violence was not confined to interceptions at sea. One revenue officer suffered a broken leg when a suspect vehicle burst through a customs roadblock and knocked him down. In July 1957 preventive officer George Kennedy, a re-employed pensioner, showed exceptional courage when, though seriously wounded and in the face of determined opposition, he thwarted a large group of armed secret society gangsters who were covering the landing of contraband cigarettes. George Kennedy was awarded the British Empire Medal.[25]

The smugglers continued to show ingenuity in their attempts to outwit the preventive service, the service its determination and intelligence in the development and use of countermeasures. From vermicelli the smugglers on the Hong Kong route switched to other cargoes. One consignment of cigarettes was concealed in a shipment of steel filing cabinets. Ashore there were constant switches in the methods of concealment. Deliveries were made to outlying islands from which they could be recovered in small boats at leisure. Another cache was excavated under a chicken house. From private cars the smugglers turned to taxis and tradesmen's vans.[26] On the Thai border the running of leaf tobacco still went on. One gang decided to avoid the roads and to carry their contraband along the cross border railway line. A customs party had hit upon the same idea and set out to lay an ambush. In mutual ignorance both parties set out to cross a railway bridge from opposite ends and met unexpectedly in the middle. In the confusion the smugglers escaped into the night but were forced to abandon over 600 lbs of tobacco.[27]

Tobacco, nevertheless, maintained its position as a major source of import duty in both Singapore and the federation. In the year of *merdeka*, 1957, the federal customs collected over M$ 294 million in import duties.[28] Of this, over M$ 104 million was from tobacco. In Singapore, with its more limited tariff, the proportion was even higher, nearly M$ 40 million from a total of just over M$ 100 million. Despite the problems of smuggling it was still, as many other governments have found, a very reliable contributor to the accounts.

The third source of import duty, common to all parts of Malaya, was petroleum. Its collection posed few problems and occupied little of the departments' time. Introduced as a war tax during the First World War, the import duty on petroleum products made only a minor contribution to revenue.[29] The Federated Malay States' annual report for 1918 records receipts of just S$ 80,365. By the 1930s the increased use of motor transport was reflected in rising imports of fuel and on 1 July 1934 the Government Monopolies Department took over from the Treasury the responsibility for the collection of petroleum duties in the Settlements.[30] In the balance of that year the department supervised the release of nearly eight million gallons of petrol and over three million gallons of kerosene. The increasing popularity of diesel fuel was doubtless the reason for the passage of the quaintly entitled Traction Engines and Motorcars Ordinance, which, from 1 July 1936, imposed a 'Special Tax on Heavy Oil Engined Vehicles', whose collection the service also undertook.[31]

Petroleum products were delivered to Malaya by sea and discharged into the tanks of secure installations operated by the major oil companies. These were licensed as petroleum depots. In 1946 there were ten in the Malayan Union. Most were located at seaports.[32] In Singapore, the Shell Company occupied its own island, Pulau Bukom, just offshore, providing a very secure facility. Although officers made occasional spot checks, dipping the tanks and examining the books, there was no reason to dispute the returns submitted by the oil companies in support of their regular payments. Since duty was paid on deliveries from the depots there was little opportunity for serious evasions. One form of traffic that did call for close monitoring was the sale of duty-free petroleum to the services and also to local flying clubs, an exemption designed to encourage amateur aviation. If the tanker drivers could disguise short deliveries to these destinations they would accumulate a balance of cheap petrol to sell to filling stations along their route. This apart, there was nothing to interest the preventive service in the petroleum business, and the tax remained cheap and easy to collect. In 1938 the revenue in the Federated Malay States amounted to S$ 16.5 million and in the Settlements to over S$ 3.8 million.[33]

After the Second World War petroleum duty collections rose rapidly as an increasing number of motor vehicles reflected the country's prosperity. In Singapore in 1958, the year the yield reached over M$ 34.5 million, the Comptroller of Customs remarked in his report on the importance of its contribution to the colony's revenue.[34] Since 1956 it had overtaken liquors as a proportion of the total and was now second only to tobacco. In the federation the 1957 yield was over M$ 56 million.[35] This, however, was a more modest share of the total revenue derived from extensive import and export tariffs.[36] These are considered in the next chapter.

13

Revenues and restrictions

In its analysis of revenue collections in 1957 the Federation of Malaya Customs and Excise report lists 12 export duties, 82 heads of import duty collections and five excise duties. The department was also responsible for 16 other federal revenue sources. The net total from all these amounted to M$ 521,684,261.03. A further 12 items contributed M$ 11,724,012.02 to the treasuries of the Malay States.[1]

With such extensive tariffs covering a wide range of very different products, the identification, classification and valuation of dutiable goods was by no means simple. This was particularly so when dealing with the ever increasing flow of imports. Malaya was a prosperous country and heavily dependent on foreign sources to meet the demands of its sophisticated market. To the comparative simplicities of liquor, tobacco and petroleum successive tariff expansions had added a number of new heads of revenue whose descriptions called for interpretation by the officers at the collection stations. Some proved to have a wider application than the legislators had probably foreseen. 'Paper products' were found to include such diverse manufactures as synthetic tabletops, roofing tiles and printers' flong. It was clearly questionable how 'musical' a 'musical instrument' should be, or where the line should be drawn between 'household utensils' and 'household and art articles'. Decisions were made on the spot and reported to head office, which reviewed and circulated its rulings to all stations. The *Rulings Book* became essential reading for the revenue branch, identifying which goods were dutiable and at which rate.

Although many revenue heads still imposed flat rate taxes, usually levied on a verifiable measure such as volume or weight, there were an increasing number of items subject to *ad valorem* duties, assessed as a percentage of value. To identification and classification there was added the task of valuation. The importer's declaration was the starting point for this process but could not be accepted without investigation. Supporting documentation in the form of invoices might well be misleading. It might be false. Even if genuine it might not represent the true value of the goods in the market. A transaction between associated parties, such as the branches of an international company or a shipment from principal to agent, might be priced to take account of other factors such as warranties, stockholding, after-sales service or advertising. It was necessary to establish a 'level playing field'.

As recorded above, this problem was tackled in 1952 by the establishment of a central assessment office and a pilot price-reporting scheme.[2] The technical adviser on piece goods, of whom more below, was attached to this office. In 1955 the department began to apply the concept of 'open market valuation' set out in Article VII of the General Agreement on Tariffs and Trade and the Brussels Valuation Convention.[3] This meant that the value for duty purposes was the price that a buyer and seller would reach if the transaction were conducted in the open market, subject to no other relationships or agreements between the two parties. It was not an easy concept and the Comptroller reported in 1957 that local traders had some difficulty in understanding it. Nevertheless, it was fair.

For the preventive staff the protection of these revenues had to thwart three forms of evasion. First, there was the physical running of goods, clandestine movements across a frontier or via an unguarded part of the coast. Second, a consignment of dutiable goods might be disguised by false declaration or by concealment in a non-dutiable shipment. Third, the goods might be openly imported subject to a false declaration, designed to reduce the tax liability. Most commonly this last method was used in attempts to secure a reduction in an *ad valorem* duty.

In both territories the preventive staff were also concerned with traffic in prohibited or controlled goods. Apart from drugs, a particular problem discussed in Chapters 8 to 10, there were, at various times, a number of imports and exports that were subject to restrictions. Arms and pornography were, of course, always liable to seizure. The movement of gold and currency was generally controlled. At times such controls were extended to other commodities. The rationing of rice in the aftermath of war necessitated restrictions on its import. Both rubber and textiles were subject to legislation that led to temporary import or export controls. Attempts to evade customs commonly involved running or concealing contraband in an apparently innocent cargo.

In the aftermath of the Second World War the clandestine movement of gold was an essential element in the complex structure of international smuggling. The traffic in drugs, arms and other commodities in short supply and high demand usually required payment at some stage in the precious metal. In his long duel with the smugglers across the Thai border Cecil Gutteridge[4] identified an inward flow of rubber to avoid the quota regulations, opium to replace the now illegal government monopoly and gold bullion to evade the exchange controls. He made seizures on the jungle tracks used by the smugglers. Towards the end of 1947 he detected an outward flow of gold in payment for imports of opium. In the form of bars measuring roughly six by two by one-and-a-half inches it was easily concealed. In Singapore in 1949 a Chinese sailor came ashore carrying 24 such bars concealed under his clothes. His load was valued at M$ 26,000.[5]

Some carriers employed ingenious methods of concealment. In Singapore an air traveller from India was found to be carrying a suitcase of which the metal frame was gold.[6] In the federation another Indian was caught smuggling gold in the handles of baskets.[7] A much larger haul fell to the Singapore customs in 1955 when they found 402 lbs of gold bullion on board a ship.[8] The forfeited gold was sold in London and the colony treasury received the proceeds, a sum of M$ 603,536.36. In the same year, when 54 lbs of gold were seized at Kallang airport, the local representative of an air operating company was declared an undesirable immigrant and denied further residence in the colony.[9] Nevertheless, the traffic continued. Seizures were recorded in the departmental reports for both territories in the years that followed.

One of the many problems the resumed British administration faced in 1945 was a serious food shortage. Rice is the regional staple and measures were taken to import it and to sell it below cost. Rationing was an essential part of the control system and illegal importation offered the prospect of large profits.[10] Rice is not easily smuggled. It is a bulky commodity. Commercial quantities could only be concealed in shipments if they were subject to false documentation, and prosecuting the principals was often a complex and lengthy process. In a case in Malacca in 1947 there were 28 prosecution witnesses and 19 for the defence. The case lasted 15 days and the culprit escaped with a fine of M$ 650, although his rice was forfeited.[11]

In Singapore a few years later Derek Mackay[12] found himself presenting a somewhat similar case before the same Mr H. A.

Forrer who once lectured Peter Burgess on the shape of pigs' tails. The case concerned a shipment of maize from Bangkok. A number of the sacks, identified by their shipping marks, contained inner bags filled with rice. The Chinese importer expressed total ignorance of this concealment and, as so often, a successful prosecution would depend on establishing his knowledge. This was largely by documentary evidence, as Derek explains.

> In his office were found a number of cables, some of which referred to a shipment of bags of 'green beans' including a specified number containing 'red beans'. The figures tallied but we were not looking for beans. Luck was on our side. The search also turned up the importer's commercial codebook. It was, of course, in Chinese, but alongside the codes for 'green beans' and 'red beans' were written the Chinese symbols for 'maize' and 'rice', terms for which the codebook already provided elsewhere.
>
> Mr Forrer's career dated back, I think, to 1915 and his temper had not improved with the years. Every case in his court was punctuated by his comments, complaints and general expressions of dissatisfaction. In the next two days as I laboriously went through the prosecution case his interventions became ever more frequent and hostile. Defence counsel concentrated his attack on my star witness, a Preventive Officer named Lim Tai Chuan.[13] Tai Chuan was a Chinese scholar, whose task it was to explain the significance of the cables and the entries in the codebook. He did so with great patience but as he stepped down from the witness box the magistrate sighed deeply and remarked that he did not know what the case was all about. Seizing his chance defence counsel assured him that he was well satisfied with that situation. The fleeting expression on Mr Forrer's face told me that my opponent had made a bad mistake. When my case closed and an adjourned date was discussed he compounded his error by announcing that he did not propose to offer any defence evidence. This was tantamount to a challenge and the magistrate accepted it.[14] On resumption he called the defence. When none was offered he convicted and sentenced. He was still on his way out of the court when defence counsel turned to me and loudly remarked that he looked forward to enjoying the written judgment against which he intended to appeal. I

doubt if he did. It demonstrated the fullest grasp of all the issues. The conviction was confirmed by the Appeal Court.

The table in Appendix XI lists the seizures by HM Customs Singapore in the years 1946 to 1949. It covers an extensive miscellany, but the departmental reports record the confiscation of many other items over the years. In 1932 and 1933 the Government Monopolies Department had to turn its attention to the smuggling of counterfeit coins and notes. It also reported the interception of large numbers of unstamped letters.[15] During 1937 it delivered to the government veterinary surgeon a number of illegally imported birds and animals.[16] By 1957 the service in Singapore was blocking imports of 'undesirable publications'.[17] These were still turning up in 1958, as were firearms, unstamped letters and animals. Most such discoveries were made in the course of routine checks but could lead to a consequent preventive investigation.

Exports were rarely of concern to the preventive service. In the federation 1957 export duties produced a yield of over M$ 180 million.[18] The bulk of this, nearly M$ 175 million, was levied on tin and rubber.

As we have seen above, tin has been mined in Malaya for centuries and taxed on export for much of that time. As described in Chapter 2, the first decade of the twentieth century witnessed a major change in mining methods and in the replacement of small-scale manual operations by mechanized extraction. This called for a level of capital investment that could only be provided by substantial joint stock companies, which were unlikely to attempt revenue evasion. Such installations, however, suffered severe damage during the Second World War and their replacement was a lengthy task. It took two years to rebuild a tin dredge.[19] Against a prewar production of 80,651 tons the industry in 1946 could only extract 8432 tons.[20] The prewar figure was not surpassed until 1950. By 1957, however, the duty collected was over M$ 54 million.[21] Tin remained a very volatile market and Malaya was a party to the international agreement by which a 'buffer stock' was maintained.[22] The department collected the contributions levied to finance this.

When the department was founded in 1910 rubber was still a small but growing trade and yielded far less customs revenue than tin. In 1915 the collection on tin was more than three times that on rubber.[23] In the years thereafter the industry expanded and by 1938 in the FMS alone there were 1,613,609 acres under rubber.[24]

Exports that year totalled approximately M$ 87 million against M$ 65 million for tin. It was not only in Malaya that such growth occurred. In Siam and the Dutch East Indies production rose. The market was over supplied and in the early 1930s the world price of rubber fell. On 7 May 1934 the three governments concerned signed an agreement to restrict exports between 1 June that year and 31 December 1938.[25] Malaya was limited to a total export of 504,000 tons in 1934, the Dutch East Indies to 352,000 tons. Expansion of the acreage under rubber was forbidden. In Malaya the customs service collected a cess of two cents a pound to finance research into alternative uses of the product. Since 1926 it had been engaged in enforcing the rubber supervision and rubber restriction enactments and now had to deal with attempts to avoid the new quota limits by various malpractices.[26] In 1934 the newly arrived Peter Burgess[27] spent three days enduring the foul smell of wet rubber from Sumatra, which he was required to check and weigh. In the Straits Settlements the Government Monopolies Department assumed similar responsibilities under the Rubber Regulation Ordinance 1934 and set up special examination stations and landing places.[28] Even after the Second World War Cecil Gutteridge[29] was faced with illegal imports across the Thai border seeking to masquerade as Malayan rubber and to take advantage of the Malayan quota.

The plantations had suffered comparatively little damage from the Japanese occupation. It is estimated that the Japanese cut down about 2.5 per cent of the 3,302,000 acres then under cultivation.[30] Unlike the tin miners the planters were able to resume production almost immediately and it expanded rapidly. By 1950 there were 3,359,251 acres in use, yielding 992,585 tons.[31] This compares with 372,000 tons in 1938. The value of this output was three times the prewar level. These were boom years for Malaya despite the emergency, earning hard currency for the sterling area and boosting the customs revenue. In 1957 the department collected over M$ 120 million in export duty and over M$ 35 million in various additional levies and cesses.[32]

There was little scope for evasion in such a structured trade. For duty purposes the base price of rubber was fixed daily. The published midday price of No.1 ribbed smoke sheet FOB in bales in Singapore was applied to duty calculations throughout the following day. Exporters could, and did, legitimately time the arrival of consignments at the port of shipment in quest of a lower value, but physical checks produced no evidence of major malpractice. In Perak Tony King[33] became aware of a considerable trade in low-quality *kampong*-produced rubber exported from Port Weld and Kuala Kurau to Sumatra. These exports were designed to disguise the much larger shipments smuggled out via a network of narrow, shallow channels in the mangroves along the coast without payment of export duty. The 'Q-boat' proved effective in intercepting a number of these illegal consignments and confining the trade to the control ports where duty was collected.

Imports of dutiable goods offered far more scope for illegal activities. The methods of physical smuggling, false descriptions and undervaluations were all employed to evade or reduce duty payment. The consolidation of mainland Malaya into the 1948 federation reduced the number of borders that had posed such problems for the customs departments before the Second World War, but they still had to cope with a northern land frontier much of which was almost inaccessible, the causeway link with Singapore carrying an ever increasing flow of road and rail traffic, the proximity of Indonesian territory, the growth of Port Swettenham as a sea port and the development of international air transport. The consequent struggle to stem the inflow of opium, liquor and tobacco has been described in earlier chapters. We turn now to other imports liable to customs duty under the tariffs in force on the mainland.

The physical running of contraband remained the method of choice on the Thai frontier. The incidence of such smuggling is hard to assess. The very remoteness of the area was a handicap to both sides in the game of hide and seek described above by Cecil Gutteridge, but the illegal movements of drugs and tobacco already described were probably matched by importations of small, high-value articles on which the smuggler could make a substantial profit. It was, however, Singapore that provided the principal source of such evasions. With its jealously guarded free port status the city was internationally renowned as the place to shop for such articles as watches, cameras and jewellery, and it was not only tourists who made their purchases there. The narrow straits between the island and mainland were well patrolled, though easily crossed by night, but the volume of road traffic across the causeway was far too great for thorough checking. Officers at the Johore Bahru post had to rely on intelligent observation and acquired instinct to identify potential offenders. A clue spotted and correctly interpreted could lead to a successful interception.

One outdoor officer walking along a queue of cars lined up in the afternoon heat was intrigued to see several passengers sweating profusely in a saloon with all its windows closed tight. A search revealed the explanation. A hundredweight of canned saccharine, dutiable at M$ 5 a pound, was packed into every hollow in the car body, including the doors. The windows could not be lowered. At the court a few days later the magistrate found it hard to believe that such a quantity could be so concealed and the officers who were there to give evidence had to repack the vehicle to satisfy him. Fortunately, they managed it.

It was not only vehicles that had to be checked. Large numbers of passengers crossed the causeway every day on public transport and entered Johore carrying such articles as watches and cameras, both of which were subject to high rates of *ad valorem* import duty. Many such were personal imports. It was obviously a temptation to a mainland resident to visit Singapore, make a purchase and on return to claim that it had been acquired long since in the federation. The onus of proof lay on the passenger, but there was often additional evidence that his or her story was untrue. The Chinese are tidy people and it was quite surprising how often the invoice for the article purchased that day in Singapore was found neatly folded in the owner's shirt pocket. On one occasion the carrier of a brand new camera was unable to prove his assertion that it had been in his possession for a considerable time and was told that it would be detained at Johore Bahru until he produced satisfactory evidence of purchase. He had already made use of the camera and requested permission to remove the exposed film. After watching for some time his unsuccessful efforts to open it the officer had to do it for him.[34]

The distance from Johore Bahru to the heart of Singapore was less than twenty miles by road and there is no doubt that many of these 'personal imports' were made on behalf of shopkeepers. A series of visits to the city could provide a stock of high value articles. No doubt some were 'smuggled to order'. In 1957 a local shoe shop proprietor hit upon an ingenious method of acquiring cheap stocks; he employed a group of children to travel frequently to Singapore barefoot and to return shod with newly purchased sandals. A customs visit to his shop brought that profitable practice to an end.[35]

It was not unusual for mainland traders to collect imports from Singapore by car or van and, aware that customs personnel at Johore Bahru were often too busy to make more than a cursory examination, there were some who tried to avoid duty by making false declarations. In 1957, for example, the proprietor of a Malacca medicine shop bought a large quantity of medicines in Singapore and at Johore Bahru presented declarations for both dutiable and non-dutiable goods. Leaving the compound after paying the small amount of duty assessed on his declarations he was stopped by officers of the preventive service. The outwardly non-dutiable cartons were packed with dutiable medicines. His attempted evasion cost him a fine of $5000 and his medicines and car, both of which were forfeited.[36]

The existence of import duty exemptions for various sections of the community could and did give rise to some abuse. The loss to the revenue was not substantial but such evasions were unfair to legitimate traders and a source of irritation to the service. When in Kelantan Tony King[37] had to clamp down on the numbers of local residents who attempted to mingle with members of the sultan's family returning from their regular shopping trips to Singapore. Later in Kuala Lumpur he found it necessary to introduce a check on passengers on the regular RAF flights from the colony.

The most persistent form of commercial malpractice was undoubtedly the underdeclaration of the value of goods subject to *ad valorem* import duties; the most frequent application was to textiles, primarily in the form of piece goods. Indeed, textiles demanded the attention of the customs service for a variety of reasons over the years and were the subject of several different kinds of offence against several different enactments. Malaya was always a major importer of cloth. The increasing prosperity of a growing population was matched by a demand for both piece goods and garments. For the collectors at the ports and frontier posts the identification and valuation of cloth became a major problem.

In 1931 the Federated Malay States imposed import duties on textiles and wearing apparel.[38] In 1933 it was found necessary to appoint a technical adviser on piece goods to provide the expertise the ordinary officers clearly lacked. Alex Boyd was the first holder of this appointment. He combined the appropriate technical ability with a lengthy experience in the industry. When he had time to spare he was able to teach young officers the basic skills of textile examination. At the SEDO he gave Peter Chattaway what Peter describes as 'a crash course' on textile recognition and valuation.

> His advice was valuable. I went out and bought a textile glass for counting the number of warp and weft threads to

> the inch (the greater the number the finer the threads and the quality of the cloth). I learnt to distinguish silk from rayon, wool from cotton, etc. Mixtures, the number of colours, printed and woven cloth – all these also affected the price.

Despite these newly acquired skills Peter applied a simple test to his own valuations. 'I developed the "squawk" test. If the importer did not challenge the assessment then I knew I had undervalued. If the reaction was an ordinary protest then I was probably correct. If there was a violent argument then I was probably too high.'[39]

An anecdote by Bicky Roualle[40] illustrates the value of Alex Boyd's experience. 'I remember in mid-1941 walking with him through the warehouse at Port Swettenham when he asked where the German blankets had come from. We were standing near a stack of hessian wrapped bales, which were clearly stencilled "MADE IN INDIA". The removal of the wrapper revealed a second, equally clearly marked "PRODUCE OF GERMANY".' Alex was to play a vital role in a number of investigations. His expert evidence in court was often decisive.

Although textiles were never dutiable in the Straits Settlements their import and export became subject to customs control in 1934 when the President of the Board of Trade announced the introduction of quotas for the importation of foreign cotton and artificial silk piece goods into all colonies and protectorates.[41] As usual, the commercial community in Singapore bitterly opposed such a restriction and the Importation of Textiles (Quotas) Ordinance 1934 was carried in the Legislative Council on the votes of the official members only. By July 1934 the federated and unfederated states had joined the system. Quotas were based on import statistics for the period 1927 to 1931. To handle the entrepôt trade, the Government Monopolies Department set up and supervised re-export depots and took responsibility for premises licensed as private re-export depots.[42] By December there were seven private depots and one public one in Singapore and a single public depot in Penang. In the second half of 1934 these depots received over 40 million yards of cloth, re-exporting some 33 million yards. Thereafter, they handled about 38 million yards a year. In 1936 the difficulties of control forced the administration to withdraw the licences from the private depots.

Limitation by quota invited both avoidance and evasion. It has been estimated that as many as seven million yards of cloth were smuggled annually into the mainland, mostly from Singapore.[43] There was also an increase in imports of made-up garments and other goods that were not subject to quota. This loophole was exploited through the entrepôt trade with the adjacent islands of the Dutch East Indies. Re-exports of cloth from Singapore to Rhio rose at a remarkable rate. Between January 1935 and February 1936 such shipments were multiplied thirty times. In Rhio the cloth was worked into manufactured articles of unusual design, trousers apparently tailored for stilt walkers and shirts with tails several yards long.[44] There were 'mosquito nets' made of close woven material, some measuring as much as forty yards in length. Loosely stitched together they could be unpicked with ease. They were shipped back through Singapore where a customs examination was unlikely to be made. This bizarre traffic was brought to an end in 1938 when the quota system was extended to made-up goods in art silk and cotton.[45] The principal source of the smuggled cloth had always been Japan and this trade died out when the Chinese community imposed a boycott on the products of their enemy.[46]

A Kuala Lumpur merchant used a similar device to evade duty on piece goods in 1938, as Bicky Roualle recounts.[47]

> For some historical reason mattress covers were not subject to import duty. One of the main textile dealers in Kuala Lumpur had submitted a declaration for non-dutiable goods specifying '10,000 mattress covers' in 100 bales. Part of the consignment had already been released without being opened for examination. The following day one of my fellow officers instructed that a couple of bales should be opened and the contents checked. Each of the so-called mattress covers was over ten feet long. They were made up of loosely tacked brocades, silks, velvets and similar expensive materials. An immediate visit to the nearby textile importer's premises revealed the contents of the bales released the previous day on sale, untacked and well pressed, as dress lengths, curtains, furnishings, etc.

The importance of imported textiles to the people of Malaya was underlined by the action of the resumed British administration immediately after the Second World War. In 1946 the government of the Malayan Union imported a million yards of cloth from India for controlled distribution to the needy.[48] The following year a further 3.5 million yards were similarly distributed and 23.5 million were released for sale. By 1954 imports of textiles, textile products, clothing and footwear into the federation alone were valued at nearly M$ 115 million.[49] The import duty yield in 1957 amounted to over M$ 20 million.[50]

Although textiles were never dutiable in Singapore Alex Boyd's services were needed there on one occasion in an investigation conducted by Cyril Williams.[51] It was a time when the US dollar was in short supply and imports from the USA were subject to a system of licensing. Neighbouring territories, including Thailand, faced the same problems and applied similar restrictions. In Malaya much of the textile trade was now in the hands of Indian merchants, of whom one, who was based in Singapore, devised a scheme to divert to Bangkok a shipment of expensive American fabric bought with sterling area dollars. To Singapore he imported worthless cotton waste, declared on arrival as the high quality goods for which the dollars had been approved. There was little chance of customs examination and, furthermore, his only offence against a law enforced by the department was a breach of the Imports Registration Ordinance for which the maximum penalty was a very modest fine. Nevertheless, Cyril was determined to expose this misuse of the colony's hard currency and with Alex as a willing accomplice he 'effected an entry' into the importer's warehouse in which they soon located a recently arrived consignment. Opening the packing cases they confirmed that the contents were so much trash. The unexpected arrival of the owner led to a few anxious minutes while they played hide-and-seek around the stacks of cloth but they finally slipped away unobserved. The proceedings in court were lengthy but a conviction was secured. Cyril had won his point and brought the malpractice to light. It was now up to the authorities to close this leak in the exchange control system.

A not insubstantial contribution to the revenue of Singapore came from entertainment duty, a charge levied on the price of admission tickets to such venues as theatres, concert halls and sporting arenas. Introduced as a temporary tax during the Second World War it was not repealed in 1945, and by 1957 its yield had topped M$ 6 million. Duty was calculated on the basis of returns submitted by licensed operators.[52] To guard against evasion all tickets had to be produced in advance to HM Customs, which registered the serial numbers and treated the tickets with a chemical that the government chemist could identify. When in

December 1952 Peter Chattaway took charge of a licensing and entertainment duty division in the colony, he found that there was rarely any reason to doubt the returns of the large cinemas, but clear evidence of evasion by the operators of the many small traditional theatres and open-air cinemas, whose reported audiences were always substantially larger on evenings when he and his officers visited the premises on inspection. There was clearly a 'leak' but it was some time before he discovered its source.

> I noticed that there were unexplained peaks of attendance on nights when no inspection had occurred and realized that they were evenings when I had left my quarters at the usual inspection times. I was living in the customs flat at the top of Fullerton Building and my car was garaged at night in the Post Office garage on the ground floor. There were always many people around and it was impossible to work out who was watching me so I started to leave the building on a regular basis several times a week, an action that caused a certain amount of consternation among the revenue cheats.

Preventive action could take many forms.

There was no lack of variety in the work of the customs departments. There were always new trades to monitor and new tricks to foil. At all levels it was not an occupation for the clock-watcher. Officers had to be ready for long and erratic hours. For the expatriate staff in particular it was seldom dull. Nor was life off-duty. Officers, their wives and children had plenty to occupy their time, activities to pursue, problems to solve and pleasures to enjoy. Some of these are described in the following chapter.

Part Five:
Off Duty

15. Customs sports day.

14
Life and leisure

Peter Burgess began his career in Singapore in 1934. After a time spent in the preventive branch there, he was looking for an opportunity to widen his experience.[1]

> My colleague Wallace Kemp, with whom I shared the house, had talked about a fine new launch, which was being built for Johore Customs at Thorneycroft's shipyard. It was much better than the largest Singapore launch and would be used to check on Japanese fishing vessels and Japanese ships loading iron ore off the east coast of Johore. Wallace speculated as to who would get this interesting and important job. 'Robin Henman should have a very good chance. He is very good with Malays. I might get it. My pater was captain of a cable ship.' I hoped. I had been on holiday to Mersing where the launch would be stationed. There was some surprise when the list of transfers was circulated and revealed I was to go in about ten days time to act as Superintendent Preventive Branch, Johore. I was summoned by my local head of department. 'You have seen the transfer list. This is an important post and the Commissioner in Johore is very anxious to see you and tell you all about it. You must go to Johore Bahru on Sunday morning. They work the Mohammedan week in Johore with Friday off and Sunday a full working day.' I felt quite excited. In Johore Bahru I went first to see the Senior Superintendent Preventive Branch. 'I don't know quite what you will do. The new launch is not yet ready and if it were you would not be able to go out much in the North East monsoon. However, the Commissioner says that several of the planters in the middle of Johore have complained of illicit rice wine. He has also arranged for you to go with the Health Officer to see opium smokers who have failed to register. I have arranged for the

> Assistant Adviser in Kluang to give you a desk in his office and he will allow you to share his house. Then after the monsoon when the launch is ready you can move to Mersing. Now the Commissioner is waiting to see you so I will take you in.' I went in and was greeted 'Ah, come in Burgess. Sit down. Now you see the position is this. Jack Dudgeon feels he must retire. He's thirty nine and feels he has gone on quite long enough.' I was puzzled. I could not think of anyone of that name due to retire so early. I must have shown my doubts as Mr Mather went on 'You know who Jack Dudgeon is don't you?' 'I don't think I do,' I replied. 'Well, you do play full back don't you?' To this I replied 'Yes'. 'Of course, now I have spoken to the Singapore Captain and he agrees that in view of your forthcoming transfer it will be quite all right for you to play in the Johore trial next Saturday.' That was my hush hush briefing.

In the European community in Malaya rugby football was a very serious business.

It was inevitable that the British should introduce their sports to Malaya. Many Malays were keen competitors in their own games and adapted easily to those in which the expatriates spent much of their leisure time.[2] It is perhaps not wholly coincidental that in the towns laid out by British officials the focal point was usually a *padang*, an open area set aside for sport. In Singapore the City Hall and St Andrew's Cathedral faced the sea across several acres of green grass, flanked by the Singapore Cricket Club on one side and the Chinese Recreation Club on the other. The principal government offices in Kuala Lumpur, a riotous concoction of pseudo-Oriental architecture, confronted the cricket pitch and the black and white buildings of the Selangor Club, whose mock Tudor exterior probably gave rise to its affectionate nickname, 'The Spotted Dog'. Such examples of British expatriate town planning were to be found in many town centres. The playing fields of Malaya were a meeting place for all its varied races and a remarkable range of sports was practised. Most large cities boasted golf clubs and swimming pools. Sailing clubs were to be found in coastal locations such as Penang, Malacca and Singapore.

Clubs played a major role in expatriate life. In the smaller towns the club would be the social centre, a place for casual meetings or formal occasions such as dances and seasonal parties. It might field teams to play football, cricket and hockey. It would most probably offer tennis courts and a swimming pool. In larger towns the clubs often specialized in particular sports or other recreational activities. Most government departments encouraged their staff to participate in sport and often entered teams in local leagues. The armed forces had their own facilities, but both individuals and teams were to be found in local competitions. Representative games between states and settlements were the top level of most team sports and attracted large numbers of spectators.

Many of the customs' expatriate officers were keen games players. Rugby football was only one of the sports in which they took part, and in which the service was well represented. Bicky Roualle[3] recalls a match in 1941 when the Klang Club XV against a regimental side included five officers from the Port Swettenham staff. Bicky played at the highest level. He was regularly picked for the annual north versus south match and in 1939 played for All-Malaya in Hong Kong. As captain of the Singapore Cricket Club against a French air force team from Saigon he found himself also acting as interpreter when the referee discovered that the visitors did not understand his English, no matter how loudly he shouted.

After joining the service at Port Swettenham in 1940 Jim Bailward[4] was soon recognized as a sportsman.

> From Port Swettenham it was 28 miles to Kuala Lumpur whither we repaired on all possible occasions. On my first visit I joined the Selangor Club ('The Dog') for whom I subsequently played many hockey and cricket matches. Quite often, when one left the office at around 4.30 p.m. on a hot day, the cloud started to build up on the drive to the capital and resulted in a tropical downpour just as one arrived. On such occasions the match had to be cancelled and drinking and liar dice became the order of the day.

John Lewis,[5] down the coast at Port Dickson, played hockey for the State. David Anderson,[6] who arrived in 1953 and was posted to Port Swettenham, played both hockey and cricket for the Selangor Club and kept goal for the Port Swettenham customs football eleven. Another successful cricketer was Johnny Johnson who represented the state of Pahang. Unsurprisingly, several officers took part in competitive sailing, notably Jack Pitt who raced dinghies from the Royal Singapore Yacht Club. Contests between local craft were also a regular spectacle along the coast.

Motor sport was introduced to Malaya before the Japanese occupation and in the postwar period flourishing motor clubs in Singapore, Selangor and Perak organized a variety of events for amateur drivers – rallies, speed trials, hill climbs, driving tests and the occasional circuit racing.[7] The sport attracted entries from all communities – British, Dutch and Australian Europeans, many Chinese as well as Malays, Indians and Eurasians. Competing cars included some remarkable locally built 'specials', and both cars and motorcycles were modified and tuned for enhanced performance. The authorities took a tolerant view of such activities and public roads were regularly closed for speed events. Singapore boasted a formidable hill climb on the outskirts of the city. For several years in succession the streets of Johore Bahru were used for a 'round the houses' race meeting for cars and motorcycles. An annual sprint event was staged on the main road through Seremban. Derek Mackay was a regular participant. In Kuala Lumpur he drove in the 'Lornie Kilo' on an occasion when his fellow competitors included the Chief Minister of the federation, Tungku Abdul Rahman, and the Minister of Transport, Che Sardon bin Haji Jubir. Such events were popular with local people and attracted substantial crowds of spectators.

Within the customs departments there was keen competition between stations and teams were fielded in almost every sport. Entrants from all areas attended the federation annual sports day, and expatriate officers and their wives were expected to play their part. Such events were also social occasions and brought together all ranks and cultures.

There was much else in Malaya to enrich the expatriate's leisure hours. Except during the dark days of the emergency the country was easily explored. There were magnificent sandy beaches and a clear warm sea. There were cool hill stations[8] offering fine golf courses, energetic walks on forest tracks and the nostalgic pleasure of evenings by an open fireplace. Throughout the country there were colourful festivals and the entertainments offered by the different cultures that flourished in the peninsula; the apparently interminable Chinese operas played to the promptings of the percussionist's drums and gongs; the Malay *wayang*s presenting traditional folk tales; the dance halls where even in the new-fangled version of the *ronggeng*, the 'joget modern', the clients maintained decorum and displayed their talents at a respectful distance from their professional partners. So spanned the racial and cultural distinctions and there w quent invitations to significant occasions. In the lengthy pr a Malay wedding the public day was the *bersanding*, when the guests filed past the newly-weds seated in regal splendour, motionless on their thrones. There were festivals to share – the parties at Chinese New Year, the feasting on Hari Raya Puasa, the end of Ramadan, and the magical illuminations of the Hindu Deepavali. Such a wealth of culture fully justified the 14 public holidays in the Malayan year.

John Lewis[9] describes life in Kelantan in 1946.

> Most of the Europeans in Kota Bahru were married so that there were about five European women there. Kelantan followed the Muslim custom of having their rest day on Fridays and all offices were closed on Thursday afternoons and Fridays. One became used to it after a time but Europeans were not able to worship on Sundays. Actually I do not think there was a church in Kota Bahru.
>
> On Fridays the European group used to go to the coast to swim at a place named in Malay 'the beach of passionate love', where incidentally the Japanese troops landed in 1941. It was a sandy beach with good swimming in the surf, which pounded the shore. There was a social club in Kota Bahru at which about five senior Malay government officers were members. One was the Grand Vizier who became the Malayan High commissioner in London after independence ten years later. As I knew him well he invited me to an official dinner in London to commemorate the event and I sat at a table next to a Russian Embassy official. When I told him who I was he could not believe that an ex-Colonial Officer had been invited to such an occasion as a friend.

John was also on good terms with the sultan and his sons and recalls a party with the Commissioner of Police, James Bell, which the sultan and one of his sons attended incognito. 'The two of them performed an old Malay dance in the sitting room in front of us.'

Most cadets began their careers in Malaya as bachelors. There were few single European women in the country but some officers did find their partners among them. It was in Taiping that Tony King[10] wooed and won Isobel Bruce, 'recently escaped from the strictures of the Girls High School in Aberdeen', back once again with her family in Malaya and 'one of the only three unmarried maidens in North Perak'. Johnny Johnson[11] met 'Nicky' in Pahang and married her in Kuala Lumpur. Most officers, however, met their future wives in the UK. For these women, marriage presented a particular challenge as they committed themselves to a new life in a very different environment.

Many newly arrived wives fell quickly under the spell of Malaya. Katharine Sim's books[12] and paintings express her delight in the countryside and its people. She writes vividly of the beauty of the sunsets, the sounds and smells of the bustling towns and villages, the colourful fashions and the goods on display in the local shops. Janey Grimwood[13] began her life in Malaya occupying a third of a bungalow in Johore Bahru, but she remembers this first home with some affection. 'Our garden at the bungalow was mainly grass surrounded by various bushes and trees. The most beautiful tree was a huge Acacia from Africa. It housed a pair of large blue kingfishers and a squirrel. In the evening sunset the tree and the squirrel turned gold.' Anne Crocker travelled by sea to Penang and married Gordon in Kuala Lumpur.[14] There was no government quarter available in Telok Anson and the Crockers' first home was a little Malay bungalow on the edge of the Perak River. They engaged an Indian cookboy who produced excellent meals on the ancient iron stove.

The pleasures of a tropical paradise come at a price. Malaya had its full share of insects, reptiles and other pests. Katharine Sim had to do battle with coconut spiders, cockroaches and fruit bats.[15] In Parit Buntar she and Stuart spent their nights within a huge mosquito net, a room within a room. The Crockers'[16] bungalow at Telok Anson was only a few feet from the river. There was a mongoose colony in the roof, cobras in the garden and the occasional visiting sea snake at high tide. Gordon records that he also found 'a pair of kraits resident in a hollow post in the corner of the ground level "bath room" (complete with PWD issue jar and bailer and a new "thunder box"). Our part-time gardener coped with the kraits by pouring boiling water down the hollow post and killing both with a blow of his spade when they reached the surface.' Mosquitoes were a problem here too. 'We sat in the evening in a colourful sack and covered our heads and hands with mosquito cream.'

A welcome lodger was the *chichak*, a small lizard that scampered across ceilings and walls, to which it clung with tiny padded feet, consuming considerable quantities of intruding insects. For

16. Port Swettenham: a typical wooden government quarter.

this service householders could forgive its occasional loss of adhesion and consequent crash-landing on the dinner table. It could turn up in unexpected places. As a member of the Malay States Volunteer Reserve (Selangor Scottish Platoon) Robert McCall took part in the King's Birthday parade in Kuala Lumpur in 1936.[17]

> As the tallest member I was right-hand marker, a position in which it was difficult to fidget. The parade was early morning, which required getting into uniform (kilt with pith helmet) in the semi-dark. All went well but, as the ceremony started, my head began to itch terribly and I could do nothing about it. Relief came with the order 'Three cheers for His Majesty. Remove headgear.' Out of my helmet fell a *chichak* and scampered away.

The frequent changes of residence required by 'the exigencies of the service' added to the difficulties of domestic life. Officers' wives had to take such sudden relocations in their stride, adapting to different environments, making the best of a variety of government quarters and establishing satisfactory relationships with new servants. These could have their eccentricities. The hospitable Pat Paterson[18] employed a cook, Ah Fong, who had never learned to speak English but delighted Pat's guests by announcing dinner with the only phrase he had mastered, 'Ma, I like your apple pie.' Bachelors generally could give only limited attention to household affairs. It was easier to accept 'adoption' by a competent *amah*, one of a breed of formidable Chinese ladies who took firm control of domestic affairs. They could be dictatorial. In Johore Bahru Derek Mackay[19] had to endure an angry tirade when he bought some pillowslips on a trip to Singapore. His *amah* sternly informed him that their manufacture was her responsibility and his purchase of the ready-made articles was seen as a reflection on her skills as a seamstress. In family homes a more balanced relationship was usually established and many lasting friendships were built between the 'mem' and her household servants.

Children could share expatriate life in their early years. Chinese *amah*s, Malay or Indian *ayah*s, were excellent nursemaids. Local facilities for health and education were more than adequate. For large families, however, the organization of home leave inevitably presented problems that increased as sons and daughters had to be sent away for their schooling. There were separations to be endured and wives might find themselves shuttling to and fro between husband and children as circumstances demanded.

Mothers might also be faced with unexpected hazards. In Port Swettenham Gordon and Anne Crocker[20] were quartered in an old bungalow on the main road through the little town. They found it noisy and dirty. Of greater concern was that their son, David, was suffering from recurrent nightmares. Gordon writes, 'We discovered that his bedroom was part of the Japanese police HQ during the war where interrogations took place. When he moved rooms the nightmares ceased.'

A more pressing physical danger faced Frankie Roualle[21] in Singapore when order broke down in the face of the Maria Hertogh riots. As she left a fashion show at the Adelphi Hotel the guests were advised that there were violent mobs of militant Muslims, Malays and Indonesians, hunting down and killing Europeans.

> I drove back to our house in Jervois Road where I had left our two daughters, aged four and two, in the care of our two Indonesian *ayah*s. On arrival I found the house deserted and dashed through to the servants' quarters. There I discovered ayah Katijah with her own four small children and my two, dressed in sarongs and made up to resemble the others, safe and sound. What a relief!

Wives, and occasionally children too, could share in som the pleasures offered by customs work. Katharine Sim often accompanied Stuart on his voyages to Pangkor island. Gordon Crocker provided similar boat trips from Telok Anson to Anne and sometimes ferried several ladies to the government resthouse at Sabak Bernam, a practice the local people interpreted as evidence of polygamy.[22] Stella[23] married Kenneth Hardaker in Malacca in November 1940 and still remembers accompanying him on patrol up the coast to One Fathom Bank and Port Swettenham. After the war they lived at Kuantan, a port on the east coast visited frequently by patrolling naval vessels. 'Kenneth, being Harbourmaster, had a lot to do with them and we went aboard some of them and entertained some of their officers, notably from HMS *Amethyst* just before she left for China. We were very sad to hear that some of them had been killed in the Yangtze "incident".'

To European women Malaya offered many opportunities for employment. They possessed the skills and academic background the country needed and they were highly valued for their integrity. Before her marriage to Tony King, Isobel Bruce was personal assistant to the head of the army field security service in Perak. Muriel Hewitt was similarly employed in the police. In Singapore Frankie Roualle was secretary to Malcolm Macdonald, the commissioner-general for Southeast Asia. Janey Grimwood[24] was a teacher in London before her marriage and soon resumed her profession in Johore Bahru.

> I had acquired a teaching post at the Convent of the Holy Infant Jesus within walking distance from my home. School began at 8.00 a.m. and continued to 11.00 a.m. when we had a break for thirty minutes. The lessons continued until 1.00 p.m. In the cool of the late afternoon we returned for sports and games actvities. I had forty eight pupils in my class, Chinese, Indian, Malay and one or two Irish. The Sultan of Johore was a patron of the school and sent some of his children as pupils. He and the Sultana visited the school on occasion.
>
> To celebrate Queen Elizabeth's coronation, sports were held on the *padang*. I ran in a teachers' race partnering a Chinese gentleman from the English college. The man ran with a piece of wool and gave it to his female partner who, armed with a needle, had to thread it before running

together to the tape. Having been brought up in England this was peanuts for me, so we received our prizes and walked off the field before the next pair had managed to thread their needle.

Frankie Roualle[25] played a rather different role in the educational system when she was living in Butterworth in 1952.

After we had been there a few months the local Government Health Officer, a Chinese, asked if I would help him with the three schools in the area, a Malay school, an Indian school and a very large Chinese school. I agreed, and after our first run in the Government van found that my duties were to visit each school, check to see whether any of the children were in need of minor medical attention which I could give, arrange for any more serious cases to be seen by a doctor and also to ensure that the Indian girls' wonderful thick hair was not crawling with nits! At the time, during the emergency, the Chinese Chung Hwa schoolteachers tended to be anti-British. I did not realize this until I drove to the Chung Hwa School to be met by a very hostile headmaster who had no intention of letting me in to see his pupils. I explained the purpose of my visit. He looked furious and held out his arm saying 'Cure that.' I looked and saw that he had appalling septic scabies sores, which must have been very painful. I opened my bag and painted the affected arm liberally with gentian violet ointment which my Health Officer had assured me cured most problems if put on twice a day. I left the ointment with him and went off hoping for the best. A couple of weeks later when passing the school I was flagged down by one of the teachers who took me to the Headmaster. I was greeted with beaming smiles and his 300 children were all lined up for inspection by the 'mem' who had cured his arm.

Two years later in Johore Bahru Frankie switched her ministrations to animals rather than children and their headmasters. She drove a van for the local RSPCA, a rather decrepit vehicle that broke down alongside an armoured personnel carrier manned by Malay soldiers. In response to her request for assistance the soldiers told her they could not leave the carrier. As she irritably peered over the side of their vehicle she discovered that they were guarding the corpses of three Chinese. Persuaded that the 'terrorists' were unlikely to escape they relented and helped Frankie on her way, so agitated that she immediately ran over a couple of ducks.

As Miss P. Nicholls, 'Nicky' Johnson[26] arrived in Malaya in the aftermath of the Japanese occupation to work as a health sister. She travelled out on a troopship to Singapore and then took the train to Kuala Lumpur, a journey facilitated by the fact that her sister was the movements officer. Posted to Raub in Pahang her task was to rebuild the public health service, which three-and-a-half years of occupation had all but destroyed. She took up residence in the resthouse at Kuala Lipis and met the local nurse who would be working with her.

> Nurse was Chinese, very good and helpful and could speak at least three dialects of Chinese, English and Malay, also a smattering of Tamil. I now learned that there were three more hospital areas in which I must set up clinics, Raub, Bentong and Mentakab. To furnish and staff with a nurse and an *ayah* it took me three months to get all this a going concern and it was certainly very, very necessary.

Nicky now embarked on her role as a travelling health sister (*missy kesihatan*). With the district officer she met the *penghulu*s.

> I soon learned what was needed after one or two visits to the odd *kampong*, for scabies, sore eyes, bowel infestations etc. I was given a very large basket, rather like a picnic basket, covered in sail cloth, the lid fastened with a padlock, and a basic amount of *ubat* (medicine) which I soon learned was not adequate and added the extras. Buckets, literally buckets of lotion to treat the scabies plus a plastering brush. Thus I painted all who came my way from neck to feet and the scabies gradually receded.
>
> Realizing I was to stay in these rural areas I acquired an army bedroll, two bush jackets and trousers, plus a small cane basket for my personal things. Thus equipped I was now ready to start the real work way out in the blue. On occasions I had to raft down the rivers, stopping at various *kampong*s, usually near the mosque on the river bank. ... Most of the ailments were malnourishment, round worm and scabies.

One expedition, on the orders of the senior medical and health officer, was to a huge swamp area, Tasek Bera, to deal with an outbreak of smallpox among the aborigines.

> I had to leave Kuala Lipis at 5.30 a.m. to travel by boat down the River Pahang to Sungei Bera and thence up river to Tasek Bera. The last three miles we had to cut through tough reeds – at least the aborigine who knew the way did so. I was beginning to feel a little apprehensive as he was rocking the boat so much and crocodiles were known to be in the swamps. However, we did arrive safely and my two boatmen soon had the Tilley lamps working to cook the rice and one of the chickens killed earlier in the day, leaving us three live chickens on the boat for future meals. As we had rock salt, tobacco and cigarette leaves on board it was decided that the boat be anchored on the water away from the bank in case wild animals caught the scent of the salt and attacked us.
>
> I had been told that there was a shack in which to shelter for nights as I should be there at least two days, but on arrival we were informed that a male elephant had passed through and taken the hut with him on his back. So the aborigines, who, I now realized, were Negritoes, piled twigs on the ground about six inches deep for me to put my bedroll on ... little sleep had I because they took it in turns to do vigil, keeping a glowing fire going all night, and with the murmur of their voices and the fear of what might pass under my bed. However, by sun up we were all alive and well. The vaccination programme went well.

Her visiting duties continued, pulling teeth, lancing boils, examining schoolchildren, vaccinating babies, giving out iron pills, vitamin pills, vitamin B and polio injections.

The emergency curtailed Nicky's activities. She was confined to the roads with a military or police escort and the villagers had to make sometimes difficult journeys to meet her there. Such restrictions were irksome but on one occasion her impatience served her well. A convoy of hussars with which she had arranged to travel to Raub failed to appear on time and, not wishing to miss an important appointment, Nicky travelled alone. She arrived safely, but the hussars, following belatedly, were ambushed. Several were killed.

17. Pahang: Nicky Johnson vaccinating aborigines.

By now Johnny Johnson was stationed at Raub. After their marriage he was posted to Singapore where Nicky soon set up a clinic for the customs staff and their families. She worked as health visitor for the Tan Toc Sen Hospital tuberculosis section and later performed a similar role for the Hansons Clinic and Trafalgar Home (for leprosy).

Katharine Sim was kept busy writing and painting. She was a regular contributor to the local press, which published her articles on the places she visited, illustrated with her line drawings. When Tony King was transferred to Kelantan the British Adviser persuaded Isobel to accept the appointment of supervisor of the Kelantan arts and crafts centre, a cooperative producing and marketing the unique Kelantan silver and woven silk cloth.[27] On examining the account books she discovered substantial bad debts, many owed by wealthy and influential members of the community who apparently subscribed to the prevailing view that the privileged should be supplied as a matter of prestige and were not obliged to pay promptly or in full. The craftsmen were naturally reluctant to accept further orders from these customers. The issue of summons, beginning with the lesser debtors, had the intended effect and the settlement of their accounts encouraged the craftsmen to resume their work.

This was timely. As Tony recounts: 'The setting up of craftsmen coincided with the Sultan's need for full ceremonial raiment for his appearance at the coronation of Elizabeth II. Despite Isobel's suggestion that fast aniline dyes from ICI would be more suitable for his many coloured sarongs and *Kain Songket* in Westminster, he insisted that local vegetable dyes be used.' On the great day he shared an open carriage with the Queen of Tonga in pouring rain. It took many months of intensive scrubbing to remove all traces of the dyes.

Those expatriate officers who stayed in the service after *merdeka* continued to play their part in local affairs. At Malacca in 1958 Gordon Crocker[28] chaired a committee to organize a pageant in celebration of the first anniversary of independence. It depicted the landing of Admiral Cheng Ho at Malacca in 1409.

> This was quite a magnificent affair involving Malays, Chinese, Indians and other races. Scrolls and speeches of welcome were taken from records. The Customs and Marine Departments were responsible for converting one of the large barges to become the Chinese Admiral's junk. Local Chinese families lent clothing, antique furniture, real gold plates and valuable china to furnish the admiral's cabin, which was open to the public after the ceremony. The junk was escorted into the landing jetty by canoes manned by Malay warriors. The junk itself was propelled by 'make believe' oarsmen, but for practical purposes powered by two of our large outboard motors concealed in the stern, with communication for steering by telephone.

This arrangement nearly led to disaster when the vessel encountered a sudden strong gust of wind as it approached the landing stage. Fortunately, this admiral, like the historical original, got safely ashore.

Most ex-officers and their families remember Malaya with affection. Some stayed in the service for several years. Many have maintained friendships with their Malaysian friends. Return visits have not been unusual. In 1994 Gordon Crocker led a small group on a tour arranged by his close friend and former colleague Tunku Adnan bin Tunku Besar Burhanuddin and were entertained to lunch at the palace by his brother-in-law, the current Yang di-Pertuan Agong.

For some expatriates, their service in Malaya was their principal career. For others who came late to the peninsula it was a comparatively brief experience of a delightful country. The world in which they worked has passed into history. Malaya has enjoyed 45 years of independence. It has been a period of great progress. Singapore has prospered as a separate state. The British administration was a brief chapter in the story of the peninsula, the contribution of the customs service little more than a footnote, but it was not untypical of that administration. It depended on a local staff drawn from all races, working with the European expatriates whose ultimate task was to pave the way to independence. Inevitably it is the latter who feature largely in this book, but credit for the achievements of the service must be shared by all. Those who had the honour to play a part in it are justifiably proud to have done so.

Epilogue

From 31 August 1957 the Federation of Malaya was a fully independent sovereign state. Singapore's progress to independence was somewhat slower.[1] Victory in the election held in April 1955 enabled David Marshall, leader of the Labour Front, to form a government. In August the legislative assembly voted for immediate self-government but a delegation that travelled to London in 1956 failed to secure this and Marshall resigned. Further all-party missions to London in 1957 and 1958 finally solved the outstanding issues and on 3 June 1959 Lee Kuan Yew, leader of the majority People's Action Party, formed the first government under the new constitution.

It was in Singapore in 1961 that Tungku Abdul Rahman floated the idea of a merger of Malaya, Singapore, North Borneo, Brunei and Sarawak. By 1962 the principles of 'Malaysia' had been largely agreed but there were difficulties ahead. Following a violent uprising in his state the Sultan of Brunei decided not to join, and in 1963 Indonesia staged its 'confrontation' and precipitated an armed conflict in the borderlands of Borneo. Following the Manila summit, a meeting of the heads of government of Malaya, Singapore and the Philippines in August, a United Nations team was sent to ascertain the wishes of the peoples of Sarawak and Sabah (formerly North Borneo). Meanwhile, on 31 August, Lee Kuan Yew formally declared the independence of Singapore, and on 16 September Malaysia came into being. The participation of Singapore was brief. On too many issues the governments in Kuala Lumpur and Singapore did not see eye to eye. In September 1964 there were race riots in Singapore between Malays and Chinese. In August 1965 Singapore seceded from Malaysia. In 2004 the two neighbours remain separate states.

They have both made great progress since independence. The economy of mainland Malaya has been transformed. Speaking to the fifty-fifth UMNO general assembly at Kuala Lumpur in 2001, the prime minister, Dr Mahathir Mohamad, was able to proclaim Malaysia 'one of the tiger economies in Asia'.[2] From an agricultural economy that depended on rubber and tin the country had become the seventeenth largest manufacturing nation in the world. Since independence per capita income had increased from US$ 300 to US$ 4000 per annum. Even Sir Stamford Raffles might be astonished at the achievements of his brainchild, Singapore. The small island now supports a population of well over four million, a density of over 6650 per square kilometre. In 2001 the port was the busiest in the world, handling 146,265 ships whose gross tonnage totalled 960 million.[3]

For the expatriate officers who served in the British administration 1957 was a year of personal decision. In effect they faced a choice of three futures. For a limited time the government departments in Malaya could still offer them employment, there remained other territories in the commonwealth to which transfers might be possible and for those who preferred to leave the service to seek new careers there was a scheme of financial compensation. Individual choice inevitably took account of personal circumstances, age, qualifications and family responsibilities, but also depended on the prospects of their replacement by local personnel. As remarked in Chapter 7, the customs service had faced difficultties in attracting suitably qualified recruits and was generally short of staff for senior appointments. Not surprisingly, a number of expatriates, including those whose retirement date was imminent, elected to stay in the service.

Most of them were to serve only a few years as the process of Malayanization accelerated. By 1961, four years after independence, the federation customs employed only 17 British officers in a total of 88 senior staff. The local officers were gradually progressing up the ladder of promotion and six of the 17 assistant comptrollers were now Asian. Nevertheless, the comptroller, his deputy and all four senior assistant comptrollers were still British.

A number of offficers continued their service in other territories. Several took up appointments in Africa, including David Anderson and Desmond Kemp. H. G. Boyce-Taylor pursued his customs career in Sarawak from 1959 to 1975, which for much of the time was part of Malaysia. But for most of those who were not yet ready for retirement the independence of Malaya was the occasion to seek a new career.[4]

Philip Merson had already left. In 1948 he decided to follow family tradition and to take up farming. Bicky Roualle settled in Norfolk and applied himself to the problems of personnel and labour relations in the television industry. His wife Frankie plunged into politics and served a term as the chair of Norfolk County Council. Tony King went into the oil business and retired as the head of marketing communications for Shell UK. Others who chose a commercial career were Cecil Gutteridge and Derek Mackay. The field of education attracted several. Jim Bailward and Peter Burgess, and Robert McCall after a few years in commerce, became teachers, and Kenneth Hellrich found his niche as a bursar. H. G. Boyce-Taylor chose to continue his working life in the East and took up a business appointment in Hong Kong. He has since retired to England but Peter Chattaway and Cyril Williams both emigrated to Australia and Vincent Lane has retired to France.

Official assistance for the job-hunting expatriates was not available until June 1957 when the Malayan Service Re-employment Bureau opened in cramped quarters in Victoria Street, London. In September that year John Lewis joined Mr R. L. Peel of the Malayan Civil Service to supervise the operation. John stayed with the Bureau until 1975. When it finally closed at the end of 1980 it had registered some 15,000 clients who had worked in many different territories of the commonwealth.

After so many years there are few survivors of those who served in the Malayan customs departments before independence and few have links now with their Asian former colleagues. For most, their time in the peninsula is now a distant memory of an age long past, a brief period in the history of Malaya, but one in which the foundations of its future prosperity and political stability were laid. These developments took place under a British administration that was never intended to be permanent. It is the common fate of a civil service that its achievements remain largely unnoticed and unsung. This book has attempted to tell a small part of the story of the British administration, to record the history and achievements of one government service and, through their reminiscences, to convey something of the lives of those British officers who served in it. Theirs was an experience that is unlikely to be repeated.

Appendix I
Statement of revenues collected in Penang, 1809/10

Heads of Revenue	*Total Revenues of 1809/10*	*Total Revenues of 1808/9*
Export duties	51,255.11¾	66,685.11½
Duties on the sale of houses and lands	625.73	1.921.52½
Quit rent	2,259	2,259.52
James Town opium farm	5,880	6,240
Beetle-leaf farm	7,440	10,920
Artap farm	2,200	2,785
George Town opium farm	33,720	38,400
George Town gaming farm	23,521	36,000
George Town arrack farm	25,320	31,200
James Town gaming farm	3,000	4,080
James Town arrack farm	2,100	3,372
Wood farm	2,340	2,760
Import duties	25,871.78¾	20,008.70½
Shop tax	1,496.25	800
Pork farm	7,388.33	6,400
Toddy and *bhang* farm	4,860	3,000
Total (in Spanish dollars)	199,357.21½	236,911.86½

Journal of the Malayan Branch Royal Asiatic Society, Vol. XXIII, Part 2, March 1950.

Appendix II

Straits Settlements: authorized establishment of the preventive service of the monopolies department, 1910

MONOPOLIES DEPARTMENT (MON: 2873/10)

The Preventive Service of the Monopolies Department is classified as follows:

1. Heads of preventive service

    Singapore, one at £420
    Penang, one at £200 p.a.
    Malacca, one at $900 p.a.

2. Supervisors

    Singapore, six at $1500, rising by annual increments of $120 to $2100 p.a.
    Penang, two (at $1440 p.a. and $900 p.a.)

Supervisors will, whenever practicable, be given free unfurnished bachelor quarters in the Monopolies Offices.

3. Senior Revenue Officers

    Grade I, salary $300 p.a.

Not to exceed, in Singapore, five, Penang, two, and Malacca, one.

    Grade II, salary $240 p.a.

Not to exceed, in Singapore, ten, in Penang, two, and, in Malacca, three.

Grade III, salary $180 p.a.

Such number as will not cause the total number of Revenue Officers in Grades I, II and III to exceed in Singapore, 40, in Penang, 12, and, in Malacca, 8.

There are also in Singapore five Special Revenue Officers at $180 p.a. each.

No one may be appointed to be a Senior Revenue Officer who cannot speak Malay and read and write his own native language. Promotion from one grade to another will depend on merit alone and will be at the discretion of the Superintendent.

4. Revenue Officers

Not to exceed 175 in Singapore, or 90 in Penang, at a salary of $108 – A12 – $144 p.a. each, and not to exceed 40 in Malacca, at a salary of $144 – A12 – $180 each.

5. Female Revenue Officers

Not to exceed four in Singapore or in Penang, at a salary of $180 – A12 – $240 each, and not to exceed two in Malacca, at a salary of $144 – A12 – $180 each.

6. All officers under this scheme, except the Heads of the Preventive Service, are eligible for rewards for good work, successful searches, or important information.

7. Officers already in the service may, on application and on the recommendation of the Superintendent, be brought on to this scheme. In the cases of officers drawing salaries at rates not in accordance with this scheme, the first increments, in appointments for which incremental rates of salary are provided, will be of such amounts as will bring their salaries into accordance with the scheme. The dates from which such increments shall be drawn will be decided by the Government in each case.

8. Any member of the preventive service may in case of emergency be required to serve in any one of the three Settlements.

Appendix III
Federated Malay States: senior appointments in the customs service, 1928

II. The authorized establishment of the Customs Service of the Federated Malay States is at present as follows, but no guarantee is given that the numbers and conditions of the appointment or the salaries attached to them will remain unaltered. Moreover, some of the posts included in these classes will not be exclusively confined to officers originally appointed as Probationers.

1 *Commissioner* (Class 1A, Malayan Civil Service).

Salary $1200 a month.

3 *Deputy Commissioners* (Customs, Excise and Chandu).

Salary $800 rising by annual increments of $25 per mensem to $950 a month.

1 *Chief Superintendent* (Preventive Branch).

Salary $600 a month rising by annual increments of $25 a month to $800 a month.

23 *Superintendents*

Salary $475 a month rising by annual increments of $25 a month to $750 a month, subject to an efficiency bar between $575 and $600 a month.

24 *Assistant Superintendents*

Salary $350 a month rising by annual increments of $25 a month to $450 a month.

Probationers

Salary $250 a month.

Extract from appointment letter of J. S. A. Lewis.

Appendix IV

Federated Malay States and Straits Settlements: senior officers during the Japanese invasion and occupation of Malaya

	Employment during hostilities	*Circumstances after 15.2.42*
Allan G.A.T.B.	287 Battalion RA	Killed in action
Allen D.J.	Aden Customs	Aden Customs
Aplin F.G.	Customs	Internee
Arnold J.L.	RNVR	POW
Auten R.K.	Food Control	Internee
Bailward J.T.	45 MT Res Coy	POW
Baker A.G.	Food Control	Internee
Barnett-Smith L.R.	RNVR	On leave
Bayley C.P.	Food Control	Internee
Bigley D.W.	RNVR	United Kingdom
Blakstad G.C.C.	Food Control	Internee
Boyd A. (Textile Advr.)	Food Control	Internee
Bradley C.R.	RNVR	Killed in action
Buckwell S.R.L.	RNVR	POW
Burgess P.H.	Food Control	Internee
Cantrell K.H.	RNVR	Australia
Capel A.H. (Op. Plant)	Food Control	Internee
Carr-Archer J.A.	Customs	Kenya
Carrel L.C.	RNVR	Australia
Clemons R.S.	Food Control	Internee
Coney D.B.	Food Control	Internee
Cooper P.H. Mc.	RNVR	Abroad, unknown where
Cooper T.G.D.A.	RAF	POW (Java)
Darby L.D.	Food Control	Internee
Dawson A.D.	Customs	Internee

Earl H.F.	Customs	Absent on leave
Elkins P.H.	Food Control	Internee
Evans E.J.	RNVR	Killed in action
Frend M.B.C.	Food Control	Internee
Ganno C.V.	Opium Packing Plant	Absent on leave
Geake F.H.	Chemist	Internee
Gilmour G.J.	Opium Packing Plant	Internee
Gordon W.	Customs	Internee
Greaves A.W.	RAF	Nigeria
Gridley A.H.	Food Control	Internee
Gutteridge G.C.	RNVR	POW
Hall D.G.	Customs	Internee
Hannigan W.H.W.	Johore Volunteer Force	POW
Hardaker K.	Army Intelligence Liaison	Internee
Harward R.L.N.	Food Control	Internee
Hellrich K.S.	Food Control	Internee
Henman O.R.T.	RNVR	POW (Sumatra)
Hide G.C.	Opium Packing Plant	Internee
Hime E.H.	RASC	POW
Holland M.B.	Customs	Internee
Jeavons A.C.	Army Intelligence	POW (d.2.9.43)
Jeffries I.I.	45 MT Res Coy	POW
Jenkins J.H.S.	Food Control	Internee
Johnston J.H.	Food Control	Internee
Keet H.G.	Food Control	Internee
Kemp J.C.W.	RNVR	POW
Langdon E.P.C.	RNVR	POW
Lawson P.D.	RASC	POW
Lewin H.G.D.	Army Intelligence	POW
Lewis J.S.A.	Food Control	Internee
Leyh S.G.H.	RNR	Australia
LLoyd H.S.J.	Customs	Absent on leave
Lock C.E.J. de R.	45 MT Res Coy	POW
McCall R.W.L.	Straits Settlements VF	POW
McKenzie Hart J.	RAF	POW
McLaren Reid C.	RAF	POW
McLaughlin J.E.	FMS VF	POW
McLaughlin W.H	Army Intelligence	POW
Marshall H.A.	45 MT Res Coy	POW
Mavor W.F.	Australian IF Intelligence	POW
Merson J.P.	RNVR	East Africa
Montgomery D.G.W.	RAF	UK
Morice J.D.G.	Customs	Internee
Palmer D.B.	Food Control	Internee
Parker J.A.	Customs	Absent on leave
Phear H.W.	Customs	Internee
Pickthall J.R.M.	RNVR	POW
Pitt G.J.G.	Food Control	Internee

Pyper J.H.	RASC	Killed in action
Richardson H. McN.W.	Customs	Absent on leave
Rickard F.S.	45 MT Res Coy	POW
Ronaldson J.T.	RNVR	Killed in action
Russell H.N.D.	Malay Regiment	Killed in action
Roualle J.F.M.	FMS VF	POW
Rowland E.C.	RNVR	Killed in action
Salter J.	Opium Packing Plant	In Singapore
Shaw G.A.T.	Army Intelligence	Australia
Sichel E.C.S.	RAOC	POW
Sim A.W.S.	RNVR	POW (Sumatra)
Steven W.G.	Food Control	Internee
Stokes D.P.	RAF	POW (Java)
Talbot A.E.S.	45 MT Res Coy	POW
Trumble D.H.	Customs	Australia
Tufnell R.S.	RNVR	Absent on leave
Wheeler A.H.L.	Australian IF	Australia
Wilbraham P.	Opium Packing Plant	In Singapore
Wicksteed E.J.K.	Food Control/RAF	POW
Williams C.O.	Food Control	Internee

Killed in action 7, POWs 30, Internees 34, Absent 20, In Singapore 2. Total 93

Research by J. S. A. Lewis.

Appendix V
HM Customs Singapore 1957: Administration

STAFF	*Establishment*	*Actual*
Senior officers	25	18
Assistant customs officers	44	34
Clerical staff	46	44
Preventive officers	9	6
Revenue officers (male)	426	393
Revenue officers (female)	12	10
Road transport staff	23	23
Marine staff	93	81
Toddy shop staff	30	29
Office boys	12	12
Watchmen	8	8
Telephone operators	2	2
Gardener	1	1
Carpenter	1	1
Office cleaners	14	13
Totals	746	675

ROAD TRANSPORT	
Bus	1
Vans and station wagons	7
Motorcars	5
Motorcycles	1

SEA TRANSPORT

Motor launches 15

(All equipped with VHF, two with radar.)

PREMISES

Headquarters	Customs House, Maxwell Road
Divisional headquarters	Keppel Road (docks) Clifford Pier (harbour) Beach Road (land) Singapore airport
Five rural substations	Bedok, Changi, Tampines, Woodlands and Sungei Tuas
Three bonded warehouses	Maxwell Road, Hare Street and Trafalgar Street

Report of the Comptroller of Customs 1957.

Appendix VI
Federation of Malaya Customs and Excise Department Organization

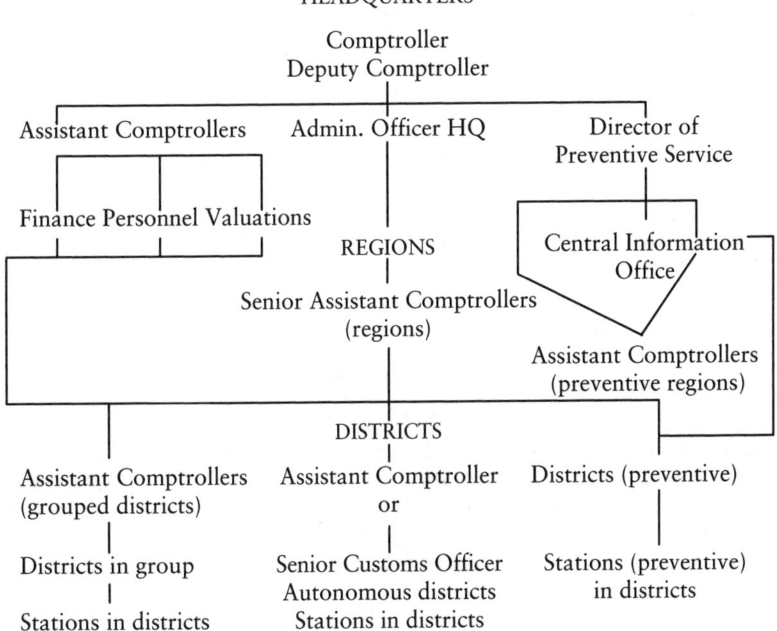

Report of the Comptroller of Customs and Excise 1957.

Appendix VII

Straits Settlements Customs Revenue 1936–38

	1936	*1937*	*1938*
Liquor	$3,371,746.38	3,924,560.46	3,862,579.33
licences	127,624.50	140,373.00	139.449.50
Tobacco	4,302,002.16	4,834,624.35	5,045,389.74
licences	31,107.00	30,680.00	30.989.50
Petroleum	3,191,223.71	3,618,081.03	3,812.490.07
licences	800.00	2,100.00	1,200.00
Sp.Tax Hy. Oil Eng Veh.	13,935.00	31,262.54	33,379.26
Opium	9,177,425.47	9,655,702.49	8,450,007.14
Textiles	9,647.43	9,124.71	12,738.81
Miscellaneous	2,668. 82	2,303.84	4,036. 34
	20,227,186.47	22,248,812.42	21,392,259.69
Rubber	333,100.02	69,753.20	59,284.09
For Malay States	3,260,479.02	4,119,047.61	3,711,771.81
	23,820,760.80	26,437,613.23	25.165,315.59
Releases of Liquor Duty Paid (galls)			
European spirits	131,621	148,439	146,286
Asian spirits	84,106	96,077	82,600
Sparkling wine	3,732	4,432	4,150
Still wine	31,300	35,044	36,264
Beer, etc.	633,350	860,210	878,758
Releases of liquor duty free to HM1 Forces (galls)			
European spirits	8,581	9,315	8,638
Wine	1,920	2,047	2,787
Beer, etc.	183,047	253,391	350,861
Releases of fuel duty paid (galls)			
Petroleum	8,717,304	9,941,333	10,503,638
Kerosene	2,803,342	2,772,280	2,724,328

Releases of fuel duty free (galls)			
HM Forces	426,093	725,077	1,484,576
Airlines	85,784	205,707	330,084

Licensed premises (1938)	*Singapore*	*Penang*	*Malacca*
Breweries	2		
Distilleries	2		1
Liquor warehouses	20	2	
Public houses	75	44	17
Retail liquor shops	139	69	23
Asian liquor shops	146	38	18
Estate toddy shops		18	39

Appendix VIII
Federation of Malaya Customs and Excise Revenues 1953–57

Imports $	*1953*	*1954*	*1955*	*1956*	*1957*
Malt liquor	21,169,862	18,892,464	22,915,105	26,069,486	25,079,160
Spirits	16,968,199	14,983,650	18,764,957	18,670,725	17,284,982
Petroleum	33,200,052	36,766,556	39,724,475	45,989,252	56,337,642
Sugar	2,952,971	7,672,853	14,149,152	16,165,800	15,667,127
Textiles	11,412,879	12,858,598	15,933,384	17,664,547	20,179,024
Tobacco	96,635,566	93,874,581	99,825,907	104,447,835	104,611,573
Other	16,016,201	20,780,348	39,585,620	47,045,055	55,434,857
	198,355,730	205,829,050	250,898,600	276,052,700	294,594,365

Note: Increase of duty rates: Petroleum 1953, 1956; sugar 1954, 1956; textiles 1956; tobacco 1953. Number of import tariff items: 1953 (40), 1954 (71), 1956 (79).

Exports					
Rubber	54,682,060	52,613,999	174,061,075	143,972,327	120,406,518
Tin/tin ore	51,257,379	53,592,692	55,794,128	60,252,016	54,242,315
Other	6,240,759	6,097,702	5,546,400,	6,152,119	5,880,986
	112,180,198	112,304,393	235,401,603	210,376,462	180,529,819

Excise

Samsu	6,601,063	5,845,975	6,808,162	6,802,528	6,405,690
Playing cards	7,567	13,595	14,006	15,192	16,694
Matches	95,683	77,709	87,583	115,168	160,530
Local tobacco	–	–	–	54,773	2,245,886
Rubber (Penang)	41,566	59,224	174,917	125,901	281,990
	6,745,879	5,996,503	7,084,668	7,113,562	9,110,790

Note: Excise duty on local leaf tobacco introduced November 1956.

State Revenue

Toddy	6,238,036	6,764,993	7,094,102	7,690,103	7,558,603
Royalty on iron-ore	1,246,484	1,699,143	3,016,962	4,327,041	2,697,837
Royalty on tin	–	–	–	–	848,360
Licences	606,498	615,867	681,087	558,386	609,657
Other	8,260	3,508	3,437	7,308	9,555
	8,099,278	9,083,511	10,795,588	12,582,838	11,724,012

Note: Prior to 1957 the royalty on tin-ore was accounted for as federal revenue.

Appendix IX
Singapore Customs and Excise Revenues 1953–57

	1953	*1954*	*1955*	*1956*	*1957*
Tobacco	$34,432,344	33,230,470	33,841,020	34,305,626	39,312,135
Petroleum	16,031,378	17,169,141	19,389,499	22,677,578	27,173,822
Liquors	21,922,433	21,224,270	23,581,215	27,156,089	28,552,981
Toddy	306,272	341,317	308,850	467,025	499,655
Entertainment duty	5,378,822	5,165,291	5,235,814	5,982,718	6,302,280
Fines/forfeits	284,725	114,703	19,309	35,292	36,175
Miscellaneous	1,448	1,887	1,709	1,166	781
	78,357,425	77,247,082	82,377,418	90,625,498	101,877,831
Christmas Island	21,127	16,821	17,640	39,892	45,115
	78,378,552	77,263,904	82,395,058	90,665,390	101,922,947
Percentages (Singapore only)					
Tobacco	43.9	43.0	41.0	37.8	38.5
Petroleum	20.4	22.2	23.5	25.0	26.7
Liquors	28.0	27.5	28.6	30.0	28.0
Ent. duty	6.9	6.7	6.4	6.6	6.2

Note: On 1 January 1958 Christmas Island passed to the jurisdiction of the Australian government.

Appendix X
The opium problem

STRAITS SETTLEMENTS: MONOPOLY BETWEEN THE WARS

(Three year annual averages)

	Monopoly sales (lbs)	*Contraband seized (lbs)*	*Prosecutions*
1918–20	140,976	3,020	Not recorded
1921–23	116,298	1,573	Not recorded
1924–26	105,754	16,764	461
1927–29	108,069	9,636	763
1930–32	61,062	5,789	1,214
1933–35	55,106	2,999	1,625
1936–38	46,028	3,792	2,863

Departmental Annual Report 1938.

SINGAPORE: THE END OF THE MONOPOLY

	1939	*1940*	*1946*	*1947*	*1948*	*1949*
Prosecutions	2,508	2,119	213	703	357	238
Charged	2,632	2,151	365	793	388	338
Convicted	2,539	2,104	360	745	318	229
Fines imposed	Not recorded		$74,921	$58,797	$10,735	$15,666
Fines paid	Not recorded		$69,875	$41,577	$8,091	$4,086
Seizures without arrest	Not recorded		22	228	322	790

Report of the Comptroller of Customs for 1949.

Appendix XI
Preventive action: Singapore

	1946	1947	1948	1949
Liquor				
Prosecutions	400	276	250	287
Persons charged	430	324	284	346
Persons convicted	371	271	250	292
Fines imposed	$126,663	$99,396	$74,327	$82,378
Fines paid	$97,405	$65,674	$42,763	$31,858
Seizures (no arrest)	54	130	338	202
Tobacco				
Prosecutions	730	295	195	106
Persons charged	1488	338	204	145
Persons convicted	1464	267	169	102
Fines imposed	$283,876	$227,099	$130,222	$62,604
Fines paid	$177,387	$85,721	$64,355	$17,852
Seizures without arrest	70	65	186	113
Confiscations				
European liquors (galls)	2,409	1,382	380	429
Chinese liquors (galls)		1,890	1,174	1,042
Fermented rice (galls)	11,203	4,268	11,942	7,162
Unlicensed stills		52	110	93
European tobacco (lbs)	160,628	6,429	2,733	2,805
Native tobacco (lbs)		80,281	14,010	5,575
Opium (lbs)	1,938	2,308	4,588	4,602
Chandu (lbs)	81	49	240	309
Chandu dross (lbs)		6	32	97
Opium pipes		2,246	1,418	3,175
Opium lamps		1,779	1,154	2,845
Opium lamp chimneys				237
Motorcars	3	5	4	3
Lorries			3	1
Jeeps		1		
Trucks		1		
Trishaws	1	5	1	2
Bicycles	23	15	11	25

Sampans	10	1	2	1
Kolehs		2		5
Motorboats		2	4	1
Bumboats	1			
Textiles (yards)	3,398			
Condensed milk (cases)	15			
Rice (tons)	19.4	14.2	7,758.9	
Biscuits		375		
Wheat (tons)		13.4	40.1	
Coconut oil		13,200		
Benzine (galls)	20,224	2,552	1,496	
English £		352	393.5	3
Australian £			300	
Malayan dollars		24,133	52,292.20	5,254.30
US gold dollars			4,205	600
Gold bars (lbs)		4	38.5	24
Indian rupees		1,575	2,500	2,330
Siamese ticals			5,146	
Dutch guilders			19,800	22,653
Dutch silver guilders			615	
Hong Kong dollars			1,500	
English sovereigns			163	
Diamonds			382	
Gold chains			1	
Gold bracelets			1	
Bayonets			6	
Guns		1		
Pistols		4	8	
Toy pistols			7	
Maize (lbs)			26,175	
Gunny sacks			50	
Firecrackers (boxes)			48	
Poison (bottles)			26	94
Cocaine (lbs)		3		
Quinine (lbs)		220		
Indian hemp (lbs)	187.69	162.75	13	
Morphine tablets		3,600	19.5	
Butter (lbs)				4,060
Preserved olives (cases)				54
Sulphate of ammonia (bags)				250
Salt (bags)				20
Onions (baskets)				12

Report of the Comptroller of Customs for 1949.

Appendix XII
Licensed premises: Straits Settlements in the early years

	1910	*1920*	*1930*
Opium warehouses	4	1	–
Smoking rooms	420	286	–
Chandu retail shops	386	548	–
Liquor warehouses	19	15	12
Distilleries	4	4	4
Liquor retailers	702	832	567
Toddy shops	109	175	165
Public houses	83	197	119
Tobacco manufacturers	–	49	17
Tobacco importers	–	268	173
Billiard rooms	44	40	47
Chemists	45	33	–

Government Monopolies Manual, 30 June 1932.

DISTRIBUTION BY SETTLEMENT, 1935

	Singapore	*Penang*	*Malacca*
Breweries	2	–	–
Distilleries	–	–	–
Liquor warehouses	15	2	–
Public houses	64	29	13
Retail shops	130	66	42
Liquor shops	157	42	28
Estate toddy shops	–	28*	40
Tobacco manufacturers	4	7	2
Government toddy shops	10	20	1

*Includes ten shops in the Dindings.

Note: Apart from estate shops all licensed toddy shops were now closed.

Annual Report of the Department of Excise 1935.

LICENSED PREMISES 1949

	Singapore	*Federation*
Breweries	2	–
Distilleries	2	15
Liquor warehouses	14	
Wholesale licences		422
Public houses	101	535
Retail shops	478	1075

Note: Singapore reported the following licences for tobacco: tobacco manufacturers (13), tobacco importers (76) and private tobacco bonds (2).

Departmental Annual Reports for 1949.

Sources

OFFICERS OF THE DEPARTMENTS AND THEIR WIVES

Bailward, J.
Bowyer-Johnson, Mr and Mrs L. J.
Boyce-Taylor, H. G.
Burgess, P. H.
Chattaway, P.
Crocker, C. G.
Grimwood, Mr and Mrs E. J.
Gutteridge, C. C.
Hardaker, Mrs S.
Hellrich, K. S.
Kemp, J.
King, A. R.
Lane, J. V.
Lewis, J. S. A.
McCall, R. W. L.
Mackay, D. J.
Merson, J. P.
Roualle, Mr and Mrs J. F. M.

TERRITORIAL REPORTS

Federated Malay States Annual Reports 1910, 1911, 1912, 1913, 1914, 1915, 1916, 1917, 1918, 1919, 1921, 1922, 1923, 1926, 1935 and 1938
Straits Settlements Annual Reports 1910, 1919, 1926 and 1938
Malayan Union Annual Reports 1946 and 1947
Federation of Malaya Annual Reports 1954 and 1956
Singapore Annual Reports 1954

DOMINION AND COLONIAL OFFICE LISTS

1911, 1912, 1926, 1940 and 1948

DEPARTMENTAL ANNUAL REPORTS

Federated Malay States 1938
Straits Settlements 1931, 1932, 1933, 1934, 1935, 1936, 1937, 1938
Malayan Union 1946, 1947
Federation of Malaya 1949, 1957

Singapore 1948, 1949, 1950, 1951, 1952, 1953, 1955, 1956, 1957, 1958

OTHER DOCUMENTS

Colonial Office Cmd. 7709 British Dependencies in the Far East 1945–9

Federation of Malaya Revenue Officers Handbook 1954

Letter of appointment J. S. A. Lewis 1928

Ph.D. thesis 1965, Margaret Julia Beng Chu Lim, 'Control of the Opium Trade in Malaya 1900–1912'

Public Record Office Files: CO.825/19/1 Malaya – Control of Opium Traffic CO.825/20/1 Malaya – Control of Opium Traffic CO.54/882/10 Opium Policy

Report of the Committee on Malayanization of the Public Service 1956

Report of the Customs Duties Committee of the Straits Settlements 1932

Report of the Straits Settlements and Federated Malay States Opium Commission, 17 June 1908

Staff Lists: Malayan Establishment 1948; Federation of Malaya 1956, 1958 and 1961

Straits Settlements Government Monopolies Manual, 30 June 1932

Straits Settlements Monopolies Department Classification of preventive service (Mon: 2873/10)

Tape recording, K. S. Hellrich, Bristol Empire & Commonwealth Museum, Bristol

ACADEMIC PAPERS

Butcher, J. G. (1982) 'The Demise of the Revenue Farm System in the Federated Malay States', paper presented at the Fourth National Conference of the Asian Studies Association of Australia, May

Cowan, C. D. (1950) 'A Note on Early Legislation in Penang: Tan Soo Chye, Governor Bannerman and the Penang Tin Scheme', *Royal Asiatic Society Malayan Branch Journal*, vol. XXIII, Part 1, February

Cowan, C. D. (compiler and editor) (1950) 'Early Penang and the Rise of Singapore', *Royal Asiatic Society Malayan Branch Journal*, vol. XXIII, Part 2, March

De Bruijn, P. G. (1953) 'Trade in the Straits of Malacca in 1785', translated by Professor Brian Harrison, *Royal Asiatic Society Malayan Branch Journal*, vol. XXVI, Part 1, July

PUBLISHED WORKS

Collis, Maurice, *Foreign Mud* (1946)

Coupland, Reginald, *Raffles of Singapore* (1946)

Donnison, F. S. V., *British Military Administration in the Far East 1943–6* (1956)

Emerson, R., *Malaysia: A Study in Direct and Indirect Rule*

Hall, D. G. E., *A History of Southeast Asia* (1981)

Heussler, R., *British Rule in Malaya*

Kratoska, Paul H., *The Japanese Occupation of Malaya 1941–45*

Mackenzie, Compton, *Eastern Epic* (1951)

Mahathir, Dr Mohamad, *Malays Forget Easily* (2001)

Millar, H., *The Story of Malaysia* (1965)

Mills, L. A., *The British in Eastern Asia*

Moore, Donald and Joanna, *The First 150 Years of Singapore* (1969)

Purcell, Victor, *The Chinese in Malaya* (1948)

Purcell, Victor, *Malaya: Outline of a Colony* (1946)

Shennan, Margaret, *Out in the Midday Sun* (2000)

Sim, Katharine, *Malayan Landscape*

Tregonning, K. G., *A History of Modern Malaya* (1964)

Turnbull, C. M., *A Short History of Malaysia, Singapore and Brunei* (1980)

West, Nigel, *Secret War* (1992)

White, Nicholas J., *Business, Government and the End of Empire Malaya 1942–7*

Winstedt, Sir Richard O., *A History of Malaya* (1935)

Winstedt, Sir Richard O., *Malaya and its History*

Notes

Chapter 1: A tropical peninsula

1. The summary of Malaya's early history is based largely on the Federation of Malaya Annual Report 1954, R. O. Winstedt's *Malaya and its History* and *History of Malaya* and Victor Purcell's *Malaya: Outline of a Colony.*
2. On Cheng Ho, see Victor Purcell's *Malaya: Outline of a Colony.*
3. On St Francis Xavier, see Sir Richard O. Winstedt's *Malaya and its History.*
4. The East India Company was founded under a charter granted by Queen Elizabeth in 1600; by the middle of the eighteenth century it had become a major power in India. Its rule eventually extended over the entire sub-continent, but, following the Indian Mutiny, the administration was passed to the Crown in 1858.
5. For Amboyna massacre, see Victor Purcell *Malaya: Outline of a Colony.*
6. On Francis Light, see D. G. E. Hall, *A History of Southeast Asia.*
7. On Pitt's Act, see R. O. Winstedt, *Malaya and its History.*
8. On Fullerton and Raffles, see D. G. E. Hall, *A History of Southeast Asia.*
9. For more on Thomas Stamford Raffles, see Reginald Coupland's *Raffles of Singapore.*
10. Francis Rawdon Hastings, Earl of Moira. He served with distinction in the American War of Independence and was appointed governor-general of India in 1812.
11. The first of these Raffles letters was to a Colonel Addenbrook (D. and J. Moore, *The First 150 Years of Singapore*) and the second was written on his second visit (R. Coupland, *Raffles of Singapore*).
12. Letter written by Stamford Raffles and quoted by Reginald Coupland, *Raffles of Singapore.*
13. On imports and exports, see Victor Purcell, *Malaya: Outline of a Colony.*
14. See C. A. Gibson-Hill, 'The Singapore Chronicle 1824–37', *Journal of Malayan branch Royal Asiatic Society*, vol. XXVI, Part 1, July 1953.
15. Sir Richard O. Winstedt, *Malaya and its History.*
16. See Donald and Joanna Moore, *The First 150 Years of Singapore.*
17. On non-intervention, see Sir Richard O. Winstedt, *Malaya and its History*; and Donald and Joanna Moore, *The First 150 Years of Singapore.*

18. D. G. E.Hall, *A History of South East Asia.*
19. Ibid.
20. Sir Richard O.Winstedt, *Malaya and its History.*
21. On Treaty of Pangkor, see Sir Richard O. Winstedt, *Malaya and its History* and D. G. E. Hall, *A History of South East Asia.*
22. On J. W. W. Birch, see Sir Richard O. Winstedt, *Malaya and its History* and D. G. E. Hall, *A History of South East Asia.*
23. D. G. E. Hall, *A History of South East Asia.*
24. Ibid.
25. Ibid.
26. On Pahang, see Sir Richard O.Winstedt, *Malaya and its History* and D. G. E. Hall, *A History of South East Asia.*
27. On Federated Malay States, see D. G. E. Hall, *A History of South East Asia.*
28. In her thesis, 'Control of the Opium Trade in Malaya, 1900–12', Margaret Lim quotes Sir Frank Swettenham in his book, *British Malaya.* 'It was Chinese energy and industry, which supplied the funds to begin construction of roads and other public wants, and to pay for all other costs of administration. They were, and still are, the pioneers of mining.'
29. Tungku Abdul Rahman, who read the proclamation of independence in the presence of the Duke of Gloucester representing the Queen, was the great, great, great grandson of the Sultan of Kedah who sold Penang to Francis Light (Harry Millar, *The Story of Malaysia*).
30. Although Singapore achieved self-government in 1959 it was not until 1963 that full independence was proclaimed. In 1959 its population totalled 1,445,929. Of these the Chinese numbered 1,090,595, Malaysians 197,060 and Indians and Pakistanis 124,084 (D. G. E. Hall, *A History of South East Asia*).
31. In the nineteenth century MCS officers might act as collectors of revenue. Such an appointment was not highly regarded. R. Heussler (*British Rule in Malaya*) quotes an observation that 'when a man got a customs job late in his career it was not a good sign.'

Chapter 2: A difficult birth

1. Victor Purcell, *The Chinese in Malaya.*
2. Ibid.
3. Ibid.
4. Ibid.
5. Reginald Coupland, *Raffles of Singapore.*
6. On Crawfurd, see Victor Purcell, *The Chinese in Malaya*, and Donald and Joanna Moore, *The First 150 Years of Singapore.*
7. Victor Purcell, *The Chinese in Malaya*; and Sir Richard O. Winstedt, *Malaya and its History.*
8. Donald and Joanna Moore, *The First 150 Years of Singapore.*
9. Donald and Joanna Moore, *The First 150 Years of Singapore.* The

Straits Times was still the leading English Language newspaper in the twentieth century.

10. The Indian Mutiny broke out in 1857.
11. Donald and Joanna Moore, *The First 150 Years of Singapore.*
12. Sir Richard O. Winstedt, *Malaya and its History.*
13. On the Chinese in Perak, see Victor Purcell, *The Chinese in Malaya.*
14. R. Heussler, *British Rule in Malaya.*
15. J. G. Butcher, *The Demise of the Revenue Farm System in the Federated Malay States.*
16. Ibid.
17. Ibid.
18. Ibid.
19. Ibid.
20. Ibid.
21. Report of the Straits Settlements and Federated Malay States Opium Commission, 1908.
22. Straits Settlements Annual Report 1910; Government Monopolies Department Annual Report 1910; Straits Settlements Government Monopolies Manual 1932 (See also Appendix II).
23. Malayan Union Customs and Excise Annual Report 1946; FMS Annual Report 1910.
24. FMS Annual Report 1910.

Chapter 3: Growing up

1. Dominion and Colonial Office List 1912.
2. Public Record Office CO.54/882/10; Straits Settlements Government Monopolies Manual 1932.
3. FMS Annual Report 1915; Malayan Union Customs and Excise Annual Report 1946.
4. John Lewis's personal account.
5. Malayan Union Customs and Excise Annual Report 1946
6. FMS Annual Report 1923; Malayan Union Customs and Excise Annual Report 1946.
7. R. Emerson, *Malaysia: A Study in Direct and Indirect Rule*; K. G. Tregonning, A *History of Modern Malaya.*
8. Personal account. On the branch line to Kelantan, Lewis writes that 'during the war the Japanese moved the equipment and rails of this branch line to Thailand to build the notorious "death railway" from Thailand to Burma using POWs and native conscripts.'
9. L. A. Mills, *The British in Eastern Asia*; K. G. Tregonning, *A History of Modern Malaya.*
10. Report of the Customs Duties Committee of the Straits Settlements 1932; L. A. Mills, *The British in Eastern Asia.*
11. Straits Settlements Government Monopolies Manual 1932; R. Emerson, *Malaysia: A Study in Direct and Indirect Rule.*
12. L. A. Mills, *The British in Eastern Asia*; R. Emerson, *Malaysia: A*

Study in Direct and Indirect Rule; Malayan Union Customs and Excise Annual Report 1946.

13. Straits Settlements Government Monopolies Manual 1932.
14. Government Monopolies Department Annual Report 1934; L. A. Mills, *The British in Eastern Asia.*
15. Government Monopolies Department Annual Report 1934; L. A. Mills, *The British in Eastern Asia.* (For evasions see also Chapter 13.)
16. Straits Settlements Government Monopolies Manual 1932.
17. Singapore Customs Annual Report 1949; Malayan Union Customs and Excise Annual Report 1946.
18. Straits Settlements Government Monopolies Manual 1932
19. Government Monopolies Department Annual Reports 1932 and 1936.
20. Government Monopolies Department Annual Report 1936.
21. Probably intended to protect the petroleum duty. Government Monopolies Department Annual Report 1937.
22. Government Monopolies Department Annual Report 1938.
23. Malayan Union Customs and Excise Annual Report 1946.
24. Ibid.
25. Ibid.
26. Ibid.
27. FMS Customs and Excise Annual Report 1938; L. A. Mills, *The British in Eastern Asia.*
28. Straits Settlements Annual Report 1938.
29. Government Monopolies Department Annual Report 1938. Although Chinese and Malays provided the bulk of the staff it also included Tamils, Sikhs, Eurasians and and Siamese.

Chapter 4: The expatriates arrive

1. From John Lewis's personal account.
2. Ibid.
3. Personal account by Peter Burgess.
4. Personal account by Robert McCall.
5. Personal account by Jean François Marie Roualle.
6. A leading authority on Malaya and its language.
7. Personal account by Philip Merson.
8. The Peninsular and Orient Steamship Company, formed under that title in 1840, operated the mail service to Australia and the East.
9. Wife of a customs officer, writer and artist.
10. Recorded interview with Kenneth Hellrich.
11. Personal account by Jim Bailward.
12. A large fleet of freighters owned by Alfred Holt & Co.
13. In 1955 the federation customs rejected a suggestion that officers be empowered to search anyone 'to ascertain if they were carrying drugs' as an infringement of personal liberty (D. J. Mackay).
14. *Federation of Malaya Revenue Officers Handbook*, 1954.

15. Government Monopolies Department Annual Report, 1938.
16. The penal and criminal procedure codes were based on, but differed in important respects from, those in India.
17. *The Voyages of Abdullah*, a Malay classic.
18. The Jawi script is based on the Arabic script but has fewer characters.
19. The Straits Steamship Company operated a fleet of small ships along the coast carrying passengers and freight.
20. Singapore Customs Annual Report 1949.
21. Malayan Union Customs and Excise Annual Report 1946.
22. Imperial Airways was the British state-aided airline formed in 1924. It regularly carried airmail to the East.
23. The security service dealing with subversion and espionage.
24. Sir William Dobbie, GOC Malaya, 1936–7.
25. Colonel Percival, then GSO1 (General Staff Officer 1) to Dobbie, returned to Malaya in 1941 as a lieutenant general and GOC (Compton Mackenzie, *Eastern Epic*).
26. 'His Excellency'. Thus were governors entitled.

Chapter 5: A violent interruption

1. On Japanese landing, see Compton Mackenzie, *Eastern Epic.*
2. Malayan Union Customs and Excise Annual Report 1946.
3. Robert McCall, personal account.
4. John Lewis, personal account.
5. Cecil Gutteridge, personal account. This and subsequent extracts are taken from the report he submitted to the Comptroller of Customs after the war.
6. An obvious move to frustrate invaders who could use local craft to outflank the defenders.
7. The ten regiments of Gurkha Rifles were then part of the Indian Army.
8. See Katharine Sim's *Malayan Landscape.*
9. Isobel Bruce, personal account. At the time of her birth the Perak River was flooded and her mother was unable to reach the hospital at Ipoh. Isobel was the first European child to be born in the Sultan's palace, the Istana Sultan Iskander Shah, in a hospital recently built for the ladies of the harem.
10. Jim Bailward, personal account.
11. Malayan Union Customs and Excise Annual Report 1946
12. Robert McCall, personal account.
13. Isobel Bruce, personal account.
14. See *Malayan Landscape.*
15. Peter Burgess, personal account.
16. Rt Hon. Alfred Duff Cooper was minister of state in the Far East, reporting to the War Cabinet. Donald and Joanna Moore discuss his mission in *The First 150 Years of Singapore.*
17. Philip Merson, personal account

18. Recorded interview with Kenneth Hellrich
19. Bicky Roualle, personal account
20. The Australian forces taking part in the defence of Malaya.
21. The principal Dutch shipping line in the Far East.
22. See, Nigel West, *Secret War*.
23. Spencer Chapman's experiences are related in his book *The Jungle is Neutral*. The Special Operations Executive was formed in 1940 to foster resistance in occupied territories.
24. For attack on Singapore, see Compton Mackenzie's *Eastern Epic*.
25. Jim Bailward, personal account
26. Compton Mackenzie, *Eastern Epic*; Donald and Joanna Moore, *The First 150 Years of Singapore*.
27. Cecil Gutteridge, personal account. For the loss of the *Giang Bee*, see also Donald and Joanna Moore, *The First 150 Years of Singapore*.
28. On customs casualties, see Appendix IV.
29. Recorded interview with Kenneth Hellrich. Account written by John Lewis during his captivity in 1942. Both report that a few officers did elect to serve under the Japanese administration. Donald and Joanna Moore in *The First 150 Years of Singapore* also describe the roundup of British civilian detainees.
30. John Lewis also records the helpfulness of the Chinese.
31. Personal account by Kenneth Hellrich.

Chapter 6: Back to work

1. Quoted by Donald and Joanna Moore in *The First 150 Years of Singapore*.
2. Malayan Union Customs and Excise Annual Report 1946; Paul H. Kratoska, *The Japanese Occupation of Malaya 1941–1945*.
3. F. S. V. Donnison *British Military Administration in the Far East 1943–6*; K. G. Tregonning, *A History of Modern Malaya*.
4. . S. V. Donnison, *British Military Administration in the Far East 1943–6*.
5. Personal accounts by K. S. Hellrich, R. W. L. McCall and C. C. Gutteridge.
6. As recounted to D. J. Mackay.
7. Personal account.
8. F. S. V. Donnison, *British Military Administration in the Far East 1953–6*.
9. F. S. V. Donnison, *British Military Administration in the Far East 1943–6*.
10. See Chapter 10.
11. Malayan Union Customs and Excise Annual Report 1946; Malayan Union Customs and Excise Annual Report 1947.
12. Malayan Union Annual Reports 1946 and 1947; Malayan Union Customs and Excise Annual Reports 1946 and 1947.
13. Malayan Union Annual Reports 1946 and 1947.
14. A Japanese 'master plan'. See Donald and Joanna Moore, *The First*

150 Years of Singapore, which also describes the crowds that cheered the British troops on return to Singapore.

15. John Lewis, personal account.
16. Cecil Gutteridge, personal account.
17. Jim Bailward, personal account.
18. Philip Merson, personal account.
19. Peter Chattaway, personal account.
20. A matrilineal society in which descent was reckoned through the female line and the traditional chiefs, the Lembagas, were elected. (Sir Richard O. Winstedt, *Malaya and its History*).
21. Derek Mackay, personal account.
22. Malayan Union Customs and Excise Annual Report 1947.
23. Singapore Customs Annual Report 1948.
24. Donald and Joanna Moore, *The First 150 Years of Singapore*.

Chapter 7: Merdeka

1. K. G. Tregonning, *A History of Modern Malaya*; Donald and Joanna Moore, *The First 150 Years of Singapore*; Federation of Malaya Annual Report 1954; D. G. E. Hall, *A History of South East Asia*.
2. Personal account.
3. Recounted by D. J. Mackay. In his *History of South East Asia*, D. G. E. Hall estimates that about two million Chinese squatters were resettled in 'new villages'. Each householder was given a 30-year lease. Eventually, there were about 550 such villages with piped water, electricity, schools and community centres.
4. Personal account.
5. Singapore Customs Annual Reports 1949 and 1950.
6. The British plea of 'not guilty' might have been understood as a total denial of the alleged facts. To claim trial was to demand the opportunity to put up a defence.
7. The law required that an accused person be produced in court at an early stage to record the charges and his pleas. A date for the trial was set on that occasion or a later 'mention'.
8. Tamil and Urdu are languages spoken in different parts of India.
9. Federation Customs and Excise Annual Report 1949.
10. Federation Customs and Excise Annual Report 1957.
11. Colonial Office Cmd.7709, *British Dependencies in the Far East 1945–9*.
12. The practice of collecting federal duties in the settlements began in 1912 (Federated Malay States Annual Report 1912).
13. Peter Chattaway, personal account.
14. Derek Mackay, personal account.
15. The Johore causeway spanned the narrow strait between Singapore and Johore, carrying the main road and railway. There were customs examination stations at each end but trains were only halted at Singapore and Johore Bahru railway stations.
16. John Lewis, personal account.

17. During the civil war in China communist forces trapped this British warship in the Yangtze River. HMS *Amethyst*'s daring escape was hailed as an epic story.
18. Singapore Annual Report 1954; Federation of Malaya Annual Report 1954; Nicholas J. White, *Business, Government and the End of Empire: Malaya 1942–57*. In *A History of Modern Malaya*, K. G. Tregonning records that income tax was tried briefly in the Straits Settlements in 1922/3 but abandoned as impossible to administer.
19. K. G. Tregonning, *A History of Modern Malaya*; Donald and Joanna Moore, *The First 150 Years of Singapore*.
20. Personal account.
21. A somewhat mocking expression applied to a senior European or 'Big Sir'.
22. Taiping as described by A. R. King
23. Federation of Malaya staff list 1956.
24. Personal account
25. Maria Hertogh was the daughter of Dutch citizens in the Dutch East Indies, left in the care of her *ayah* when her parents became prisoners of the Japanese. Traced to Malaya she became the subject of legal proceedings in the Singapore courts to decide a dispute over custody. When this was awarded to the natural parents the peace of Singapore was shattered by rioting Muslim extremists, who turned to killing Europeans.
26. Personal account.
27. Federation of Malaya Annual Report 1954; Federation Customs Annual Report 1957; personal account by D. J. Mackay then at Customs HQ.
28. From 1955 federation customs and excise applied the concept of open market valuation set out in Article VII of the General Agreement on Tariffs and Trade and in the Brussels Valuation Convention. Federation Customs and Excise Annual Report 1957.
29. The Singapore Customs Annual Report 1948 states that a total of 164 officers attended 15 courses. The establishment of the Training School at Malacca is recorded in Federation Customs and Excise Annual Report 1957.
30. Personal account.
31. Federation Customs and Excise Annual Report 1957; Singapore Customs Annual Report 1958.
32. Federation Customs and Excise Annual Report 1957. An organization chart appears in Appendix VI.
33. D. J. Mackay's personal account.
34. Federation Customs and Excise Annual Report 1957.
35. Singapore Customs Annual Report 1958.
36. Federation Customs and Excise Annual Report 1957; Singapore Customs Annual Report 1958.
37. Report of the Committee on Malayanization of the Public Service 1956, kindly provided by J. M. Gullick.

38. K. G. Tregonning, *A History of Modern Malaya*; Donald and Joanna Moore, *The First 150 Years of Singapore.*

Chapter 8: Wholesale monopoly

1. Personal account.
2. M. Lim, *Control of the Opium Trade in Malaya 1900–12.*
3. Victor Purcell, *The Chinese in South East Asia.*
4. In 1839 the European merchants in Canton were forced to surrender their illegal stocks of opium for destruction. Together with their families they boarded ships that were denied supplies on the orders of commissioner Lin Tsê-hsü. The arrival of naval support precipitated a conflict that ended with the Treaty of Nanking in 1841. Hong Kong was ceded to Great Britain and five 'treaty ports' were opened to trade. Although China was forced to pay compensation for the merchants' losses, the treaty avoided any reference to the future of the opium trade (Maurice Collis, *Foreign Mud*).
5. Victor Purcell, *The Chinese in Malaya.*
6. P. G. de Bruijn (translated by Professor Brian Harrison), 'Trade in the Straits of Malacca in 1785', *Malayan Branch Royal Asiatic Society Journal*, vol. XXVI, Part 1, July 1953.
7. Victor Purcell, *The Chinese in Malaya.*
8. C. D. Cowan, 'Early Penang and the Rise of Singapore, *Malayan Branch Royal Asiatic Society Journal*, vol. XXIII, Part 2, March 1950.
9. Donald and Joanna Moore, *The First 150 Years of Singapore.*
10. C. D. Cowan, 'Early Penang and the Rise of Singapore, *Malayan Branch Royal Asiatic Society Journal*, vol. XXIII, Part 2, March 1950.
11. Donald and Joanna Moore, *The First 150 Years of Singapore.*
12. J. G. Butcher, *The Demise of the Revenue Farm System in the Federated Malay States;* M. Lim, *Control of the Opium Trade in Malaya 1900–12.*
13. J. G. Butcher, *The Demise of the Revenue Farm System in the Federated Malay States.*
14. M. Lim, *Control of the Opium Trade in Malaya 1900–12.*
15. Ibid.
16. Donald and Joanna Moore, *The First 150 Years of Singapore.*
17. M. Lim, *Control of the Opium Trade in Malaya 1900–12.*
18. Ibid.
19. Ibid.
20. Ibid.
21. K. G. Tregonning, *A History of Modern Malaya.*
22. Ibid.
23. Government Monopolies Department Annual Report 1910.
24. Report of the Straits Settlements and Federated Malay States Opium Commission; Donald and Joanna Moore, *The First 150 Years of Singapore.*
25. The percentage had been increasing. In 1898 the revenue from

opium was S$ 2,332,186 out of a total of S$ 5,071,281 (45.9 per cent). By 1904 it peaked at S$ 6,357,727 out of S$ 10,746,517 (59.1 per cent) and even in 1906 it was still S$ 5,125,506 out of S$ 9,618,312 (53.3 per cent). (Victor Purcell, *The Chinese in Malaya*).

26. Victor Purcell, *The Chinese in Malaya.*
27. Ibid.
28. M. Lim, *Control of the Opium Trade in Malaya 1900–12.*
29. Ibid.
30. Ibid.
31. Government Monopolies Manual 1932; Government Monopolies Department Annual Report 1910; Straits Settlements Annual Report 1910; Federated Malay States Annual Report 1910.
32. Government Monopolies Department Annual Report 1910; Malayan Union Customs and Excise Annual Report 1946.
33. Government Monopolies Manual 1932.
34. Government Monopolies Manual 1932.
35. Federated Malay States Annual Report 1911.
36. Federated Malay States Annual Report 1912.
37. Victor Purcell, *The Chinese in Malaya.*
38. Government Monopolies Department Annual Report 1920.
39. Victor Purcell, *The Chinese in Malaya.*
40. Public Record Office File CO.54/882/10 'Opium Policy'.
41. Straits Settlements Annual Report 1919.
42. Victor Purcell, *The Chinese in Malaya.*
43. Ibid.
44. Public Records Office File CO.54/882/10 'Opium Policy'.
45. Ibid.
46. Ibid.
47. Federated Malay States Annual Report 1926.
48. Public Records Office File CO.54/882/10 'Opium Policy'.
49. Ibid.
50. Malayan Union Customs and Excise Annual Report 1946.
51. Government Monopolies Manual 1932.
52. Personal account.
53. Government Monopolies Department Annual Report 1931; K. S. Hellrich personal account.
54. John Lewis, personal account.
55. Government Monopolies Department Annual Report 1932.
56. Ibid.
57. Ibid.

Chapter 9: Retail monopoly

1. Federated Malay States Annual Reports 1926, 1935 and 1938.
2. Government Monopolies Manual 1932.
3. Ibid.
4. Public Record Office File CO.825/19/1 'Malaya: Control of Opium Traffic'.

5. Ibid.
6. Personal account.
7. Personal account.
8. Public Record Office File CO.825/19/1 'Malaya: Control of Opium Traffic'.
9. Ibid.
10. Ibid.
11. Ibid.
12. Straits Settlements Department of Excise Annual Report 1935.
13. Straits Settlements Department of Excise Annual Report 1938; Victor Purcell, *The Chinese in Malaya.*
14. Straits Settlements Department of Excise Annual Report 1938.
15. Victor Purcell, *The Chinese in Malaya*; Straits Settlements Department of Excise Annual Report 1936.
16. Personal account.
17. Straits Settlements Department of Excise Annual Report 1935.
18. Straits Settlements Department of Excise Annual Report 1937.
19. Straits Settlements Customs and Excise Annual Report 1938.
20 Ibid.
21. Personal account.
22. C. C. Gutteridge personal account.
23. K. G. Tregonning, *A History of Modern Malaya*; Straits Settlements Department of Excise Annual Report 1938.
24. Malayan Union Customs and Excise Annual Report 1946; Singapore Customs Annual Report 1956.

Chapter 10: Prohibition

1. Singapore Customs Annual Report 1956; Malayan Union Customs and Excise Annual Report 1946.
2. Victor Purcell, *The Chinese in Malaya*; F. S. V. Donnison, *British Military Administration in the Far East 1943–6.*
3. Colonial Office Cmd.7709 'British Dependencies in the Far East 1945–9'.
4. Malaya Union Customs and Excise Annual Report 1946
5. Singapore Customs Annual Report 1956; Federation of Malaya Annual Report 1954.
6. D. J. Mackay personal comments.
7. Personal account.
8. Singapore Customs Annual Report 1956.
9. D. J. Mackay personal account; J. F. M. Roualle personal account; Singapore Customs Annual Report 1950.
10. Singapore Customs Annual Report 1956.
11. Extract from *The Weekender*, 3 February 1956.
12. D. J. Mackay personal account.
13. Singapore Customs Annual Report 1957.
14. Singapore Customs Annual Report 1958.
15. D. J. Mackay personal account.

16. Malayan Union Customs and Excise Annual Reports 1946 and 1947; C. C. Gutteridge personal account.
17. Malayan Union Customs and Excise Annual Report 1947.
18. Personal account.
19. D. J. Mackay personal account.
20. Singapore Customs Annual Reports 1949, 1950, 1953 and 1956; *The Free Press*, 20 July 1953; D. J. Mackay personal account.
21. Personal account.
22. Personal account.
23. Extract from *The Free Press*, 20 July 1953.
24. Singapore Customs Annual Report 1955.
25. Singapore Customs Annual Report 1956.
26. D. J. Mackay personal account.
27. Singapore Customs Annual Report 1956.
28. D. J. Mackay personal account.
29. Personal account.
30. D. J. Mackay personal account.
31. D. J. Mackay personal account. In 1949 Singapore customs reported 1571 known saloons and 969 raids on such premises.
32. D. J. Mackay personal account.
33. Singapore Customs Annual Report 1953.
34. Singapore Customs Annual Report 1953.
35. Federation Customs and Excise Annual Report 1957.
36. Federation of Malaya Annual Report 1954; Federation Customs and Excise Annual Report 1957.
37. Singapore Customs Annual Report 1955.
38. D. J. Mackay personal account.
39. Singapore Customs Annual Reports 1957 and 1958.
40. Singapore Customs Annual Report 1956.
41. Ibid.
42. The government opium treatment centre was established on St John's Island, Singapore in 1954. It had accommodation for 800 patients. Treatment took from three to twelve months and was voluntary. The prisons and medical departments ran the centre jointly and the social welfare department offered follow-up aftercare (see Singapore Annual Report 1954 and the Singapore Customs Annual Reports for 1956, 1957 and 1958).

Chapter 11: The demon drink

1. Government Monopolies Department Annual Report 1909.
2. The opium and liquor farms were abolished in Perak in 1909, Selangor and Negri Sembilan in 1910 and Pahang in 1911 (Malayan Union Customs and Excise Annual Report 1946).
3. A small portable instrument used to ascertain the strength of spirits by measuring their density. The reading was converted to proof by reference to a standard table.
4. Alcohol for use other than human consumption, such as industrial

processes, had to be rendered 'non-potable' and was then non-dutiable. The common form is methylated spirit.

5. There are various ways of measuring and expressing the strength of alcohol. The British measure of 'proof', used in Malaya, was expressed as a percentage of a spirit, which, at 51°Fahrenheit, weighed twelve-thirteenths of an equal measure of distilled water.
6. The system of bonded warehouses enabled an importer to defer payment of duty until he drew stock from the bond. The security of such stores was a major concern for the customs departments.
7. Derek Mackay, personal account.
8. The supply of duty-free goods to service personnel was a long-established practice.
9. Personal account.
10. Singapore Customs Annual Report 1956.
11. Singapore Customs Annual Report 1958.
12. Malayan Union Customs and Excise Annual Report 1946.
13. Straits Settlements Annual Report 1910; Government Monopolies Department Annual Report 1932; Singapore Customs Annual Report 1949; FMS Customs and Excise Annual Report 1938.
14. Malayan Union Customs and Excise Annual Report 1946.
15. Malayan Union Customs and Excise Annual Report 1947.
16. Peter Chattaway, personal account.
17. Philip Merson, personal account.
18. Robert McCall, personal account.
19. Tony King, personal account.
20. See illustration on p. 186.
21. Government Monopolies Department Annual Report 1933; Straits Settlements Customs and Excise Annual Report 1938; FMS Customs and Excise Annual Report 1938; Malayan Union Customs and Excise Annual Reports 1946 and 1947; Singapore Customs Annual Report 1956; Federation of Malaya Customs and Excise Annual Report 1957.
22. John Lewis, personal account.
23. Peter Burgess, personal account.
24. John Lewis, personal account.
25. Bicky Roualle, personal account.
26. John Lewis, personal account.
27. Derek Mackay, personal account.
28. See illustration on p. 175.
29. Peter Burgess, personal account.
30. Singapore Customs Annual Report 1956; Malayan Union Customs and Excise Annual Report 1947.
31. FMS Customs and Excise Annual Report 1938.
32. Johnny Johnson, personal account.
33. Federation of Malaya Customs and Excise Annual Report 1949.
34. Singapore Customs Annual Report 1956.
35. Singapore Customs Annual Report 1956.
36. Singapore Customs Annual Report 1958.

37. Government Monopolies Department Annual Reports 1932 and 1933; Malayan Breweries produced 'Tiger', ABC Brewery 'Anchor'.
38. Singapore Customs Annual Report 1949.
39. Federation of Malaya Customs and Excise Annual Report 1957.
40. In 1910 the Government Monopolies Department reported that the liquors supervisor was a member of the board!
41. Government Monopolies Department Annual Report 1932; Straits Settlements Customs and Excise Annual Report 1938.
42. Derek Mackay, personal account.
43. The milky liquid tapped from the palm tree naturally ferments to produce an alcoholic beverage that was popular in many parts of East Asia.
44. Government Monopolies Manual 1932; Straits Settlements Department of Excise Annual Report 1935.
45. Malayan Union Customs and Excise Annual Report 1947.
46. Peter Chattaway, personal account.
47. Johnny Johnson, personal account.
48. Federations of Malaya Customs and Excise Annual Report 1957; Singapore Customs Annual Report 1957.

Chapter 12: Up in smoke

1. FMS Annual Report 1915; Government Monopolies Manual 1932.
2. Straits Settlements Annual Report 1919.
3. Government Monopolies Manual 1932; Government Monopolies Department Annual Report 1933.
4. Straits Settlements Excise Department Annual Report 1935.
5. Straits Settlements Annual Report 1919.
6. Government Monopolies Manual 1932.
7. Ibid.
8. Straits Settlements Excise Department Annual Report 1935.
9. Government Monopolies Department Annual Report 1932.
10. Government Monopolies Department Annual Report 1933.
11. Straits Settlements Excise Department Annual Reports 1936 and 1937; Straits Settlements Customs and Excise Annual Report 1938.
12. Malayan Union Customs and Excise Annual Report 1946.
13. Singapore Customs Annual Report 1949.
14. Singapore Customs Annual Report 1949.
15. Bicky Roualle, personal account.
16. Tony King, personal account.
17. H. G. Boyce-Taylor, personal account.
18. Derek Mackay, personal account.
19. Federation of Malaya Customs and Excise Annual Report 1957.
20. Singapore Customs Annual Report 1952.
21. Singapore Customs Annual Report 1956.
22. Singapore Customs Annual Report 1957.
23. Singapore Customs Annual Report 1958.
24. Ibid.

25. Singapore Customs Annual Report 1957.
26. Singapore Customs Annual Report 1958.
27. Federation of Malaya Customs and Excise Annual Report 1957.
28. Federation of Malaya Customs and Excise Annual Report 1957; Singapore Customs Annual Report 1957.
29. Malayan Union Customs and Excise Annual Report 1946.
30. Government Monopolies Department Annual Report 1934.
31. Straits Settlements Excise Department Annual Report 1937.
32. Malayan Union Customs and Excise Annual Report 1946.
33. FMS Customs and Excise Annual Report 1938; Straits Settlements Customs and Excise Annual Report 1938.
34. Singapore Customs Annual Report 1958.
35. Federation of Malaya Customs and Excise Annual Report 1957.
36. Federation of Malaya Customs and Excise Annual Report 1957.

Chapter 13: Revenues and restrictions

1. Federation of Malaya Customs and Excise Annual Report 1957.
2. Ibid.
3. Ibid. Malaya was bound by the provisions of international treaties such as the General Agreement on Tariffs and Trade.
4. Cecil Gutteridge, personal account.
5. Customs Annual Report 1949.
6. Derek Mackay, personal account.
7. Federation of Malaya Customs and Excise Annual Report 1949.
8. Singapore Customs Annual Report 1956.
9. Ibid.
10. D. G. E. Hall, *A History of South East Asia*.
11. Malayan Union Customs and Excise Annual Report 1947.
12. Derek Mackay, personal account.
13. Philip Merson had previously found Lim Tai Chuan invaluable during his time in food control.
14. In criminal proceedings the prosecution case is presented first. Under Malayan law the magistrate could only call on the defence if he were satisfied that, in the absence of any reply, he could safely convict on the prosecution evidence alone.
15. Government Monopolies Department Annual Reports 1932 and 1933.
16. Straits Settlements Excise Department Annual Report 1937.
17. During the emergency this description was applied to materials that could be regarded as subversive.
18. Federation of Malaya Customs and Excise Annual Report 1957.
19. D. G. E. Hall, *A History of South East Asia*.
20. Ibid.
21. Federation of Malaya Customs and Excise Annual Report 1957.
22. Commodity markets are often volatile. The heavy investment required in tin mining made it desirable to temper fluctuations in demand (and price) by an international agreement to maintain

'buffer stocks' to absorb excess production.
23. FMS Annual Report 1915.
24. FMS Annual Report 1938.
25. L. A. Mills, *The British in Eastern Asia*.
26. FMS Annual Report 1926.
27. Peter Burgess, personal account.
28. Government Monopolies Department Annual Report 1934.
29. Cecil Gutteridge, personal account.
30. D. G. E. Hall, *A History of South East Asia*. In Chapter 5 Peter Burgess records his meeting with Duff Cooper who had discovered how difficult it was to destroy old rubber trees.
31. D. G. E. Hall, *A History of South East Asia*.
32. Federation of Malaya Customs and Excise Annual Report 1957.
33. Tony King, personal account.
34. Derek Mackay and Bicky Roualle personal accounts.
35. Federation of Malaya Customs and Excise Annual Report 1957.
36. Ibid.
37. Tony King, personal account.
38. Malayan Union Customs and Excise Annual Report 1946.
39. Peter Chattaway, personal account.
40. Bicky Roualle, personal account.
41. Government Monopolies Department Annual Report 1934; L. A. Mills, *The British in Eastern Asia*.
42. L. A. Mills, *The British in Eastern Asia*; Government Monopolies Department Annual Report 1934.
43. L. A. Mills, *The British in Eastern Asia*.
44. In *The British in Eastern Asia* L. A. Mills records that in 1935 a number of Chinese tailors emigrated from Singapore to Rhio. They returned when the traffic in 'garments' ceased.
45. Straits Settlements Customs and Excise Annual Report 1938.
46. L. A. Mills, *The British in Eastern Asia*.
47. Bicky Roualle, personal account.
48. Malayan Union Customs and Excise Annual Reports 1946 and 1947.
49. Federation of Malaya Annual Report 1954.
50. Federation of Malaya Customs and Excise Annual Report 1957.
51. Derek Mackay, personal account.
52. Introduced with the war duties in 1940 it was retained as a revenue source after the restoration of the British administration in 1945. In Singapore in 1956 the yield was S$ 5,982,718.91 (Singapore Customs Annual Reports 1949 and 1956).

Chapter 14: Life and leisure

1. Peter Burgess, personal account.
2. In her account of the British in Malaya, *Out in the Midday Sun*, Margaret Shennan records the importance of sport in the lives of the expatriates and its value in bringing the races together.

3. Bicky Roualle, personal account. Robert McCall was also a member of the team that played Hong Kong in 1939.
4. Jim Bailward, personal account
5. John Lewis, personal account
6. David Anderson, personal account.
7. Derek Mackay, personal account.
8. At altitudes of over 4000 feet they could offer nostalgic reminders of Britain. The principal locations were at Maxwell's Hill, Fraser's Hill and Cameron Highlands, where 'The Smoke House', a mock Tudor pub, boasted pewter tankards and (allegedly) a lawn of Cumberland turf. See also Margaret Shennan, *Out in the Midday Sun.*
9. John Lewis, personal account.
10. Tony King, personal account.
11. Johnny Johnson, personal account.
12. See Katharine Sim, *Malayan Landscape.*
13. Janey Grimwood, personal account.
14. Gordon and Anne Crocker, personal account.
15. See Katharine Sim, *Malayan Landscape.*
16. Gordon and Anne Crocker, personal account.
17. Robert McCall, personal account.
18. Recalled by Gordon Crocker.
19. Derek Mackay, personal account.
20. Gordon and Anne Crocker, personal account.
21. Frankie Roualle, personal account.
22. Gordon discovered that he was known locally as '*Itu Tuan customs dengan dua atau tiga isteri*' (that customs officer with two or three wives).
23. Stella Hardaker, personal account.
24. Janey Grimwood, personal account.
25. Frankie Roualle, personal account.
26. Nicky Johnson, personal account.
27. Tony and Isobel King, personal accounts.
28. Gordon Crocker, personal account.

Epilogue

1. K. G. Tregonning, *A History of Modern Malaya*; D. G. E. Hall, *A History of South East Asia.*
2. Speech published under the title 'Malays forget easily'.
3. Statistics supplied by the Singapore Ministry of Information, Communication and the Arts (*Singapore Facts and Pictures 2002*). The ministry also reports that in 2001 the customs and excise collected over S$ 1.8 billion in revenue, clearing 1,159,503 containers and 3,862,725 inward consignments.
4. Personal accounts.

Index